DA

The Multinational Corporation and Social Change

edited by
**David E. Apter
Louis Wolf Goodman**

The Praeger Special Studies program—
utilizing the most modern and efficient book
production techniques and a selective
worldwide distribution network—makes
available to the academic, government, and
business communities significant, timely
research in U.S. and international economic, social, and political development.

The Multinational Corporation and Social Change

PRAEGER SPECIAL STUDIES IN INTERNATIONAL ECONOMICS AND DEVELOPMENT

Praeger Publishers New York Washington London

Library of Congress Cataloging in Publication Data
Main entry under title:

The Multinational corporation and social change.

(Praeger special studies in international economics
and development)
Includes bibliographical references and index.
1. Underdeveloped areas—International business
enterprises—Addresses, essays, lectures. 2. International business enterprises—Addresses, essays,
lectures. I. Apter, David Ernest, 1924-
II. Goodman, Louis Wolf.
HD2755.5.M833   338.8'8'091724   75-1989
ISBN 0-275-23020-1

PRAEGER PUBLISHERS
111 Fourth Avenue, New York, N.Y. 10003, U.S.A.

Published in the United States of America in 1976
by Praeger Publishers, Inc.

To the Memory of Stephen Hymer

CONTENTS

		Page
Chapter		

The multinational corporation has in recent years become an object of immense concern. The reasons for this are many and obvious. Its organizational power and fiscal flexibility have affected societies all over the world in ways so manifest that the corporation appears to be the dominant influence in public affairs, largely independent of control by national governments. Multinationals are the creatures of advanced industrial societies. Their influence within a metropole allows them to reinforce their own domination of peripheral countries with the prestige and power of metropolitan governments. As privileged organizations, they hold a unique position among growth-inducing institutions able to affect the direction of development. Connections between metropolitan power, multinational, and periphery nations, already complex, are ever more ramified.

It is not surprising then that such matters should become a prime focus of research and review. A basic question for researchers is: "To what extent is the multinational corporation an autonomous or independent power in the world, acting in terms of its own needs, without regard to national sovereignties or controls?" Yet so intricate are the actual legal, jurisdictional, and other issues and so diverse the institutional arrangements, that a precise assessment is difficult. That the multinationals have exceptional power to act as independent entities is without question. No one doubts that their organizational flexibility, management methods, and economic power affect national decision-making autonomy in ways that even large-scale domestic enterprises do not enjoy. Multinationals seek outlets which, as much as possible, will enable them to avoid inhibitions to their economic freedom such as union activity, bureaucratic regulations, national taxation, and other restrictions unavoidable for firms operating within a domestic context. Nevertheless, just how fast and loose the multinational firm plays with the world economy has been overstated. A good deal of the "scare literature" exaggerates and oversimplifies the picture.

These essays have been selected from a number of papers presented in 1974 at a conference on the multinational corporation at Yale University. The conference was held under the auspices of the Institution for Social and Policy Studies, Yale University. The authors would like to express their gratitude to the institution and its director, Professor C. E. Lindblom, for support and facilities, and to Professor John Perry Miller, the former director.

The extent to which the multinationals can dominate the metropolitan center whence they have largely sprung is to some extent a problem of magnitude. The question of business control over policy per se is a hardy perennial. What is novel about the multinational corporation is the extent to which its organization, functions, and needs will be taken into account by government policymakers. A multinational enterprise, able to obtain tax relief and concessions, guarantees of compensation in the face of possible nationalization, or other legalized and therefore legitimate preferential benefits, may soon produce unwanted and unanticipated burdens as well as other consequences over which citizens can be expected to exercise little control or judgement.

Thus it is not the autonomous power exercised by the MNC which is the main object of concern but the diversity of functions it performs for metropole and periphery alike. Multinationals are not really so difficult to control if a government wants to do it. The OPEC countries have shown how even periphery nations can work with MNCs for mutual benefit. Multinationals are not simply instruments of metropolitan domination. Indeed, the occasion may arise when the multinational will act as the instrument of the periphery within the metropole, its Trojan horse.

It is the mixture of power, flexibility, organizational efficiency, and functional convenience which needs further exploration. The recent literature has sent up warning flags. Investigations are now under way at all levels. The United Nations has mounted a long-term review of the role of multinational corporations. So too in the United States a number of agencies have sponsored investigations. University based researchers are engaged in exploring many aspects of multinational behavior.

Such studies are beginning to bear fruit. A good deal more is known about the multinationals than a few years ago. A large literature already exists. To assess such progress and, most particularly, the developmental implications of the MNC, the Institution for Social and Policy Studies of Yale University organized a conference in May 1974. Participants were drawn from academic and research centers, universities, government, and the United Nations. The papers presented for discussion (of which about half have been selected for inclusion in the present volume) focused on the multinational corporation as in instrument of development in both developing countries and metropolitan centers. The seven essays in this volume represent the broad range of perspectives present in the literature and in this inference.

The first essay considers the structural history of international enterprise in the context of development. The role of the MNC in a given host country is very much a function of its level of industrialization and historical circumstances. With this focus, and comparing MNCs with charter companies and cartels, David Apter suggests that there is likely to be a continuing role for MNCs not only as a new form of international business but as an adaptive instrument by means of which metropolitan technologies and organizational skills effect structural changes on the political and social life in periphery countries.

Raymond Vernon's essay continues this theme by showing how managerial technology affects state-firm relations. He indicates why, with modern productive processes, the MNC serves as an extremely flexible instrument for worldwide international business operations. The antique forerunners of the MNC, operating at a distance from their chartering agents, controlled the areas in which they did business. Today, MNCs need to cooperate with home and host governments and rarely have exclusive power in a geographical area. The potential volatility of such relations causes Vernon to review the concepts "dependency" and "interdependence." Evaluating the utility of each concept for describing relations between corporations and nation states, he concludes that no matter what the real impact of the multinational corporation, its sheer size and flexibility will continue to cause great uneasiness until it is in some way made more accountable.

In the volume's third essay, Goodman points out that there is not just one type of MNC but many. He distinguishes among multinationals in terms of the base of their worldwide headquarters (for example, United States, Japan, Western Europe, Eastern Europe, or Third World), their products (mining, agribusiness, manufacturing, or service), their use of factors of production (whether capital or labor intensive) and the markets in which they buy and sell goods (whether they are relatively oligopolistic or relatively competitive). Such characteristics are important predictors of how MNCs arrange financing and carry out research and development, production, and marketing. Goodman focuses on the goals and behavior of top policy makers and tries to show how they determine the roles played by lower level MNC managers and how they, in turn, are affected by forces within the firm, within host and home countries, and by their competition. Scant attention has been paid in the literature to differences among types of multinationals and types of managers. The result is "overgeneralization" of research, imputing to all MNCs and MNC managers characteristics which are appropriate only to a more limited set.

This discussion of types of MNCs and the forces which shape their behavior is put in a dynamic perspective in the essay by Gustav Ranis. Ranis uses ideal typical descriptions of MNCs and host countries to show how they interrelate in the evolution of international business. In this essay it becomes clear that although MNCs are very powerful in today's world their power is far from complete. Few things exist that multinationals have the power to shape completely but, since they always must work in concert with other social forces, operating through compromise and negotiations much like all other important social actors, the issue of strategy and decision-making is particularly important. The difference between MNCs and other social actors is that the former are, more often than not, more powerful than the forces with which they must deal. It takes a compensatory political strategy and national determination to overcome that power. Precisely because the strategies and impact are so varied, it is necessary to examine the experience of MNCs in particular nations, contrasting the reality with the ideal type Ranis describes. Deviations from his expected pattern give clues to unusual MNC or nation state expectations or to the importance of considering the impact of other institutions.

The next essays examine the behavior of multinational corporations in particular geographical contexts. Yoshihiro Tsurumi suggests some of the differences between Japanese multinationals and those of the United States. Japanese firms are likely to be smaller than the average U.S. firm and characteristically go abroad in search of cheaper labor or to locate new sources of raw materials. American MNCs, on the other hand, have tended to seek out and hold foreign markets. Tsurumi points out that the Japanese multinational strategy makes it extremely difficult for Japanese nationals to be absent from any supervisory roles. In contrast, U.S. multinationals can more easily employ host country nationals. Tsurumi sees Japan as highly dependent upon the spread of its multinationals but increasingly vulnerable due to the high visibility of Japanese firms which produces growing negative reactions from Japan's Asian neighbors.

Walter Goldstein, discussing the impact of the multinational corporation on developed nations concludes that "*dependencia* is already a fact of life in the wealthier economies of the developed world." Corporations can retain flexibility in the pursuit of their economic goals by playing off the interest of one nation state against another. He does not foresee, at least in the short-term, either meaningful MNC social accountability or effective cooperation between developed nations capable of regulating MNC activities. MNC influence on world trade and development will serve only the interests of a few individuals—most particularly managers, employees, and stockholders of the MNCs themselves.

Ronald Müller focuses on the impact of the multinational on socioeconomic stability and national planning in the United States. He concludes that, even in this most developed nation, a lack of systematic national planning results in global competition of multinationals having more impact on the shape of U.S. society than do programs structured by the nation state. This chapter makes it clear that the topic of "the multinational corporation and development" is not the exclusive interest of the Third World, and that serious steps both within and among all nations are necessary to deal with the global transformations that have been worked by the rise of the multinational.

The final essay considers the multinational corporation as a logical stage in the evolution of capitalist enterprise. Magdoff, tracing the evolution of global capitalist competition, Magdoff closes his chapter with a discussion of the necessity and difficulties of building a world that gives greater priority to improving the lot of the impoverished majority of the world's population.

These are some of the main themes of the essays. Many other questions are raised. Müller and Magdoff are not only concerned with who benefits and who loses but also with long and short run consequences. Several of the essays deal with the behavior of MNC managers, showing their relationships to planners in host nations, and the effects of MNCs on traditional elites, and blue collar workers in both metropole and periphery.

The chapters by Apter, Ranis, and Goldstein discuss the impact of the MNC on the state and society. Having destroyed artisan industry with its relatively low material productivity, what happens when new automated industry employs fewer workers at higher wages and higher productivity? How does this relate to the question of possible transitions from capitalism to socialism? Or does the MNC introduce "capitalist" elements in socialist societies? With what world system are MNCs most compatible? Apter deals with the question of whether the MNC is only congenial to a world capitalist system or if it is an organizational form as useful in socialist national systems as capitalist ones. Müller points out that MNCs require neither capitalism or socialism per se but economic concentration. Such compatabilities depend more particularly on the ways the MNC can mold and react to its environment—matters treated by Goldstein, Magdoff, and Vernon.

The MNC is thus intimately connected to broad issues of development, modernization, dependence, and metropole-periphery relationships. The MNC was once seen as a specialized and privileged instrument of capitalist penetration. The oil crisis has suggested some of the ways periphery in combination with MNCs can pressure metropole, especially if the latter cannot reduce its burgeoning demands for raw materials. Does dependence on raw material suppliers, aggravated by simultaneous inflation and recession in the United States, Europe, and Japan weaken the ability of the metropolitan powers to impose their will on the periphery? If so, what effect will this have on the system of global interdependence based on the hegemonic propensities of metropolitan powers (whose appetites have appeared to be held in check only by the mutual bargaining accompanying the growth of investment and trade)?

The answers to such questions are vastly complicated. The metropolitan industrial nations have been caught off guard by unanticipated economic crisis. The question is whether or not they are only temporarily nonplussed by events including actions of the OPEC countries. For the moment, Third World governments with raw materials reserves have improved their bargaining capacity in making deals with multinationals. A developing country can thus on occasion use the multinational as its interest group in the metropole. Faced with the prospect of depression or deep recession at home and rising political pressure abroad, an MNC is increasingly dependent on emergency strategies. It will save its own skin without excessive regard for the *situs* of ownership. Large capital investments all over the world make MNC strategies contingent on terms which have little regard to black or white, rich or poor, capitalist or Communist. In this view the MNC is an influential, independent, but vulnerable broker no longer the exclusive instrument of the Western metropolitan nations. Evidence for this can be found in the increasing number of arrangements with the Communist world, and the active collaboration of petroleum MNCs and oil nations since the rise of OPEC.

As multinationals cooperate with socialist and/or Communist countries, they call to question the view that the multinational corporation is unique to high capitalism. Some regard the MNC as an instrument by which capitalism is detached from its national place of origin and becomes truly international. But if the MNC no longer acts as the agent of, say, U.S. capitalism, does this mean it acts as the agent of capitalism in general with governments serving a capitalist class detached from its national roots, a "highest stage" of imperialism? Or is this picture of multinationals and imperialism too "overdetermined"? Does this mean that the socialism of the modern Communist metropole is a form of state capitalism and mercantilism? Is the MNC like the giant cartel? Is the socialist combine a parallel to the old capitalist charter, for example, agents of government which link trade and empire? Such matters are not merely definitional but are of great speculative interest.

Ultimately, the question centers about the utility of conventional "capitalist" and "socialist" distinctions. The issue of the nature of global systems and the place of the MNC within it may be too complex for such terms. International economic affairs are not governed by "capitalism" or "socialism" but by thousands of loosely linked oligopolistic bargains struck by nation states, multinational corporations, and other transnational actors. Within such a system, the impact of MNCs on development, national planning, or any social process is a function of the behaviors and constraints imposed by all of the actors involved at a given moment. There is plenty of room for maneuver.

The Multinational Corporation and Social Change

CHARTERS, CARTELS, AND MULTINATIONALS— SOME COLONIAL AND IMPERIAL QUESTIONS
David E. Apter

Scholars interested in the multinational corporation have followed two main lines of inquiry. One seeks to locate the place, role, and function of the corporation within the general pattern of technological and organizational evolution, focusing on the impact of multinational enterprises upon the total pattern of social life. The world is defined as a single "developmental space," a relationship between dynamic metropole and derivative periphery. Such a view provides a context for change in history and provides a *problemmatique* for theory. Out of the diverse features of development certain trends, tendencies, and patterns of growth are revealed. The multinational corporation, located within history, becomes one among several decisive forces. As a phenomenon it can be compared with earlier prototypes, its contemporary roles evaluated and, depending on the preferred theoretical emphasis, presented for good or ill as a crucial instrument in the process of development.

The second emphasis treats the multinational corporation as a thing in itself, seeking to define its organizational forms, patterns of decision-making, the extent of its rationality, the methods it uses both to define its goals and pursue them. Questions include how MNCs operate with respect to subsidiaries, governments, the treatment of conflict and threats to their autonomy, the extent of flexibility and centralization or decentralization in policy-making, production, pricing, technology flows, deployment of

This article was written while the author was a member of the Institute for Advanced Study at Princeton; funds were from a National Science Foundation grant.

expertise, localization of management, credit and tax policies, and mixed private and public enterprise strategies and arrangements.

We propose discussing both, considering the multinational corporation in the context of developmental change and contrasting two predominant views about it, liberal and socialist. We will suggest some of the problems socialist-minded poor countries have encountered when seeking alternatives to the multinational corporation, and why advanced socialist countries can work with them to their own advantage. The conflict between the two positions is less and less clearly defined. Indeed, liberals—who might be expected to favor the multinational corporation as a rational method of organizing enterprise with reasonable efficiency, and involving fewer complicated political arrangements than government to government agreements—are in some ways more disturbed about MNCs than are socialists. Indeed, the USSR now has a number of MNCs with headquarters in Brussels.

LIBERAL AND SOCIALIST INTERPRETATIONS

Everyone agrees that the multinational corporation is not simply a big firm. Both liberals and socialists consider the MNC an agent in the regionalization and internationalization of metropolitan enterprise. It is a means of expanding a particular system of relationships between nation states, by means of a private network, the market. Insofar as the international market is dominated by metropolitan agencies so their activities affect the political autonomy of nations. Clientcy and other relationships inhibit or constrain national prospects and agenda-setting possibilities. Liberals, concerned that the market is not free, but manipulated, bemoan the loss of self-regulating features of which the national policies of states would be important but by no means exclusive factors.

To free themselves from constraints imposed by multinational corporations, nations seek remedial strategies or compensatory national policies. The effect is to politicize the economic marketplace. The market is less and less economic and more and more political. Economic gains are negotiated by political bargaining and not competitive regulation. At some point the network of international exchanges is so mediated by political considerations that realpolitik replaces comparative advantage. So distorted is the common negotiation that ordinary economic rationality disappears. Lack of discretion is a consequence of overwhelming power and poorer countries need to find ways to protect themselves against MNCs. Their only means is political. An example is the Lagos Agreement of 1973 designed to improve the bargaining positions of African nations by collective and mutual arrangements. As Curry and Rothchild put it, "If governments harmonize certain of their policies, then they can present a 'united front' to a multinational company that is deciding in which country to invest. This concept was central to the Lagos agreement in 1973 when 39 African nations agreed to bargain jointly for trade concessions in their Brussels meeting with the European Economic Community. It was also evident in the program of economic action declared by the non-aligned countries at their Algiers meeting of 1973—they called for the formation of producer associations 'in order to halt degradation of their terms of trade, to eliminate unhealthy competition, to prevent harmful activities by multinational companies and to reinforce their negotiating power.' "[1]

Such agreements are responses to the power of the multinational corporation and their "unhealthy" impact on competition. The multinational corporation, too dominant a force in the market, generates a political counterforce. From a liberal point of view, then, the power of the multinational corporation needs to be curbed by means other than compensatory political actions. The liberal view is close to the old antitrust idea. Big combinations need to be decentralized. Productive units ought to be separated from financial ones. Such localization, a changed method of capitalization, and fostering more competitive entry into the market would strengthen the economic interdependency of countries around the world, thus increasing the likelihood of mutual cooperation and obligation while reducing the manipulated or "neomercantilist" aspect of such interdependency by allowing greater scope to the factors of production, comparative advantage, and competitive efficiency.

A good many Marxists would agree about the problem while disagreeing with the conclusions. In a socialist view, uneven development results from dominated and hegemonic enterprise. The multinational corporation, an instrument of capitalist power, extends hegemony by means of the market, organizing it, and creating a mutual interdependency on its own terms. It thus dominates the periphery. Such domination results in metropolitan exportation of capitalist crisis and determines periphery policy which can only respond rather than initiate action on its own behalf. Hence the appropriateness of state rather than private enterprise as a means of internal development by periphery countries. Ghana under Nkrumah, Guinea, Algeria, and Tanzania represent examples of countries trying to free themselves from such conditions. In Algeria for example the government eliminated competition with the state sector by severely limiting private investment by Algerian nationals. It nationalized foreign private industries. In 1968, government took over all companies selling oil and gas, as well as firms manufacturing construction materials, fertilizers, machinery, electrical supplies, textiles, and so on. A few banks avoided outright nationalization by means of agreements, but by the end of 1968, 80 percent of the industrial sector had been taken over by the state.[2]

The successful prototype of a socialist solution to the problem of external economic hegemony is "transformational socialism." This relies on state enterprise. The Soviet Union, Yugoslavia, China, and Cuba are examples. Quite irrespective of how one regarded Stalinism, it is clear that methods of socialist enterprise in developing countries have been workable alternatives to the crises and contradictions imposed by capitalist ways. Both socialists and liberals see a common problem arising from MNC domination, the politicization of the market. Each draws different remedial conclusions. To channel that politicization in a socialist direction and provide for a collective public power is one important object for developmental socialists. In this regard the multinational corporation can represent a step along the way or a key instrument of neomercantilism or corporatism.

Diagnostic agreement and divergent conclusions among liberals and socialists is by no means new. Lenin quoted Hobson with approval. Both deplored the decline of competition characteristic of early capitalism and the emergence of a form of monopoly control which combined industrial and finance capitalism, internationalizing large-scale enterprises which formed cartels and holding companies which, appearing to be in the national interest, in fact worked to its detriment.[3]

Such agreement between liberals and socialists does not extend to solutions. Liberals not only want to restore competition by breaking up controlling enterprises but they also wish to work toward a more perfect market. They are afraid of Stalinism in any form, corporatist or socialist. Socialists believe that it is impossible to go backwards to a competitive economic market. It is against the nature of modern technology. Indeed, the forces which make the multinational enterprise efficient and powerful cannot be undone by such primitive solutions. The problem is to point the enterprise in the direction of socialism to create a much needed information market. Such an information market is a function of decentralized control. The multinational is one form such decentralization might take.

Today, more liberals are becoming convinced of the persuasiveness of the socialist line of argument. It is not possible to return to competition in the market place. The world is so interdependent and the organization of highly technologically sophisticated forms of production is so concentrated that what has occurred is irreversible. Much European and increasingly American democratic socialism is of this variety.

Both liberals and socialists are unilinearists. They see development as proceeding in stages. The stages, together, constitute a process—from the limited internal market to the ramified international one, from parochial localism to sophisticated multilevel exchange. The process goes in one direction stimulated by a secular transition from lower forms of technology (using primitive means of labor and energy) to the highest forms of capital intensive enterprise. For the liberal this produces a new power role—that of the modern industrial technocrat who as an international actor uses the currency of modern scientific knowledge. Such technocrats serve managements, whether within the civil service or as the agent of private management. Either way they act as agents of their own power.

Because knowledge is tied to the productive process, and the productive process is continuously competitive in terms of the application of scientific information gathering and its application, so these, the management-scientists, engineers, advanced systems research people, have autonomous authority, the main venue for which is the budgetary allocation for research and development and the main criterion an improved efficiency in output resulting in more competitive strategies. Fiscal economies, product differentiation, costing, and all feasible strategies of evaluation are part of the calculation. Nor is the object simply to make as much money as possible. It is aimed at striking an optimal balance between short-term gains and long-term "infrastructure stability" (including political factors). All these become part of a world managerial design calculus. Everywhere becomes somewhere. Nowhere is nowhere. And the mobilities of enterprise, whether in search of tax shelters or cheap labor, treat the world as a singular development space. Gains are calculated not only within the terms of reference of the enterprise itself but the environment too. The market of wants serves to show how well the market of decisions is working. This, a universalizing, assimilating, developing, and unilinear process may produce unfortunate leads and lags. Nevertheless, it is essentially progressive.

Socialists who share such views are particularly concerned with lead-lag social costs. Such costs represent crucial political criteria relevant to an evaluation of performance. Liberals are more inclined to consider the market as the primary method of adjudication with a necessary and hopefully effective social welfare policy by government to cushion more painful discrepancies between investment and social equity. Their fear is bureaucracy and excessive reliance on planning.[4]

Whatever the criteria, most liberals and socialists increasingly agree that the more prosperous countries are those with the largest proportion of multinational enterprises, yet it is these which experience the most severe political and social "contradictions." These contradictions may be superimposed on modernizing countries, compounding their internal discontinuities. Modernizing societies thus bear a double burden.

Despite such eventualities, few modernizing governments are willing to prevent MNC investment. They continue to offer them inducements, preferring immediate gains and the likelihood of postponed problems, to postponed gains which hopefully might never materialize. Because multinational corporations are able to operate in situations of considerable political uncertainty they offer more immediate advantages to modernizing governments.

What are some of the accrued social overhead costs? Perhaps the easiest way to answer the question is by establishing as a cost criterion the proportion of the population which becomes superfluous or marginal to the economy. The MNC may not be alone responsible for marginality. Its connection to the problem is that by utilizing resources and establishing developmental priorities, a form of agenda setting is undertaken. With government the only mediating instrumentality, the result is likely to be dismal because most governments are unable to cushion the shock of marginality, unemployment, and large urban squatter populations. They lack the funds or the personnel to do much about such matters. Examples are Argentina, Chile, Peru, and other Latin American countries where there is today a virtual replication of nineteenth-century class relationships. Indeed the situation may be worse. In Europe, industrial enterprise was labor intensive. Trade unionism, and the growing politicization of the labor force, the emergence of labor and socialist parties, all forced government action leading to reform. But contemporary multinational-based enterprise is capital intensive. It requires a small work force, uses foreign highly educated technicians, and a larger local group of middle management and clerical personnel. Instead of a large working class, some scholars have argued there is "an industrial reserve army."[5] The result is extremism punctuated by repression, corporatism rather than democracy.

THE UNILINEAR MODEL OF DEVELOPMENT

To summarize briefly, liberals and socialists agree on development as a generally unilinear process. For liberals the appropriate counterbalance to the power of the multinational corporation is international competition. For that, it is necessary to break up the most dominating and powerful firms, but liberals do not know how to accomplish this. For socialists what is required is nationalization, planning, and decentralization. The object is an information market. Whatever the view preferred, the linear model can be described as follows.

The industrial process has evolved in several stages. The primary stage marked the beginning of the industrial revolution. The intermediate stage, represented by the outward shift of metropolitan trade into colonialism and imperialism, created a stable environment for increasingly internationalized capitalism. This stability broke down in two world wars and depression. The third stage is marked by the emergence of the modern multinational corporation while a fourth, not in the model as described here, is where socialists and liberals would disagree, and where socialists argue among themselves.

The multinational corporation is a third-stage phenomenon. Exceptionally dynamic, it is a world unto itself. It contrasts sharply with the other two. The first led to colonialism, for example, metropolitan powers taking over real estate. The second produced a "cartelization" of the world. It resulted in imperialism and world conflict between main hegemonic centers. The third stage leads to the provincialization of the periphery which becomes a residual area in terms of decisions made in a few multinational centers. But this provincialization also opens up opportunities. Periphery and center become integrated into a single global system in which, if the dependency of more and more of the world turns on fewer and fewer main centers of multinational control, those centers can become hostage to an organized periphery.

As a tertiary stage phenomenon, the multinational corporation is the advance guard of private development. But it could serve the same function under socialism. Its chief weapons are credit and technology both, not the one or the other. Its reality is the spread of institutions functional to industrialization even though, as Müller and others have pointed out, it may not always be the most efficient economic device. Especially under conditions of high modernization, the multinational corporation constitutes a powerful subsystem of industrial capitalism, an exportable technostructure. Such technostructures, more or less well institutionalized, are systems of management based on secrecy, operations research, global resource control and deployment. Such a technostructure, the multinational enterprise, is a national corporation which has transcended itself through the internationalization of its operations, dominating the means of production where it can, and sustaining transfers of income for its own benefit and primarily at its own discretion.[6]

So far we have introduced a developmental perspective. Each stage represents a substantial change in the character of capitalism as a system of private enterprise. The secular transformation is the extension of the market from metropole to periphery, drawing all societies into a single network. Stage one of the process is associated with the charter company as its unique instrument, stage two the cartel. Stage three is characterized by the multinational corporation. Changing forms of productivity and enterprise make the transition from one stage to another, from commercial to productive operations, the combination of industrial and financial enterprises, a growing scientific and technical competition between firms, and capital intensive rather than labor and periphery increasingly intertwined, but the roles of science, technology, and management become more and more central. How to develop equivalent expertise is a particular problem of periphery countries which remain vulnerable to the increasing pace of scientific innovation and its application through a technological infrastructure.[7]

We now want to discuss this three-stage unilinear model in order to show how the MNC is the culmination of an organizational evolution; we also wish to show its political role as an exceptionally dynamic instrument.

Both liberals and socialists tend to agree about this model. It corresponds with their general evolutionary and developmental perspective. It also suggests the critical significance of economic factors in the social transformation of societies. (1) In contemporary life, modernization facilitates role transfers from metropole to periphery. (2) Roles generate institutional linkages. (3) In the more advanced stages of modernization one of the most important forms of role transfer and institution-building is the multinational corporation. (4) This stimulates other role and institutional networks, educational, commercial, fiscal, and technical. (5) Such stimulation reinforces host country-metropole networks.

Primary Stage Capitalist Development

Primary stage development was a function of charter companies. These instrumentalities helped create the modern international market. They represented the first organized or institutional means of imposing metropole on periphery by large-scale economic transfers. In both liberal and socialist thought they are associated with the emergence of modern capitalism, with Spain (or Spanish charters) representing a last gasp of mercantilism (a system in which political considerations dictated economic activities and economic activities were pursued to further political goals).[8] English and Dutch charters were associated with the emergence of modern capitalism and the creation of an international market in which economic gain was a self-regarding and legitimate enterprise. The mercantilists proscribed competition and relied on regulation under a hierarchical and bureaucratic system of control. Charters were competitive enterprises between each other but attempted to reduce competition within territorial jurisdictions.

Charters were, like the multinational corporation of today, peculiarly "transportable." They were highly mobile arrangements of economic and political power. With them it was possible to undertake exploration in far places then follow it with investment, consolidate a supporting infrastructure of commercial and bureaucratic arrangements, and establish a marketing system regulated by administrative controls under conditions of exceptional risk. We have said that charters took two main forms, bureaucratic and mercantilist, serving the purposes of national metropolitan governments which exercised a monopoly, as in Spain, and entrepreneurial and capitalist in which individual "adventurers," some of whom were little more than pirates and freebooters, acted under company supervision, with special warrants from government. They were given free reign to act as they saw fit.

Both methods embodied quite different networks of roles, markets, and linkages between metropole and periphery as conduits for further modernization. In the Spanish case this took the form of an elaborate and bureaucratic structure of settlement. Urbanization quickly followed centralized administration. Administrators linked vast territories abroad with the urban centers in each area. In the English case a century later, enclave communities were established which drew more and more local peoples into contact. In this way, charters established new behavioral networks.[9]

Charter companies were corporate joint stock enterprises "licensed" to operate abroad. They began in medieval times, "chartered" mainly by municipalities.[10] Companies of "merchant adventurers," combining an exceptional entrepreneurial daring with a talent for mercantile organization, they were "willing to take a chance, to hazard one's life for one's goods in an enterprise that might bring a worthwhile reward." The organizational form followed. "It was a very usual practice in the Middle Ages for merchants in one city, or from a group of cities, doing business in some foreign mart to form a 'fellowship' or 'hanse' to further their common interests. Thus associated, they could jointly negotiate concessions which would assure them favorable conditions for trade, such as freedom from vexatious restrictions, permission to set up an authority of their own to order their affairs and settle disputes among themselves, and power to exclude from the trade any of their fellow townsmen who were not of their fellowship."[11]

Note the objects, freedom from restrictions, autonomous authority, monopoly privileges, and so forth. Money, transformed from a "noble metal" under mercantilism into an instrument of banking and credit, formed the basis for capitalist commercial and lending associations.[12] As capital markets increased so did the search for new product markets. Explorers and discoverers were employed by joint stock companies, operating under mixed state and private financial arrangements, these "entrepreneurs" being little more than pirates in the king's trade. "Adventurers" in the classic sense (or conquistadores), they staked out national claims to unexplored real estate at great personal risk. The biggest and most successful charter companies, like the African Company of Adventurers operating in West Africa, or the British East Indies Company or the Dutch East Indies Company, combined the entrepreneurial with the bureaucratic. Instruments of both rule and trade, they regulated themselves, imposed their control over their environment, and had their own soldiers and officers.[13]

Dutch and English companies, coming into world commerce somewhat later than the Spaniards, operated as "Crown agents." Largely autonomous, there was little supervision by home parliaments. The Spanish case was the reverse. Subject to direct royal control from Castile, empire was a remarkably well-organized system of trade, linking Manila, Havana, and Lima, the main entrepots and territorial viceroyalties with Seville. Networks of relay and garrison towns were settled, trade strictly regulated, with a reserved royal fifth or seventh. The organization of trade was equalled in thoroughness only by the organization of social life in the territories.[14]

Initially, of course, the Spanish case was a tremendous success. Yet, like its lumbering galleons, it could not sustain such a large and expensive empire. In Latin America it eventually was subject to political demands by free trading Creole nationalists. Corruption, too much bureaucratic restrictiveness, not to speak of the actual practices of mercantilism which relied on the accumulation of bullion, all helped to pull Spain down and build up her capitalist competitors. Wealth extracted from the Spanish Indies was used to buy ships and equipment in Genoa, Holland, and England, stimulating their industries and financial organization. The costs of empire then were, under mercantilism, so high that Spain sank into decline, its ships prey to the corsairs of the English, its technology, increasingly quaint, relegated to the museum of tail-end medievalism. Elsewhere mercantilism evolved. Within the shell of the chartering system there emerged a more capitalist form of enterprise.

In the Caribbean, West Africa, and the Indies, the Dutch, French, and British charters pioneered a new pattern. Wherever extraordinarily difficult health conditions prevailed, and with few good harbors and a largely unexplored hinterland, the charter company became a strategic instrument of penetration. Let us consider the West African example. "Charter companies were prominent during the early phase of sea-borne trade with West Africa, and especially during the seventeenth century. These companies were given trading monopolies over various sections of the African coast in return for fulfilling certain obligations. In the Netherlands the leading officially-sponsored firm was the Dutch West India Company (1621) which, besides having interests in the Caribbean, was also active along the West African coast during the seventeenth century. The most important French companies were the Compagnie des Indes Occidentales (1664), founded by Colbert on ideas formulated by Richelieu, the Compagnie du Senegal (1673), and the Compagnie du Guinee (1684). The principal English concern was the Royal African Company (1672), which succeeded the aptly named and unbusinesslike Royal Adventurers into Africa (1660). The presence of joint-stock companies in some branches of foreign commerce was mainly a result of the desire of subscribers to share the risks of African trade, which was notorious for its uncertainty, though in part it was also a response to the capital requirements of long distance trade, especially the need to invest fixed capital, such as forts and ships. The state issued charters because it saw the companies as useful agents of foreign policy, and hopefully, as a means of enriching the rulers too. The promoters sought government patronage as a means of attracting capital and eliminating competition. Interdependence was the basis of mercantilism: the power of the state was increased by measures designed to achieve a favorable balance of trade; at the same time particular interest groups sought to use state power as a means to private gain."[15]

Despite their political successes, the chartered companies, protagonists in the struggle for international power waged by nations, were in the end faulty economic bodies. They required large state subsidies. A growing overhead investment in ships, garrisons, arms, and other equipment, as well as a staff which required supervision and control in the end could not compete with high risk, low cost entrepreneurial traders. "They were asked to perform the most difficult of all commercial feats, the reconciliation of the capitalist ethic with public duty (an expectation which survives today only in certain nationalized industries). Their main achievements were as frontier agencies of the old colonial system, opening up markets which others were to exploit more effectively later on."[16]

Capitalist Charter companies eventually declined in favor of much more autonomous capitalist enterprises. Just as mercantilist charters had given way to capitalist ones, expatriate firms, following the railroads and administration,

> from being relatively small concerns dominated by one man or by a partnership, began to form limited liability companies. A few of many possible examples will suffice to illustrate this development, which began at the close of the nineteenth century: John Holt & Co. became a limited company in 1897; Cheri Peyrissac in 1880; R. & W. King, founded at the close of the seventeenth century, followed suit in 1911; and Maurel et Prom in 1919. Second, there was a move towards concentration. Many small businesses were eliminated, and the survivors amalgamated to produce a handful of very large firms. This trend was already apparent in the 1880's, and it developed still further during the first phase of colonial rule, until by 1930 there were three outstanding firms (The United Africa Company, the Compagnie Francaise de l'Afrique Occidentale, and the Societie Commerciale de l'Oest Africain). Between them these giants handled roughly two-thirds to three-quarters of West Africa's overseas trade, and their commercial network may be compared in size and importance with the administrative system operated by the colonial powers. Indeed, sometimes the 'District Officer' of U.A.C. had more local influence (and was certainly better paid) than the 'branch manager' of His Majesty's Government.[17]

Historically, then, although charters soon became too unwieldy and impossible to control, they stimulated a variety of local initiatives. Local capitalism led to the disappearance of the charter as a state trading combine. New marketing arrangements made possible new and larger scale economic investment opportunities. In the case of countries possessing a special commodity like bauxite, or iron ore, raw materials investment quickly became integrated into a much more complex system of economic relations. (The way it worked in West Africa has been described as follows. "The most prominent of the three firms was the United African Company which alone handled nearly half of West Africa's overseas trade in the 1930s. U.A.C. dominated British West Africa, and its subsidiaries bought and shipped about a quarter of the principal exports of French West Africa. U.A.C. was the weighty off-spring of two sizable parents: the Royal Niger Company, which was formed in 1886, and the African Association, which was established three years later. Although the Niger Company lost its royal charter in 1900, it continued to trade on a large scale, and in 1920 was bought by W. H. Lever, the soap magnate...."[18]

Colonialism was a way to connect innovative roles from the metropole with traditional ones by means of an ever more ramified network of marketing arrangements with commercial and mercantile roles spreading out from enclaves where they first began, to the furthest territorial boundaries.[19] The connection between territories was kept to a minimum while the interaction between metropole and territorial periphery intensified all the time. Increasingly, too, traditional groups, and most particularly ethnic ones, pursued their own interests within this sphere, sometimes separatist, more often parochial, occasionally acted virtually as an ethnic class vis-a-vis other classes. These, transformed into interest groups based on primordial loyalties, served to support rival claims for shares in the markets and more generally in the benefits of modernization.

In turn, a large class of mercantile compradores evolved, middlemen and entrepreneurs connected innovative institutions with the local ones, mediating, modifying. So the entire social structure changed. Rival claims over distribution of goods and services becoming politicized, resulted in a search for overarching political institutions.

Intermediate Stage Capitalist Crisis

What the primary stage of capitalism showed was how the charter company created a network of international systems linked into nationally dominated markets. The mercantilist system had failed. It was replaced by the British, Dutch, and French commercial networks which carved up world markets in terms of real estate. Eventually, charters became too cumbersome. They stimulated localized and small-scale activities which penetrated into the hinterlands, producing local trading and marketing facilities and above all extending the domestic market on which the international depended. Then came a period of classic imperialism and metropolitan crisis. War between the metropoles, followed by depression, seemed to fulfill the Marxist prophecy. What was happening in this intermediate stage seemed to follow precisely what Marx had described.

"(1) Concentration of means of production in few hands, whereby they cease to appear as the property of the immediate laborers and turn into social production capacities, even if initially they are the private property of capitalists. These are the trustees of bourgeois society, but they pocket all the proceeds of this trusteeship.

(2) Organization of labor itself into social labor: through cooperation, division of labor, and the uniting of labor with the natural sciences.

In these two senses, the capitalist mode of production abolished private property and private labor, even though in contradictory forms.

(3) Creation of the world-market.

The stupendous productivity developing under the capitalist mode of production relative to population, and the increase, if not in the same proportion, of capital-values (not just of their material substance), which grow much more rapidly than the population, contradict the basis, which constantly narrows in relation to the expanding wealth, and for which all this immense productiveness works. They also contradict the conditions under which this welling capital augments its value. Hence the crises."[20]

Marx thus pointed to the importance of productivity, the transformation of property, the privatization of expropriation of what was increasingly a social product and the universalization of this on a world scale. Lenin gave this an even more explicit organizational form. Translating the process of capitalism into instrumentalities, he says: "Monopoly capitalist combines—cartels, syndicates, trusts—divide among themselves, first of all, the whole internal market of a country, and impose their control, more or less completely, upon the industry of that country. But under capitalism the home market is inevitably bound up with the foreign market. As the export of capital increased and as the foreign and colonial relations and the 'spheres of influence' of the big monopolist combines expanded, things 'naturally' gravitated towards an international agreement among these combines, and towards the formation of international cartels.

"This is a new stage of world concentration of capital and production, incomparably higher than the preceding stages."[21]

The intermediate stage of capitalism, the "cartelization period" was one of intense competition and conflict between main metropolitan centers, between those with and without empire who wanted larger ones, that is, Imperial Germany, as well as between interlocking combines and trusts. This ambiguous situation, of polarized political conflict combined with internationalized finance intensified internal capitalist crises. This, according to the Marxists. Nor did liberals entirely disagree. They too regarded World

War I as a struggle for markets. They too saw the ensuing depression as producing polarization, driving out weak firms, with Fascism an extreme response to a thoroughly impossible economic situation. Where they differed with socialists was over cures rather than causes. Depression was a result of fundamental imbalances in the consumption function, interest, and labor supply. The liberal solution was monetary, not structural. Take Keynes for example. Keynes argued that Marx offered nothing but empty controversy.[22] In his *General Theory of Employment, Interest and Money* he mentions Marx only three times and these are passing references. Yet in his views about the causes of war, the character of European conflict, the nature of underconsumption (rather than Marx's overproduction), and a host of other factors, he was closer to Marx in his critique of capitalism than he acknowledged. The liberal solution, Keynesian economics plus democracy was not far removed from some of the views of socialists, particularly democratic ones.

The critique of cartels, monopolies, and restrictive practices under capitalism and its poor performance between the two wars, seemed to fit reasonably well the criticism of Marxists, Leninists, Socialist revisionists, and Keynesians. The latter made the least radical demands upon capitalism, calling not for its overthrow but for new employment and interest policies. None of the "liberal" solutions seriously envisaged the breaking up of large-scale enterprises and the return to competitive conditions of the market place. Rather, the modern liberal critique consisted of emphasizing changes in fiscal policy to stimulate investment and employment at home, and greater enterprise abroad. It involved the intervention of the state.

The great cartels which Lenin had forseen as the highest stage of capitalism were vulnerable to the depression just as the great charters were vulnerable to the nature of the market they created. Cartels did survive, and indeed some of them prospered, like I. G. Farben and other huge European corporations.[23] But the great depression turned the emphasis inwards towards political solutions. After World War II capitalism was given a new lease on life. The decline of colonialism, the emergence of new forms of technology and a global system of management came to the fore in the modern multinational corporation. Capitalist enterprise, which some had considered to be obsolescent if not obsolete took a great leap forward and surprised even its own advocates.

The intermediate period of capitalism then is characterized by crisis, war, state intervention, and fiscal policy. Before World War II public finances were too small a part of the total economy to make fiscal policy significant. But it is the growth of the public finance sector which affected national budgeting and merged public finance with international trade, payments, wages and incomes, money, and credit that characterizes the intermediate stage. Such facilities provided the basis for a growing domestic policy-making power by metropolitan governments. In the third stage, however, it is the expropriation of fiscal power and productive power by international private agencies which characterizes high capitalism, and indeed prejudices the domestic policy-making capacities of governments.[24]

Tertiary Capitalism and the Multinational Corporation

Despite all the predictions about mature capitalism and its likely failure, the period since World War II until the present recession has been one of unparalleled growth. The so-called backward parts of the world have been drawn into the world economy. Politically, there is a world of interdependent nations to replace the old mixtures of colonialism and imperialism. The problem now is one of so tightly integrated a network of monetary and credit flows, division of labor and technology in the manufacturing process, and the growth of scientific machines for "thinking," programming, and the application of science to technology that the previous stages of capitalism seem primitive by comparison. Just as the charter company at the early stage of capitalism was a rough and ready method of reducing risk for foreign enterprise while bringing to bear appropriate commercial techniques, and the cartel was an instrument of indirect national policy during the intermediate period of capitalism, so scientific innovation at exceptionally high rates and its application to a technological infrastructure has become the hallmark of high levels of industrialization. The market is more and more a system of informational bits, not only about buyers' wants and sellers' gains but also many other items. Included are evaluations of priority, public and private, which, reducing the significance of ownership itself, deal with calculations of sectoral intermesh. Fiscal and credit coordination requires predictions about international monetary flows. In such a context, the multinational corporation begins to be more of a problem for liberals than socialists. Socialists see the multinational corporation as an instrument able to dominate individual capitalist countries. They welcome the secular growth of large scale organization and its capacity to "socialize" industrial life. This helps pave the way to modern socialist economies. Moreover, the multinational form can be "progressive" vis-a-vis socialist systems by replacing the combine and cartel forms of organization characteristic of state capitalism. Such forms are now obsolete. Planning is too complex. Bottleneck information is insufficient and is no substitute for an information market. The problem of passing from intermediate to high industrialization is a major one for socialist countries because they are stuck at the cartel stage of organization while trying to avoid a market system or its equivalent. For them the multinational corporation is an interesting and attractive possibility as a way out of bureaucratic central control.

For liberals, the situation is reversed. Precisely because of the high degree of credit, monetary, and productive integration, and the extent to which policies of national governments are affected by the decisions of powerful multinational corporations, some means of controlling them has become critical. In the liberal view, so powerful have the multinational corporations become that effects of MNC decision-making jeopardizes the ability of governments to make decisive national policy. As a predominantly private enterprise, which operates, controls, or owns strategic productive facilities in more than one country, it is capable of a great many alternative strategies and shifting lines of product differentiation. Its enterprises are both productive and financial and its agents are of more than a single nationality, capable of operating in tandem and forging contractual relationships with governments according to various agreements. Because multinationals possess an

TABLE 1

Multinational Corporations in the World Economy (1971)
billions of U.S. dollars

Country	Direct Investment Abroad	Sales from Production Abroad*	Total Exports of Country
United States	86.0	172.0	43.5
Britain	24.0	48.0	22.4
France	9.5	19.1	20.4
West Germany	7.3	14.5	39.0
Switzerland	6.8	13.5	5.7
Canada	5.9	11.9	17.6
Japan	4.5	9.0	24.0
Netherlands	3.6	7.2	13.9
Sweden	3.5	6.9	7.5
Italy	3.4	6.7	15.1
Belgium	3.3	6.5	12.4
Other	7.4	14.7	90.4
Total	165.0	330.0	311.9

*Estimated to be twice the accumulated value of direct investment abroad.

Source: New York Times, August 13, 1974.

exceptional access to financial credit and productive facilities, which are controlled and exploited by means of highly mobile yet centralized managerial decision-making, their collective consequences are more powerful all the time. They are able to establish a modernizing agenda in some developing countries as no other single entity. Such "agenda setting" enables metropolitan centers not only to influence economic and social policies strongly in modernizing countries but do this over long enough periods of time. A rough guide to their relative significance by metropoles is provided by Table 1.

In this context, the United States and Britain remain powerful "imperial" countries. (West Germany and Japan, despite the fuss made about their astounding overall economic performance fall far behind.) In the United States alone, annual sales for home based multinationals are more than $1 billion. Of the ten largest multinational firms in the world, eight are American based, of which one fourth are located in developing countries and about 70 percent of that in Central and South America. Evidence of direct interference in the internal affairs of other nations was revealed in Chile where International Telephone and Telegraph and Kennecott Copper, firms whose property was nationalized, attempted to prevent the Allende regime from coming to office. If modernizing nations do not simply dance to the tune of the multinational directorate it is not for lack of the MNCs trying.

Hence, in the liberal view, huge enterprises, conglomerates, ever more international, form entirely new jurisdictions and financial empires. The bargains between nations and corporations have consistently favored the latter. One does not need to be a Marxist to believe that behind giant financial and productive conglomerates are their governments. As long as they are organizationally relatively efficient, reducing the element of risk in development, maximizing a flow of information, and able to mobilize resources not readily available to any particular country, they can serve as instruments of metropole foreign economic policy. Compared to other modes of development, whether the self-help project, the command economy, or the mixed private-public corporation, they are by far the most economically efficient.

The multinational corporation is a peculiarly transposable part of the huge financial infrastructure of trade, commerce, and credit of the Western world. Its organizational mobility is like that of migrants who reconstitute their social life wherever they go. The point is that the multinational corporation, enclave or octopus, represents a unique international social structure of productive relations. Eminently transferable, a flexible, functional unit, composed of a system of interlocking roles with a capacity to universalize productive processes, it contains both the problems and advantages of industrial life, both of which it generates in modernizing societies. To put the matter a little differently, the multinational corporation, in its variety of forms, is an historically distinct subsystem. Although it remains the most dynamic and autonomous part of capitalist industrial societies, it subsists on symbiotic relationships with nonindustrial societies by creating its own supporting social infrastructure. It is a breeder. Such a self-generating capacity leads both to greater dependency on the part of modernizing society, and it also holds out the prospects of greater long-run autonomy, depending a good deal upon opportunities, political strategies, and other situational and strategic factors.[25]

Technical progress provides the drive toward the structural international-ization of enterprises, while technical advances are likely to raise the optim-al scale of an enterprise for the realization of its minimum unit costs. The broadening of a field of action undertaken by an enterprise depends upon the progress made in the information and communication sciences. These make possible the simultaneous decentralization of its activities, and increasing control by a single decision-making center over many different independent economic entities. This pattern of deployment of information-using facilities affects the worldwide behavior of multinational corporations and allows them greater independence from the conventional controls of the market-place. At the same time that it is able to use market mechanisms to its own advantage or to extend its control, it is also able to facilitate expansion with-out reducing its flexibility. Hence the market and innovation within it be-comes the essential arena of effective action. The multinational corporation is able to use foreign markets as a natural extension of its own national market without being subject to ordinary restrictions. It thus obtains the ca-pacity for exceptional power, flexibility, and control. "In this way the exter-nal creativity of an economy, that it is to say, the ability of enterprises within it to project and establish their activities outside the national territory, is be-coming ever more a measure of the overall competitivity of an industrial system."[26]

Prebisch, considering the social effects of such production techniques developed in the industrial metropoles, showed how new productive organizations twist the tail of the economy and with it the bodies social and politic. Nor could he find a way out of this situation, "which frequently leads to conflict between the interests of the individual entrepreneur and the interest of the community...."[27] Appeals to the multinationals themselves are fruit-less. As Vernon puts it, "To the extent that multinational enterprises see a problem, it is the unremitting nipping at their flanks by governments, as the enterprises try to expand and prosper in the world environment."[28]

So far we have discussed the stages of capitalism suggesting how both liberals and Marxists view its evolution. For liberals, the problem is the power of monopolistic international firms over the domestic policy-making of governments, and the need for governmental interventions as a way of compensating for this development. To avoid both, the solution is to introduce more competition and decentralization by private firms and to find international fiscal and monetary arrangements appropriate to this end. For the socialists the evolution of the multinational corporation is negative as an instrument of metropolitan power upon periphery and positive as a stage in the transition from capitalism to socialism as well as freeing up or decentralizing bureaucratic control.

We now want to apply the same model to *modernization*. In this regard the model is no longer historical but contemporary, delineating stages of modernization according to systems of roles locked into the industrial network. Modernization is a function of such networks. What we are then dealing with is the following situation. The multinational corporation as a tertiary stage capitalist phenomenon has different impacts upon periphery countries according to what stage of development they are in. In countries at a primary stage of modernization they are likely to take the form of enclaves with little interaction with the rest of a population but highly significant for local governments and economics. At a high stage of development, on the contrary, they are likely to be intermeshed throughout the entire social and political network prevailing in a country and to have indirect impacts for which they take few responsibilities.[29]

THE LINEAR MODEL OF MODERNIZATION

Before turning to these matters it will be useful to define more precisely what we mean by modernization. Modernization occurs when roles developed in industrial metropoles are transferred to nonindustrial peripheries. The effect is dynamic. Such roles develop into institutional networks. There can be no bureaucrat without an administration, no soldier without an army, no teacher without an educational system, and so on. Modernization then is a spreading of key roles functional to industrial centers universalizing themselves institutionally in new settings. We call this process "institutional transfer."[30] The alternative is "boot-strapping," creating wholly self-generated institutional networks as occurred in the Soviet Union. Such a process is difficult for most countries to undertake, which is one reason why metropolitan institutional links are maintained.

Multinationals, purveyors of high technology, prime agents in institutional transfer, have an exceptional capacity to re-create or reproduce networks in a novel environment. They establish the conditions for their own functioning. The result is a network suitable for their prosperity locking a host country into a complex international system of reinforcing social institutions: financial, educational, technological. The dynamism of the MNC enables it to be an agenda-setting instrumentality. Balancing priorities according to developmental needs is affected by the institutional network, the transferred roles which blend with those of the host country. The MNC may work through legal channels, but from the standpoint of any national system it cannot exercise responsibility consonant with power. It can never be fully legitimate in this special sense whether or not it operates entirely by legitimate means or uses more unsavory methods.

Moreover, as the multinational corporation tries to influence political decisions, or alter the policies of a government in its favor, these efforts for the most part will be without the consent of the governed. The United Nations Commission has rightly emphasized the need for an equivalently multinational agency to control its effects. But no such agency now exists and it is not likely that there will be one able to do the job.[31]

For the moment, at any rate, the MNC is anything but a paper tiger. Whether its fortunes go up or down it will continue to exert an enormous effect on the political and economic life of nations. If it declines, the consequence will be catastrophic for the stability of world fiscal and monetary conditions. If it goes up, the impact of powerful private decisions on public social and economic life and national sovereignties will be tremendous.

This suggests that in the seesaw relationship between governments and the various forms of enterprise characteristic of each stage of capitalist development, there is an accumulation of private power which stimulates compensatory public policy. The strategy today for most poor countries whose governments are fragile due to the circumstances of primary modernization, is to gain the advantages of multinationals without paying the price of imposed tertiary stage capitalism. In highly modernized societies, the problem is to mediate a range of economic factors which engage society at every point.

In terms of a unilinear model, primary stage modernization in conjunction with tertiary stage capitalism produces exogamous enclaves. Usually, these develop extractive industries such as aluminum in Guinea, a primary stage modernizing country. In an intermediate stage of modernization, the MNC is larger than an enclave but not yet fully integrated into the network of domestic productive roles, thus forming an identifiable sector. In the tertiary stage of modernization, there is an elaboration of the MNC so great that it is interleaved with the entire network of economic and social roles to an extent where it is universalized, virtually invisible, and often taken for granted as for example U.S. multinationals in Canada. In terms of our model we can describe these situations as follows in Figure 1.

Zero industrialization we call "traditional." Traditional roles and networks include tribal systems or any other forms which predate industrial entry. Historically, the first inputs of modernity into so-called traditional societies were by means of charter companies. However, today we can consider countries to be scattered along the modernization continuum according to institutional role transfers. The impact of industrial societies will of course be extremely varied. Enclaving and sectoring are different from

FIGURE 1

Stages of Modernization of Multinational Corporations

Traditional   Industrial

Primary	Secondary	Tertiary

Roles and
Networks

MNC   MNC   MNC
Enclave   Sectors   Integration

Roles and
Networks

Industrial   Traditional

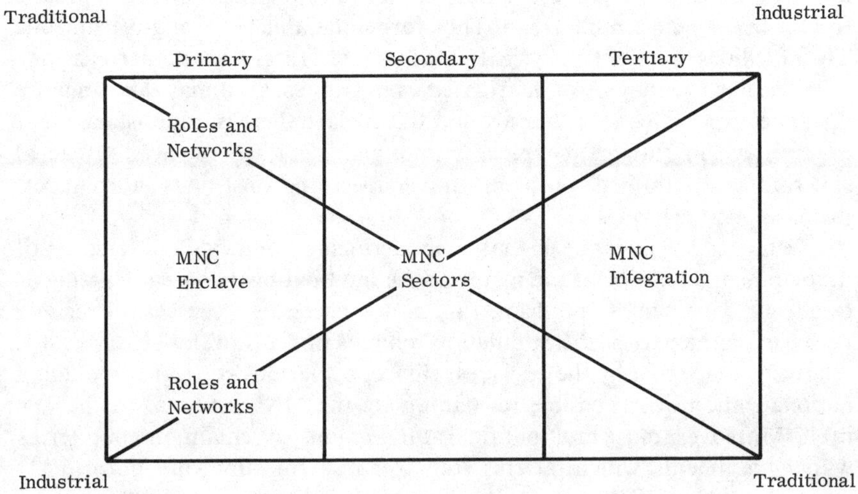

integration. An enclave can be taken over. So can a sector, although with greater difficulty. Once integration has occurred, the situation is very different. It can be argued that the greater the degree of modernization in a society the more vulnerable it is to industrial societies and most particularly to the multinational corporation.

Let us consider more fully the multinational corporation at each level of modernization.

Primary Modernization—"Enclaving"

Countries which we regard to be at the primary modernization stage are those where a large proportion of economic activity and social life remains in the traditional sector. They are not much integrated into world commercial markets for commodities or industrial products. Most primary modernizing countries are in Africa, although certainly not exclusively so. Bangladesh is in this stage. So is Burma.

For such primary stage modernizers, multinational corporations offer great advantages. By providing an external technology and expertise, as well as efficient methods of infrastructure development, they represent a form of economic organization which we have called "enclaving." Enclaving is the importation of role networks associated with productive enterprise which on the whole remain independent of the local population. Such methods of exploitation of resources are varied and can be undertaken alone, as a joint private venture with other forms or in collaboration with governments. Such enclaves build basic infrastructure feeder installations, which stimulate further investment from abroad. They form a taxable base for governments. Their facilities represent a physical growth "stock" for further modernization.

The enclave may be quite isolated as in Guinea. Or it may take on more dynamic social effects so that around the enclave there is established a new class in which foreign technicians and managers are replaced by local supernumaries trained both in universities and institutes abroad or, increasingly, local ones.

While it would appear that a modernizing country in this stage of development would be at the mercy of the multinational company acting as the agent of tertiary capitalism, this is not necessarily the case. Precisely because a large part of the population remains in the traditional sector, it is relatively unaffected by the enclaves. Hence, by various strategies, including nationalization, it is possible to manipulate the MNC and make it behave itself. Moreover, most multinationals are anxious to remain on good terms with governments which, at this stage of modernization, are notoriously unstable. Hence, if they enter into negotiations with one, they may find themselves dealing with another and a quite hostile one, shortly thereafter.

The MNC enclave offers a relatively efficient and manageable route to development in countries at a low level of modernization. It provides governments with financial resources. It opens up the economy to world trade. It expands opportunities. Its main difficulty is that in societies where resources are scarce, every decision to engage in a certain line of economic activity, and which requires some construction of facilities by governments, or provision of certain rebates, advantages of location, and so forth, is a decision not to do something else. Hence the agenda-setting power of the MNC is extremely important in primary stage developing countries less by design than by default. Governments at this stage of modernization simply cannot do many things, and a decision to do one thing is likely to preclude an alternative option.

Most African nations remain primary modernizers. MNC enclaving represents the only relatively efficient, easily available means to exploit raw materials: bauxite, as in Guinea; rubber and iron ore, as in Liberia; oil, as in Nigeria. Political means have been found in some African countries to control the MNC either by threats of nationalization or through mixed nationalization and corporation associations. Both Zambia and Zaire have been extremely successful in dismantling powerful multinational corporations by means of nationalization and leasing arrangements. In Guinea, the foreign corporations exploiting bauxite have had to be extremely circumspect.[32]

As we have suggested, countries in the primary stages of modernization are in one sense extremely vulnerable to the economic and financial power of the multinational corporation and in another less so than later stage modernizers. To control their specific policies, a country only needs the political determination to do so because in primary stage modernization where the multinational company remains an enclave, not yet thoroughly intermeshed in the role network, subsistence or near subsistence farming and other traditional modes of work still remain economically significant. There is a smaller press of the newly marginal and consequently less of a welfare burden for governments to contend with. Moreover, people may lead double or even triple lives, putting their farms or some other property in the care of family members while they participate in the commercial or industrial sector, perhaps becoming a migrant to a new town yet without losing rural security. Little is irrevocable. This contrasts with true marginals in intermediate or tertiary stage modernization societies where they can't go home again. Having burned their bridges they become utterly dependent on new occupations.

Intermediate Modernizing—"Sectoring"

Most countries today fall into the category of intermediate modernization. Some African countries are entering this stage, such as Nigeria. Many Latin American countries are in this condition, such as Peru. Countries at this stage characteristically find themselves less able to control the social effects of modernization than in primary modernization and the multinational corporation becomes a catering body for a compradore middle class. At the same time, by helping to stimulate an irreversible flow of populations out of the traditional sectors and into urban areas, without providing jobs, the multinational corporation creates latent dysfunctions in the form of high social overhead costs. Responsible for a large economic sector, it is maximally disruptive from a social point of view. The only solution is more modernization rather than less, more industry, more technological infrastructure.

It is in such circumstances that the multinational corporation becomes identified as an instrument of underdevelopment. Precisely because it helps to create conditions for which it assumes no responsibility (the formation of large marginal populations, for example,) it produces vast inequalities in income, wealth, life style, and power. This may in turn be so harmful that to deal with MNC-produced disparities requires a radicalization from above, where governments nationalize multinationals and integrate previously differentiated sectors of the society into a single unity, more socially homogenous.[33]

The object then is to pursue development and industrialization and enlarge the proportion of roles functional to growth, without the penalties and exogamous institutional mechanisms of control and dependency or gross inequities, both of which are associated with MNCs whose key developmental decisions are made outside the country and on the basis of factors which may be of limited relevance to the country itself and capitalism which is associated with inequality.

However, what might be called the "Algerian solution" of extensive nationalization is not so easily accomplished. Enclaves can easily be taken over and, if not run by the government, handed over to a consortium. But where MNC domination affects an entire sector, such as large-scale fabrication plants, or petrochemicals, the problem is that the efficiency of the operation, the profits of the firm, are a function of an international network of pricing, tax rebates, labor agreements abroad, and so forth. To nationalize the part of the organization operating in a particular country is not to nationalize the network. Hence, unless the multinational sector consists of subsidiaries in which there is virtually no connection to the productive and financial facilities of the rest of the firm, the Algerian solution is very awkward, leading to inefficiencies, bureaucracy, and a different set of social overhead costs. Dependency then, is built into intermediate modernization. Control cannot simply be a function of nationalization or any stock-in-trade solutions. No one can nationalize the metropolitan impact, the world market, the pricing and transfer policies.[34]

The problem is a serious one if as Furtado put it, "As external induction increases monetary income, the profit of the industrial nucleus linked with the domestic market also grows; increased investment within that nucleus follows, increasing further the level of money income."[35] Further expansion will then continue to favor the metropole resulting in severe disequilibria.

Furthermore, during intermediate modernization, countries receive certain kinds of multinational enterprises in parts rather than wholes. An automobile assembly plant may have some of its components built in West Germany, others in the United States, and still others somewhere else. Taking over the plant changes very little with respect to the determination of company policy. A satellite remains a satellite and there is not much which can be done about it as long as its products are desired.

As we have said, dependency is a consequence of the extent to which the profitability of an enterprise is a function of its total operation on the world market, its transfer pricing, and the organization of economies including tax shelters abroad, diversification to low labor cost countries for the production of parts, not to speak of the credit arrangements, debt servicing, and flows of monetary papers and discounting, all of which constitute total calculations of the MNC but which can never be controlled by means of nationalization. Hence, for example, nationalization of copper in Chile did not mean that the profits of the copper companies could automatically be realized by the Allende government.

MNC economic efficiency then is a function of the internationalization and deployment of the factors of production from the standpoint of the firm and not any single country. A country can introduce more factors into the calculus by the intervention of regulatory demands, but sheer nationalization can be very difficult.

Tertiary Stage Modernization—"Integrating"

Countries in tertiary stages of modernization show a dual aspect. They are maximally vulnerable to high capitalism and the multinational corporation. At the same time, they can—because of their high level of technological development and infrastructure growth—go it alone, assuming they have the resources and the population. The Soviet Union, China, and Cuba were countries with highly modernized sectors despite their general condition of backwardness. They had reallocatable surpluses and could in effect create a system of socialist bootstrapping by means of national planning and forced draft industrialization. Countries like Mexico, Argentina, and Brazil could all make great economic progress by following bootstrap methods and benefit from socialist revolutions like that of Cuba.

One reason why communist solutions are rare is that a high level of modernization also creates a large middle class which is dependent on the intermediate level roles supported by multinationals. The middle class is thus the instrument of MNC integration—totally involving it in a complex market and commercial network created by that same middle class. We say middle class rather than working class since most multinational enterprise is capital rather than labor intensive. It produces few semi- or unskilled jobs. It does provide local technocratic, clerical, and administrative posts, middle level managerial positions, and supply and servicing jobs for private contractors and small firms.

If radicalization or the growth of an effective labor movement which might threaten the autonomy of the MNC should occur, then the solution would be to make an alliance with middle class political parties. Barring that the preferred solution is to support governments in which labor, the MNC, and other business are all part of the same scheme of things, that is, corporatist states. Since the higher the input of multinational investment, the greater the degree of inequality in society, the political problem is to prevent inequality from degenerating into violence against property. Governments as much as the MNCs have a stake in the control of conflict.

Where such cooperation cannot be worked out, the problem of how to deal with the MNC at a tertiary level of modernization is a very difficult one. Simple nationalization does not work. The big alternative is to go into a totalistic socialism in which control over every aspect of social and political life becomes a prerequisite and in which planning is a substitute for the market. Other alternatives are limited. The preferred one is a democratic and liberal regime with large middle class support. The less preferred one is a corporatist regime.

Is policy by multinational corporations increasingly determined by such political considerations? There is greater caution exercised today than ever before. The experiences of ITT and other large scale enterprises have resulted in very bad publicity. There is increased political wariness on the part of political leaders. But behind the picture of multinational domination and threats that an elaborated and integrated form of penetration suggests (and which we in the United States are just beginning to be aware of as Arab and Iranian oil producing countries begin to buy into U.S. firms and purchase large real estate and other holdings), there is a quite different one in the minds of the managers themselves. They regard their operations with pride and point to efficiencies under circumstances which would otherwise conspire against a well-run operation. They may support artistic and other good works as Kaiser did in Cordoba. Officials are often proud of their companies including the physical entity, the plant itself, the symbol of dynamic enterprise and modernity. These, often attractively designed, are not at all like the factories of old-fashioned labor intensive industries. Indeed, modern MNCs produce little of the ugliness of factory towns.[36] More likely, the MNC has its office in an architecturally dramatic building, with well-landscaped lawns and gardens. Production facilities are often established away from the center of towns or in thinly populated areas. If, as sometimes happens, they should be enveloped by squatter populations, the picture changes radically. The gardens will be surrounded by protective steelmesh fences, patrolled by armed guards and dogs. Outside the gates, in the *barriadas* a hostile and sullen population, only semiemployed, stares at them in resentment. This grotesque neighborliness between the people and the multinational corporation is not uncommon.

Perhaps this puts the matter too dramatistically. But it enables us to visualize the paradoxes we have tried to describe, that is, the social overhead costs of multinational development. At its worst, the result is a "surveillance society" with everyone watching everyone else. Security conscious officers of multinational corporations, with all their property to protect, curry favor with friendly political leaders and parties. They attempt to eliminate "radicals" and other hostile elements.

Perhaps here is the most extreme paradox of all. Security for the MNC is security of property, security of access to markets and decisions of government. But it does not extend very far to security of tenure for workers, or appropriate welfare considerations. Of course, health schemes and pension plans exist. But rarely can they provide for the community in which the social impact of the multinational corporation is greatest. Hence, the need for the first kind of security, political, arises because the second is ignored. Multinationals have a limited liability in that regard. Yet it is precisely where social change is the most rapid and where the need for cushioning the shock through social security is the greatest.[37]

Multinationals are exceptionally security minded. Since a great deal of their operation depends on high capital investment, to protect that investment is uppermost in their minds. But, because they are not heavily dependent on labor, MNCs do not need to worry much about strikes or other labor action. Where the marginals are available so is a ready alternative labor supply. Managerial and factory personnel can be brought in from the outside and they remain subservient to the interests of the firm.

This is why so many political regimes in tertiary stage modernization tend not only to act on behalf of the multinational corporation but, sharing in the common desire for political security, opt for some form of corporatism. Then a tandem relationship is possible. The multinationals bring growth and, by "investing and marketing abroad, the company not only can start new growth from a low market share but also can usually make acquisitions to facilitate its entry. It can easily export its management and technological know-how by moving only a tiny group of employees abroad. By operating a full-fledged company in the foreign country, it can offer a full line of service and managerial backup to the marketing effort. Profitability as well as growth may be higher in the foreign affiliate than at home. IBM is a prime example of this approach, all over the world."[38]

In turn, multinationals favor regimes which will impose stability on the political environment, help in the recruitment of outside personnel, and contribute important infrastructure facilities, ports, transportation, real estate, housing for personnel, and so forth. Corporate regimes tend to offer special conditions to attract multinationals, ensure them high return on investments, favorable and controlled supply of labor, tax rebates, and other fiscal advantages. Hence, tertiary stage modernization and corporatism go together.

If our assumptions are correct, then the greater the degree of modernization, the more political instability. The more instability the more the multinational corporations are forced into the position of trying to control it. In this respect their political meddling is not simply ideological. It becomes necessary if they are to protect and enlarge their investment. For them the optimal arrangement is when metropole and periphery collaborate in mutual security and technical exchange. If the security people can hold down political instability, the technical people can promote further industrialization.[39] If this can be done "democratically" so much the better.

SOCIALIST AND NEO-MERCANTILIST ALTERNATIVES

The simplest way for a modernizing country to avoid these consequences is to opt for socialist alternative modes of development. The trouble is that the socialist alternative offers other problems. Most socialist criticisms of how capitalism works are better than their solutions. One of the major shortcomings of socialism as a program of development in a tertiary stage modernizing country is that socialism cannot be transferred piecemeal. As a system of institutional transfer either the whole country must become socialist in some meaningful political sense, or the enterprises run by socialists or socialist sectors of a nonsocialist economy are likely to be bureaucratic and inefficient. Most people in tertiary stage modernizing countries are not eager for a "Cuba solution." They are not willing to undertake the "Totalization" of the political and social structure. The dead hand of Stalinism is less preferred than the hiding hand of capitalism.[40]

Most of what passes for socialism in primary and intermediate stage modernizing societies is what Dumont calls "proto-socialism."[41] It is far less efficient than the multinational corporation. It results from bureaucratization and "ossification." Its hidden costs are not the growth of a middle consuming class riding on the backs of marginals but a bureaucratic parasitism. As emphasis shifts from an economic to a political one, as under socialism it must, so administrative functions take precedent. As the need for planning and control assumes a higher priority, mistakes become more costly and the political aspects become more important than the productive decisions themselves. As Hirschman has observed, "As soon as we move from the sphere of production to that of administration, tasks lose their definiteness and achievement its 'testability.' It is therefore to be expected and is indeed widely confirmed by observation and experience that efficiency will be higher in the plant than in the office-operations of industrial firms."[42] Magnify these circumstances on a governmental level and with political administrative cadres and we begin to gain some perspective into the social overhead costs of modernizing socialism.

The modernizing society is thus damned if it does and damned if it doesn't. If the multinational corporation under high modernization presents us with the spectre of corporatism and military regimes, directed against incipient radicalization, the socialist alternative presents us with incipient bureaucratism and the dangers of what can best be called "proto-Stalinism"(or what Ali Mazrui called a Leninist-Czar). Neither prospect is particularly agreeable. Moreover, both the industrial capitalist and socialist metropoles are hostile to socialist economic development when it is combined with democratic political systems. For example, by using socialist ends and democratic means, Chile under Allende outraged both "camps."[43]

Socialist forms of production require a huge bureaucratic overhead. Because there is little separation between economic and political arrangements, the socialist state itself acts in a sense as a potential multinational corporation or state capitalist enterprise which as Dumont has stated, can be politically dangerous as well as extremely inefficient.[44] The social cost of rising unrest and the latent or unplanned and unforeseen structural consequences of planning can lead to a socialist form of imperialism. Such forms of development bring their own dangers, as virtually every third world political leader is aware. More and more the preferred political strategy is a mixed solution; becoming "socialist" in name but preferring the narrow economic efficiency and large social inefficiency, of the multinational corporation in practice. As we have suggested, the MNC does not like such strategies. It prefers political corporatism or as Huntington calls them praetorian regimes, especially under conditions of high modernization. "In the world of oligarchy, the soldier is a radical; in the middle class world he is a participant and arbiter; as the mass society looms on the horizon he becomes the conservative guardian of the existing order. Thus, paradoxically but understandably, the more backward a society is, the more progressive the role of its military."[45]

It is perhaps also true that in a world of modernization, the larger the consuming middle class, the more likely the degree of political competition, conflict, bargaining and corruption, and the more likely the soldier is to be a modernizing oligarch, providing the political control which makes investment by multinational firms more attractive, and policies which favor their activities. Corporatism then is the political result of the hidden hand, the consequence of tertiary capitalist development in modernizing societies, the social overhead costs of which include political instability and social dislocation.

Aside from socialist or neomercantilist alternatives, both of which affect liberals, what other means of MNC control or affiliation are possible? As a growing force, the multinationals will not be stopped by international cooperation such as proposed by the UN and groups of well-meaning citizens. Nor will they be controlled from within excepting under the conditions described. An "OPEC" solution is only possible in the short run as the demand for conventional raw materials and energy supplies increases. In the long run, product innovation will likely generate its own form of import substitution, leaving the raw materials exporting countries with surpluses.

With its universalizing impulses conditioned to fit local conditions but basically too powerful for most modernizing countries to check, and with advantages too close at hand to be ignored by host governments, the multinational corporations can only be controlled by strong government. They make take the form of corporatist bureaucratic regimes, which we have elsewhere described as "neomercantilist."[46] Neomercantilist systems have the following characteristics. They are development minded, that is, they have an ideological predisposition for growth. They favor efficiency. They have an idea of organizational autonomy. They distinguish between policy and planning and favor the former over the latter. They utilize the market. They do not map out detailed programmatic goals but rather prefer to remain flexible, sustaining policies which prove to pay off. They are autocratic. They tend to tolerate token opposition and facade parliaments but repress dissidents. They use government resources and facilities in collaboration with multinational corporations to expand the technologically proficient cadres at the expense of intellectuals (who are tolerated as long as they are compliant). At the same time, neomercantilist systems cater to a network of functional interest groups. They use trade unions to control and discipline labor and provide labor bureaucracies with security. The labor bureaucracies are not only instruments to control labor, they bargain for welfare benefits. Neomercantilist systems can be reformist and antiaristocratic. They may promulgate land reforms. They maintain the support of a consuming middle class while manipulating a jingoistic labor. The most successful neomercantilist systems are those which provide an expanding middle for the working class to enter while controlling the marginals by punitive measures and the dole.

Neomercantilism in tandem with the multinational corporation is a method of control of modernization which has become more common as modernization itself proceeds. It is the main alternative to some form of socialism. Neomercantilism provides political controls, mobilizes basic resources, establishes technical and fiscal networks, and has the power to generate an institutional infrastructure favorable to the multinationals. Hence, our original proposition that the greater the degree of modernization, the greater the likelihood of either the socialist model or the neomercantilist model. China and Cuba represent the socialist alternative. Brazil is the prototype of the neomercantilist model.[47]

Are international controls feasible? Some look to the United Nations as a way of getting the best of both possible worlds, that is, control of the multinationals without political intervention. A recent study group has recommended that "in order to encourage true internationalization and international responsibility of MNCs, supranational corporations could be chartered by the United Nations or a special agent set up for that purpose. Tax revenue could then go to the international body."[48]

The success of this proposal is doubtful. There are too many competing political pressures and interests at work in the UN. Moreover, there is likely to be little agreement about how to monitor MNC activities. As more socialist countries employ MNCs in the conduct of their own affairs, international control over MNCs may be interpreted as interference in national policy making.

The most useful purpose the United Nations can serve, aside from providing some gainful employment for its more earnest civil servants, is to expose the scope of multinational activities. A team working on the implications of the multinational corporation, under the overall direction of Under-Secretary-General Philippe de Seynes, recommended in 1975 that a permanent United Nations body keep the MNCs under continuous review, establish data centers about their activities, and provide a corps of technicians and administrators to help governments in their dealings with MNCs.

The UN report that recommends the internationalization of control over MNCs[49] (a likelihood about as effective as UN peacekeeping activities) uses language exceptionally weak even for that body. A commission on multinational corporations should be established under the Economic end Social Council with a "code of conduct for governments and multinational corporations to be considered and adopted by the Economic and Social Council...."[50]

Putting the matter in this light seems to offer two unhappy choices to countries at the third stage of modernization. Either they become the subjects of "administrative kulaks" who mostly do not know what they are doing but rather are experts at bureaucratic survival and competition, or they are victims of externally controlled MNCs who are content to let the social chips fall where they may, and hope for tough regimes to prevent the wrong people from picking them up.

THE MNC AND INDUSTRIAL ORGANIZATION

Some of the difficulties described are the common concern of liberals and socialists. There are at least two problems with both points of view which stem directly from the unilinear model itself. Liberals see the need to control the multinational corporation by political means or by breaking them up. Socialists regard the MNC as a function of tertiary capitalism which will give way to socialism.

One problem with both points of view is that they pay insufficient attention to the multinational corporation as a thing in itself. As an instrument of certain technological factors, it can work under both socialism and capitalism. In the case of industrial socialist countries, failure to find equivalents for the market which in capitalist countries provides information through a complex system of competitive arrangements has produced a condition in Eastern Europe where relative growth is declining and internal inefficiencies mounting. The search for a market formula under conditions of socialism is a continuous one in the Soviet Union and, although debate is muted, this is because the issues are potentially explosive. When alternatives emerge, such as in Yugoslavia or Czechoslovakia under Dubcek, the reaction is intense. While political unrest may not be tolerated in the Soviet Union, "the whole intricate mechanism of relations between 'the state' and 'the economy' needs mending. Similarly, sociologists have observed the sluggishness of the labor force, or the working class, its restless turnover, 'lack of discipline', and escape in alcohol, which directly concerned the 'state' as employer and the party as 'guide'. Youth has been a multifaceted problem. The growing numbers of high school graduates are frustrated when they find themselves on jobs without adequate compensation and mechanization, the results of the slowness of economic development and inadequacy of industrial organization."[51]

From the standpoint of linearity, the problems of tertiary capitalism and high socialism are pretty much the same. So intricate is high industrialization that the advantages of central planning disappear. Marx and Engels and their successors in socialist countries "had no inkling of how difficult it was going to be to collect realistic information about the state of the economy and its enterprises, to process this information and hand down orders to enterprises in an intelligible form. The processing was done in the form of 'material balances', a very crude way, but there was no other available at least at that time. Information processed by this method arrived at the center garbled, partly because they were not able to produce it or were not asked the right questions. Orders issued after the processing, which could make them coherent let alone optimal, were incomplete because they could not be anything else if they were to be issued in technical terms."[52]

Socialist countries are coming to rely on the multinational corporation. The MNC can be separated from its connection to capitalism. Socialist countries are turning to Western companies. "Already there are more than a thousand agreements between Western corporations and Communist countries. Many of these are simple arrangements for 'turn-key' plants. (A multinational corporation builds a plant, turns it over to the Communist government, and is paid out of future production.) But a number of Communist countries in Eastern Europe have found that long-term involvement by the multinational corporation is a better way to insure continuous inputs of managerial and technological resources. Now some East European governments, particularly Yugoslavia, have followed this logic a step further, and to insure full access to the latest generation of technology have invested abroad, often in joint ventures with multinationals. Should this trend continue, it would require ideologists to reinterpret their view of imperialism as the transfer of labor's surplus value across national borders and raise questions about the simple equation of multinational corporations, capitalism and imperialism."[53]

It now appears that the MNC is very much a feature of high industrialization, socialist or capitalist. This should turn attention to some of its internal characteristics and features rather than its place in history. A good deal of the work now concentrated on the multinational corporation deals with it as an entity which is not likely to disappear quickly, is not exclusive to capitalism, is changeable, and which can be employed by modernizing countries as well as industrial ones.

THE MNC AS AN INSTRUMENT OF METROPOLE DEPENDENCY

Whatever one's views, the ability of the MNC to survive in an increasingly uncertain economic and political climate, and its capacity to serve various masters, tells us a good deal both about the future of capitalism and socialism. To the extent to which it functions autonomously or becomes available to communist countries, it raises the question of whether or not the multinational corporation is a uniquely suitable device for mobilizing high technology and resources for productive purposes under any circumstances. Moreover, if the OPEC countries are in any way an indication, MNCs may also be instruments of a reverse economic vulnerability and dependency. There is no reason why, at least in the short run, the multinational corporation cannot be converted from an instrument of a metropolitan power into one which, in the face of increased profits, will serve any country holding out the promise of its survival.[54]

The OPEC countries have obtained multinational acquiescence to co-ordinated pricing arrangements, and succeeded in raising the 1974 price of a barrel of oil four times over its 1973 level. Early predictions of a $600 billion dollar income to oil-producing countries over the next five years may prove to have been too high. It is doubtful too that the final result will be sufficiently substantial to represent a drastic worldwide reallocation of wealth. But only in primary stage modernizing societies where they represent enclaves can they easily be nationalized or transformed into mixed state-private enterprises controlled by periphery not metropole.[55]

However, continuing scarcities and the stagflation of the 1970s made the largest MNCs particularly vulnerable to political pressure abroad because they had so much to lose at home. It was thought, in the mid-1970s, moreover, that similar conditions could eventually prevail in other enclave situations such as Zambian copper and other raw materials products. To reverse such a trend in the short run would require that the Western world drastically lower its levels of consumption. But this would reduce industrial momentum concurrently with sharp increases in unemployment. With worldwide shortages looming larger all the time, conservation plus sustained domestic industrial production would require the kind of harsh planning and controls we associate with wartime economics or socialism. Both solutions are, in the West, politically unappetizing, involving decisions for the long run which governments are anxious to avoid.

Under such circumstances, the assumption that the MNC is necessarily the instrument of the metropole rather than a modernizing periphery has become somewhat moot. It might also become a Trojan horse inside metropolitan gates. Should this happen on a large scale, the multinational corporation might be transformed into a weapon in the hands of formerly dependent countries. But in the long run this is unlikely.

SOME SPECULATIVE CONCLUSIONS

The only thing that can be said with any certainty is that such a situation would be politically dangerous. However, we are not predicting such a reversal. More likely the power of the multinational corporation will be used, like that of a double agent, both ways. What makes the modern MNC so interesting and so difficult to fathom is precisely its lack of intrinsic relationships to any capitalism or any metropolitan society.[56] The Marxist view is that the multinational corporation is a feature of advanced or mature capitalism, making available for export capital intensive industry and combining in an exceptionally efficient way two forms of capitalism which Marx in his day saw as separate: industrial and financial. The multinational corporation, although a unique "carrier," or organizational synthesis of the two, represents not only the high water mark of capitalism but of industrial organization. Marx believed that the industrial side of capitalism would create or generate an industrial proletariat which would have a revolutionary potentiality. But the typical multinational corporation is capital rather than labor intensive. It does not generate much of a proletariat so much as a counterpart bourgeoisie. It does not stimulate revolution in capitalist societies and it does produce a middle class in socialist ones. It is thus an instrument of a universalized bureaucratic middle which has certain well-defined characteristics including a preference for consumerism. It represents a culture of commodities, precisely the sort of thing for which Marx reserved his greatest contempt.[57]

The multinational corporation then is a particular form of enterprise characterizing modern industrial expansion. Under situations of high risk investment, a condition common in developing countries, where instability and uncertain markets discourage smaller and more vulnerable investors and enterprise it offers certain advantages. It has an exceptional capacity to redesign and direct technology flows and investment across national boundaries. By stimulating national development it also fosters a more genuine interdependency among nations. In short, what Marxists consider to be the source of the problem, liberal theorists consider to be its solution.[58]

Who is more right is in some ways not an empirical question but a matter of which pictures of the world one prefers to carry in his head.

Internationalization and mutual dependency may appear as a triumph of liberalism, a necessity for the survival of capitalism, or a method by which the rich nations exploit the poor. They may appear to be a foundation for a network of genuinely collaborative relations in which production-elites from metropole and periphery plan joint development efforts or the very core of clientcy and dependence. Present jurisdictions and boundaries, blurred by a more elaborated system of negotiated associations—regional and multilateral—may be perceived either as a form of the new internationalism or the new imperialism. In these regards, the role of an agency such as the multinational corporation must remain very much in the eye of the beholder.[59]

Whatever one's views about such matters, what is clear is that the MNC is no mere epiphenomenon. The common concern is its special and autonomous status. Sitting foursquare in a world of nations, MNCs appear to be able to make and use rules for their own benefit. Recent disclosures about the political behavior of the worst mannered and cavalier of them (like the ITT) have aroused even stronger reactions than documentation of their economic activities.[60] Many of those who countenance the MNC as an appropriate form of efficient development will still condemn its political activities. Both liberals and Marxists tend to agree that even if the MNC represents an evolving extraterritorial capitalism, it still provides certain advantages such as technological innovation and managerial flexibility (although these may now be suffering from hardening of the arteries brought on by a more depressed economic environment). Both recognize that these bring on political demands as well.

What then are our conclusions? We have suggested that the multinational corporation, despite the inequalities and instabilities it generates, is an efficient alternative to bootstrapping, indeed, perhaps the only one. We have suggested that socialism in modernizing societies produces a huge bureaucratic overhead with which the social overhead of the MNC must be compared. We have indicated that multinational corporations might be of great benefit in highly industrial socialist societies. We have suggested that, no matter what its role, however, the multinational corporation will be extremely difficult to control and under circumstances of high modernization will tend toward corporatist or neomercantilist political solutions.

Because these are such important questions, the multinational corporation will continue to be of more than scholarly interest. The literature on the subject of MNCs deals with the general impact of large economic organizations "on the nature and structure of the interrelationships between economics and politics," and has attracted much scholarly research and writing from several disciplines. It has received attention from scholars across the board, from law to journalism, economics to sociology. Studying the multinational corporation shows how strategic it is intellectually because it reveals weaknesses in our theories and understanding of organized agenda-setting in modern life. It requires an interdisciplinary analysis. "Economic theory is deficient both in describing an economy based on and controlled by corporate actors and in explaining the actions and impact of these actors. The study of the MNC's is, therefore, an important field for cross-disciplinary research. Because of the large interface between corporations and governments, its study has to draw on both economics and political science."[61]

Much remains to be done. The MNC still needs to be "located" in a more powerful theoretical framework. Work along these lines is being undertaken by scholars as diverse as Fernando Henrique Cardoso, Philippe Schmitter, Jose Nun, and Guillermo O'Donnell on the one hand, and Raymond Vernon, Jack Behrman, and the Committee on Finance of the U.S. Senate[62] on the other. Such diversity attests to an exceptional conceptual liveliness.

Still required, however, is much more intensive and probing research on the multinational corporation itself as a universalized instrument of high industrialization. Our consideration has been primarily in terms of tertiary capitalism and the impact of the MNC upon countries at various stages of modernization. That, however, is only a beginning. There are many more ramifications to be explored.

NOTES

1. See R. L. Curry and D. Rothchild, "On Economic Bargaining Between African Governments and Multinational Corporations," *Modern African Studies,* vol. 12, no. 2 (June 1974): 184.

2. See David and Marina Ottaway, *Algeria, the Politics of a Socialist Revolution* (Berkeley: University of California Press, 1970), pp. 225-26. At this time the Algerians were interested in Yugoslavian experiments, with worker-management committees, and very strongly influenced by Trotskyites.

3. See V. I. Lenin, *Imperialism* (New York: International Publishers, 1939), passim. Lenin, drawing on Marx, speaks of this process as the concentration of production, that is, "the monopoly arising therefrom; the merging or coalescence of banking with industry—this is the history of the rise of finance capital and what gives the term 'finance capital' its content." (p. 48)

4. See Albert O. Hirschman, *The Strategy of Economic Development* (New Haven: Yale University Press, 1958), passim.

5. See Jose Nun, "Superpoblacion relativa, e jercito industrial de reserva y masa marginal," in *Revista Latino Americana de Sociologia,* no. 2, (July 1969): 178-235.

6. Among the best known examples are GM, Unilever, IBM, ITT, Exxon, and Ford. See R. Vernon, *Sovereignty at Bay* (New York: Basic Books, 1971), pp. 132-33.

7. Ibid., p. 88. See also Robin Murray, "The Internationalization of Capital and the Nation State," in John H. Dunning, ed., *The Multinational Enterprise* (New York: Praeger, 1971), pp. 265-88.

8. See Eli F. Heckscher, *Mercantilism* (London: George Allen and Unwin, 1955), p. 21. See also R. Trevor Davies, *The Golden Century of Spain* (London: Macmillan and Co., 1961), and C. H. Haring, *The Spanish Empire in America* (New York: Harcourt, Brace, and World, 1963).

9. See Magali Sarfatti, *Spanish Bureaucratic-Patrimonialism in America* (Berkeley: Institute of International Studies, 1966), passim. See also Rosemary Arnold, "A Port of Trade: Whydah on

the Guinea Coast," in Karl Polany et al., *Trade and Market in the Early Empires* (Glencoe: The Free Press, 1957).

10. See Eleanore Carus-Wilson, *Medieval Merchant Adventurers* (London: Methuen, 1954), p. xii.

11. Ibid., p. xiii.

12. See Max Weber, *General Economic History* (Glencoe: The Free Press, 1950).

13. For useful discussions of these see Clive Day, *The Policy and Administration of the Dutch in Java* (London: Oxford University Press, 1966).

14. Perhaps the most detailed analysis of the Spanish system is Robert Bigelow Merriman, *The Rise of the Spanish Empire in the Old World and the New* (New York: Cooper Square Publishers, 1962), four volumes. The best short study is C. H. Haring, *The Spanish Empire in America* (New York: Harcourt, Brace and World, Harbinger Book Edition, 1963).

15. See A. G. Hopkins, *An Economic History of West Africa* (New York: Columbia University Press, 1973), p. 92. See also Edward Reynolds, *Trade and Economic Change on the Gold Coast 1807-1874* (London: Longman, Inc. 1974).

16. Ibid., p. 93.

17. Ibid.

18. Ibid., p. 199.

19. See P. T. Bauer and B. S. Yamey, *The Economics of Underdeveloped Countries* (Cambridge: James Nisbet and the Cambridge Press, 1957).

20. See Karl Marx, *Capital* (Moscow: Foreign Languages Publishing House, 1962), vol. III, "Excess Capital and Excess Population," pp.1-261.

21. See Lenin, op. cit., p. 69.

22. See his letter to George Bernard Shaw, 1st January 1935, quoted in R. F. Harrod, *The Life of John Maynard Keynes* (London: Macmillan, 1951), p. 462.

23. See Vernon, op. cit., pp. 81-86.

24. For a discussion of this intermediate period see Gunnar Myrdal, *Beyond the Welfare State* (New Haven: Yale University Press, 1960), pp. 70-71.

25. See G. O'Donnell and D. Linck, *Dependencia y autonomia,* (Buenos Aires: Amorrortu, 1974), passim.

26. See Bruno Colle, "Private Supranational Power (Multinational Enterprises and European Integration)," *Lo Spettatore Internazionale,* vol. IX, no. 1 (January-March, 1974): 25. 25.

27. See Raul Prebisch, *Change and Development*; Report Submitted to the Inter-American Development Bank (Washington, D. C., 1970), p. 192.

28. See Raymond Vernon, *Sovereignty at Bay* (New York: Basic Books, 1971), p. 261.

29. See Harry G. Johnson "The Ideology of Economic Policy in the New States," in Harry G. Johnson ed., *Economic Nationalism in Old and New States* (London: George Allen and Unwin, 1968), pp. 124-41.

30. See D. E. Apter, *Ghana in Transition* (Princeton: Princeton University Press, sec. rev. ed. 1973), passim.

31. See Jack N. Behrman, "Governmental Policy Alternatives and the Problem of International Sharing," in John H. Dunnings ed., *The Multinational Enterprise* (New York: Praeger, 1971), pp. 293-94.

32. See the interesting discussion of such matters in Julius K. Nyerere, *Freedom and Unity* (London: Oxford University Press, 1967), pp. 209-11.

33. See William B. Quandt, *Revolution and Political Leadership: Algeria, 1954-1968* (Cambridge: The MIT Press, 1969), p. 272. Quandt says, "An important manifestation of nationalism in Algerian political culture is seen in the idea that the state has a right to intervene in many areas of national life. In particular the state must control its own resources and territory. While xenophobia is virtually absent in Algeria, there is strong insistence that foreigners should not influence her internal politics."

34. See Maurice Halperin, "Growth and Crisis in the Latin American Economy," in James Petras and Maurice Zeitlin, *Latin America, Reform or Revolution* (New York: Fawcett Publications, 1968), pp. 44-75.

35. See Celso Furtado, *Development and Underdevelopment* (Berkeley: University of California Press, 1964).

36. See Prebisch, op. cit., p. 193.

37. See Guy Perrin, "The Need for Security in the Advanced Societies of Today and Tomorrow," *Bulletin,* International Institute for Labour Studies, no. 8 (1971): 3-25.

38. Senate Finance Committee, *Implications of Multinational Firms for World Trade and Investment and for U.S. Trade and Labor* (Washington, D. C.: GPO., 1973), p. 121.

39. See Robert A. Packenham, *Liberal America and the Third World* (Princeton: Princeton University Press, 1973).

40. Debates about "Totalization" underlie much of the discussion going on among socialists within the Soviet Union about decentralization. See the discussion of Bukharinism and Stalinism and its modern counterparts in Moshe Lewin, *Political Undercurrents in Soviet Economic Debates* (Princeton: Princeton University Press, 1973), passim.

41. See Rene Dumont, *Socialism and Development* (New York: Praeger, 1973), p. 110.

42. See Albert O. Hirschman, *The Strategy of Economic Development* (New Haven: Yale University Press, 1938), p. 154.

43. The outrage was of course considerably more than that. The cooperation of the CIA and the ITT to "destabilize" the Allende regime is only one example of the way in which multinationals and metropolitan power can service each other. See Richard Fagen, "The United States and Chile: Roots and Branches," *Foreign Affairs*, Vol. 53, no. 2 (January 1972): 297-313.

44. Dumont, op. cit., p. 110.

45. See Samuel Huntington, *Political Order in Changing Societies* (New Haven: Yale University Press, 1938), p. 221.

46. See D. E. Apter, *The Politics of Modernization* (Chicago: The University of Chicago Press, 1965), passim.

47. See Fernando Henrique Cardoso, "Associated-Dependent Development: Theoretical and Practical Implications," in Alfred Stepan ed., *Authoritarian Brazil* (New Haven: Yale University Press, 1973), pp. 142-76.

48. Conference Report, "Strategies for Peace" (Muscatine, Iowa: the Stanley Foundation, 1973).

49. See United Nations Economic and Social Council, Report of the Group of Eminent Persons, "The Impact of Multinational Corporations on the Development Process and on International Relations" (New York: United Nations, Document E/5500, May 1974).

50. See United Nations, *The Impact of Multinational Corporations on the Development Process and on International Relations* (United Nations: Report on the Secretary-General, June 14, 1972), E/5000), p. 5.

51. See Moshe Lewin, *Political Undercurrents in Soviet Economic Debates* (Princeton: Princeton University Press, 1974), pp. 338-39.

52. See Ljubo Sirc, "Socialism and Ownership" in Leszek Kolakowski and Stuart Hampshire eds., *The Socialist Idea* (London: Weidenfeld and Nicolson, 1974), p. 177.

53. See Joseph S. Nye, Jr., "Multinational Corporations in World Politics," *Foreign Affairs,* vol. 53, no. 1 (October 1974): 165-66.

54. See *New York Times,* January 12, 1975, "Excerpts from Oil Allocations Report."

55. See Khodadad Farmanfarmian, et al., "How Can the World Afford OPEC Oil?" in *Foreign Affairs,* vol. 53, no. 2 (January 1975): 201-22.

56. See J. K. Galbraith, *The New Industrial State* (London: Penguin, 1967), passim.

57. "The finance aristocracy is nothing but the rebirth of the lumpen proletariat on the heights of bourgeois society," ibid., p. 142.

58. See Karl Marx, *The Class Struggles in France* in *Selected Works* (Moscow: Foreign Languages Publishing House, 1962), pp. 118-242.

59. See Dennis Kavanaugh, "Beyond Autonomy? The Politics of Corporations," in G. Ionescu ed., *Between Sovereignty and Integration* (London: Croom Helm, 1974), pp. 46-47.

60. See Anthony Sampson, *The Sovereign State* (London: Hodder and Stoughton, 1973), passim.

61. See Helga Hernes, "The Visible Hand of the Multinational Corporation," *European Journal of Political Research,* vol. I, 1973, p. 266.

62. See the United States Senate Finance Committee Report, *Implications of Multinational Firms for World Trade and Investment and for U.S. Trade and Labor* (Washington, D.C.: U.S. Government Printing Office, 1973), vol. 1, pp. 153-63. See also Fernando Henrique Cardoso, "Associated Dependent Development: Theoretical and Practical Implications" in A. Stepan ed., *Authoritarian Brazil* (New Haven: Yale University Press, 1973).

2

MULTINATIONAL ENTERPRISES IN DEVELOPING COUNTRIES: ISSUES IN DEPENDENCY AND INTERDEPENDENCE
Raymond Vernon

The idea of dependency, of *dependencia*, a condition that is thought to be hobbling the development of the world's poor countries[1] and the idea of interdependence among nation states, a condition that is thought endemic to practically all countries, rich and poor,[2] are currently being explored by many of the world's leading social scientists and international policy makers.

The multinational enterprise has figured prominently in discussions of both these concepts. The reason is obvious. Such enterprises generally consist of a parent firm that is located in one country and a network of affiliates located in many other countries. As a rule, such a network disposes of a common pool of information and financial resources, is joined in a common organization, and responds to a common strategy. Networks of this sort have come to be responsible for about a third of the non-Communist world's industrial output and for a considerable proportion of the world's international trade and international capital movements. Whatever dependency or interdependence may mean, the multinational enterprise is presumptively involved.

The word dependency, as it turns out, appears in many contexts with different implications. As a rule, it includes the idea of an unbalanced relation between nation states and an unbalanced relation between classes, and it lays the causes of imbalance on the processes of international capitalism. There may be growth of output in the dependent country, but it is likely to be growth

The research on which this paper is based was financed by grants from the Ford Foundation to the Harvard Business School and the Harvard Center for International Affairs.

of the wrong products. There may be growth of income, but for those that need the income least. There may be growth even in political power, but for purposes that serve no useful social end. Accordingly, those who stress the problems of dependency generally assume that under the existing system of relations between rich and poor countries, the gains to the poor countries are not so great as to preclude radical experiments with other forms of relationship. The assumption is that if Indonesia sharply curtailed the operations of Japanese firms in its territory, if the Ivory Coast impeded the entry of French firms, or if Brazil restrained the activity of U.S. firms, this would probably be a good thing for the poorer country.

The concept of interdependence, on the other hand, tends to emphasize a somewhat different set of problems. To an increasing extent, the economic, political, and social lives of nations have become intermeshed. Nations draw more heavily on one another for the sources of their material and intellectual growth. This may seem a good thing at times from the viewpoint of the poor country. But the result is that when any big country sneezes, all the other countries catch cold. Here the image is more horizontal than vertical; questions of dominance and submission are not for the moment at issue. There is a longing for autonomy, but a fear of its cost. The central question, therefore, is whether alternative international policies can be devised that increase the benefits and reduce the drawbacks of the interdependence.

The ideas of dependency and interdependence clearly have some bearing on any discussion of the multinational enterprise. But they suffer from a common weakness when they are used as pegs on which to hang a serious discussion. As used in the literature, both concepts evoke a model of political behavior in which nation states are the only significant actors.[3] When Pechiney persuades de Gaulle to speak on its behalf in order to get a subsidiary established in Greece, the interests of Pechiney are thought to be subsumed inside the system of the French state. When Exxon collaborates with British Petroleum in its negotiations with Iraq, the U.S. state system and the British state system are thought to be in collaboration. In short, there is a strong tendency to analyze international relations principally by reference to the power and purpose of the nation states, without giving much weight to the distinctive motivations and resources of multinational enterprises themselves.

That such a tendency should exist is understandable. First of all, the idea of a state-centered world was reasonably consistent with reality up to, say, 1950 or 1960; indeed, for the analysis of most phenomena in international relations, such a model continues to represent the most useful starting point. Second, the state-centered model is in keeping with the basic ideas that dominate the study of economics and politics; it is, in short, compatible with Plato and Machiavelli, as well as with Marx, Marshall, and Keynes.

But the state-centered model has gross limitations in any discussion of the multinational enterprise, especially in a discussion focused on the concepts of dependency and interdependence. I intend, therefore, to try to break out of the subtle molds imposed by the model. An effort of this sort always runs a certain risk. It generally suggests more complex ways of looking at a phenomenon that may have seemed clear enough under simpler and more evocative rubrics. But simplicity in this instance is a dubious virtue because it leads to a view of the world that does not have much to do with the way things actually are.

SHRINKAGE OF INTERNATIONAL SPACE

Let me begin with the self-evident. In recent decades, space has shrunk; in economic terms, the cost of overcoming the obstacles imposed by space has declined in relation to the cost of most other things. The shrinkage, however, has not been uniform for all kinds of space. In the hearts of old cities, we do not travel end communicate faster or more easily than we did some decades ago. Our speed and ease of travel and communication inside the developed countries have increased only moderately. It is in the open empty spaces, and especially in the international spaces, that the spectacular shrinkages have occurred.

A temptation exists for those like myself, trained in economics, to measure and embroider this statement with the use of some simple numerical measure, such as cost per passenger mile. But any such description grossly understates the economic and social implications of the trend. The importance of the improvements in international travel and communication is that they have been embodied in routine, predictable, standardized services. That has been achieved with the introduction of scheduled international airlines, reliable cable and radio transmission, the near abolition of the visa, the routine clearance of hand luggage, the negotiability of the traveller's check, and all the thousand and one institutional devices that whittle away at the distinction between domestic and international travel. Human and institutional horizons have been stretched across international space in a way that no unit-cost-of-travel measure could begin to capture.

The shrinkage of international space has had still another effect in the enlargement of horizons. The reach of a man's social or economic horizon is not only influenced by predictability and by cost; it is also constrained by time, a constraint that is often absolute in character. For the man with a two-week vacation, the only pleasure spots to be considered are those that fit the two-week constraint. The businessman who needs a loan within a week cannot negotiate with sources that are ten days away. The toy distributor who sends out his designs for execution in June with an eye to the Christmas trade cannot weigh the merits of a producer who is unable to deliver before Christmas.

With the decline in space, a powerful set of homogenizing forces has been set in motion. The differences in consumer tastes and in productive technologies prevailing in different countries have been greatly narrowed. Of course, in most countries there had always been some social classes whose tastes in food, clothing, shelter, and recreation were based upon alien standards of some sort. During the nineteenth century, the *haute monde* and the high officialdom of Mexico City, Buenos Aires, Montevideo, and Delhi associated themselves more closely with the prevailing tastes of their peers in London or Paris than with their poorer compatriots. But the homogenizing phenomenon after World War II has applied to a mass consumption. In automobiles, Toyota, Ford, and Volkswagen have become the universal standard; in food, the pizza, the hamburger, and the ice cream stick are articles of near universal consumption. Plastic pails, aluminum roofing, radios, cameras, and hi-fi sets are indistinguishable by national origin.

For those who are repelled by the idea of a universal mass life, it is a matter of some comfort that the convergence of mass tastes through international contact seems to have given ordinary people more variety not less. Though the ordinary consumer in Accra or Rio or Chicago now relies for his clothing upon the mass-producing textile mills of an international culture, his choice has been widened to include the dashiki, the pullover, and the cotton shirt.

In any event, as national consumer tastes have come to cover a wider spectrum and as the various national spectrums have come to overlap, the homogenization of industrial technologies also appears to have proceeded rapidly. In part, this has been speeded by the growing similarities in consumer tastes; when the same plastic material or the same automobile parts satisfy prevailing tastes in many countries, one reason for different technological emphases goes by the boards. What is more, the convergence of technical norms to some extent feeds on itself. A technology that has been applied successfully can be applied a second time with fewer errors and false starts. This reflects, partly, the well-known phenomenon of the learning curve. Besides, where machinery is involved, a standard machine produced in large quantities is likely to be less costly and more troublefree than one that is designed to the individual situation.

The result has been that the technologies applied in developing areas have tended to be determined largely by existing international standards. Local adaptations of such standards have occurred, of course, often on a fairly large scale.[4] But brand new technologies, created to respond to the particular conditions of poor countries, have been rare.

The economic consequences of the dominance of international standards are not very clear. If the development of new technologies entailed neither uncertainty nor cost, it would be easy to conclude that each environment should be addressed *de novo* for the design of an optimum technology. But the costs and uncertainties of creating and applying new technologies from scratch are generally quite high and have to be borne by some entity, business or government. The institutions that are required to make decisions on a choice of technology, such as business firms and government agencies, are generally in no position to recapture the full cost or assume the full risk of such adventures.* If they did have that capability and assumed the necessary risk, it is not clear that either private costs or social costs would be lowered. So the homogenizing trend continues.

In a world of homogenizing tastes and convergent technologies, trade names and trademarks also tend to move easily across international boundaries. The cost of extending a well-known trade name into a new area is generally lower than the cost of establishing a new one in that area, because the conditioning of buyers' responses to the well-established name has already been taking place. Today, the name of IBM or Datsun or Philips is already well known in a new market even before the market opens up, thereby presenting a difficult handicap to any competitor.

Some of the effects of the shrinkage in international space are strongly apparent in the routine statistics on international trade and international payments.[5] In the period after World War II, international trade grew much faster than the internal trade of most nations. In the dozen years following 1960, international trade in the non-Communist world rose by about 8 percent a year in physical terms, while the total output of goods rose only 5.5 percent a year.[6] In the same period, the annual flow of foreign direct investment among the developed countries was rising at a rate of nearly 12 percent, a growth rate far higher than that for business investment inside those countries.[7] Quite apart from the rising levels, however, international trade and investment have also changed in direction and content.

Until World War II, a considerable part of international trade consisted of the traditional mercantilist exchange—a swap of raw materials for finished products between countries that were quite unequal in industrial capabilities and in commercial power. As a rule, the function of the weaker country was confined simply to production, while the jobs of transporting, processing, and delivering the products lay in the hands of business interests in the stronger country. The sugar and coffee plantations of Latin America and Africa, the livestock ranches of Argentina and New Zealand, therefore, could be seen as mere adjuncts or outreaches from the importing country, the metropole.

---

*Note that some of the most spectacular technological innovations designed to respond to local conditions have been undertaken and financed by nonprofit organizations. The improved seeds and related technologies associated with the green revolution were originally brought into existence through the efforts of the Ford Foundation and the Rockefeller Foundation.

That situation has changed in various respects. First, raw material trade as a whole has lost its relative importance;[8] and despite the current world shortages in the 1970s in such materials—or perhaps because of those shortages—the trade in such materials is likely to continue to decline in statistical importance in the future. In addition, the poor countries are not the passive participants they once were. These countries have been playing a much more active hand in determining who shall do the international shipping and overseas distribution of the products. For some types of products, local enterprises or government bureaus have taken over some of the job.

Meanwhile, international trade in manufactures has been changing in ways that reflect more intimate interrelationships among the economies involved. Specialization and crosshauling in manufactured products, which had been expanding rapidly among the rich countries for some time, has begun to involve the poorer countries as well. Spain, Brazil, Mexico, Korea, and other such countries have developed significant positions in the international exchange of manufactured products. That change has meant that producers in the advanced countries have had to make much more durable and even irreversible commitments to production facilities in the developing world.

Apart from international trade and payments, the evidence of shrinking international space is also to be found in the accelerated shuttling of ideas and information across international boundaries. International tourist expenditures have grown annually at a rate of about 10 percent since 1960.[9] Patents granted by the major industrial countries to foreigners—a particularly sensitive measure—increased spectacularly. In the case of U.S. patents, the proportion granted to foreigners has risen from about 13 percent before World War II to over 30 percent in 1972. In the case of patents issued by the leading European countries, the foreigners' share has risen from about one-half in the 1930s to over three-quarters in 1972.[10] Various signs point, therefore, to the conclusion that the world of interests and ideas has been shrinking rapidly.

THE MULTINATIONAL ENTERPRISE AS AN INSTITUTIONAL RESPONSE

One of the more significant implications of the shrinkage in international space is its effect on the size and shape of the organizations that operate in more than one country.

International organizations, whether public or private, are, of course, a well-established historical phenomenon. Centuries ago, a few religious orders, banking houses, and communities of scholars had solved the problems of successful international organization. Where the sharing of resources such as money or knowledge offered net gains to all the participants, a major incentive to the creation of such organizations was created.

The problems of conducting a business with production units spread all over the globe, however, have been fairly formidable, more difficult perhaps than those faced by international churchmen, bankers, and scholars. But the advantages have been very great as well. Apart from the well-known efficiencies associated with specialization and scale, big enterprises have discovered the advantages of drawing on diversified sources for their raw materials and relying on many different markets for their sales.

With the improvements in international communication and the easing of international travel, the problems of operating and controlling multinational enterprises have sharply declined. The standardizing of systems and operating procedures has become practical over a wider range of activities and thus has brought new organizational economies of scale.[11] Like the standard machine and the standard production process, these standard procedures are sometimes modified to local conditions, especially if the adaptation can be done without impairing the basic strategy and structure of the system; personnel policies and marketing policies, for instance, are commonly tailored to the local scene.[12]

The operations of a multinational enterprise in any national environment, therefore, generally represents a mixture of national influences. Up to a point, there is local adaptation. But anyone wandering through Volkswagen's Sao Paolo plant almost at once feels transported back to Germany; Fiat's plants in Argentina exude the atmosphere of Turin; and there is no mistaking the American origins of an IBM facility located anywhere.[13]

The "foreign" aspect of the multinational enterprise can sometimes be identified in fairly explicit terms. One U.K. study indicates, for instance, that U.S.-controlled subsidiaries in the United Kingdom differ from their British counterparts in various respects: less labor strife, less willingness to recognize unions, and more willingness to enter into agreements that relate wages to productivity.[14] A number of studies indicate a disposition for multinational enterprises to pay higher wages and provide better working conditions than their local counterparts.[15] An occasional study, such as one covering the practices of the International Petroleum Company in Peru during the 1960s, reports some self-conscious efforts to introduce social values and practices of an "enlightened" sort, such as the modification of local paternalistic employment practices—activities that would be quite unlikely to be initiated by local firms.[16]

According to most versions of the dependency theory, the introduction of new national norms through a foreign-owned enterprise is presumptively undesirable. The question is not so much whether such an enterprise seems to be making a welfare contribution to the economy; more to the point is the fact that a foreign enterprise is involved. Because the underlying objectives of the foreign contributor are thought at variance with those of the state, it is assumed that national gain will eventually be turned into national loss. Take, for instance, the tendency of multinational enterprises to pay higher wages. Borrowing a leaf from Lenin's views on why industrialists sometimes share their monopoly profits with labor, some observers have speculated that multinational enterprises which follow such a practice may be trying to win friends and influence people, and may be driving wedges in the solidarity of different local interests.[17]

It would be astonishing if that kind of strategy had never occurred to the managers of multinational enterprises. But in a less pejorative vein, it might be enough to observe that business managers, like most managers in a bureaucracy, place a heavy weight on questions of survival, continuity, and efficiency. With these criteria dominating, the disposition of the multinational enterprise is to reduce any risk that can readily be reduced.

In their efforts to improve their chances at survival and continuity, multinational enterprises generally try to remain as unobtrusive as possible in the local economy. Commonly, however, that objective is compromised by two kinds of forces. One is the requirements of successful local marketing; these often call for copious advertising and emphasis on a well-known international trademark. Another is the inability of the enterprise consistently to avoid being identified with one local faction or another. In Ghana, for instance, does one hire from an Ashanti tribe or from the Ewe? Where occupation castes exist, should local custom be breached or should it be allowed to govern? When the ruling party solicits a fat political contribution, is the solicitation to be disregarded? Indeed, should the enterprise itself follow local practice by taking the initiative and searching for local political support? Although most multinational enterprises devoutly wish that problems of this sort would go away, that wish is not always granted; whether they like it or not, multinational enterprises are sometimes identified with one side or another in a local struggle.

The behavior of multinational enterprises, therefore, may be seen as influenced by two groups of conditioning forces: those in their home cultures and those in the local economy. Yet neither of these forces, in my opinion, are as important as the imperatives that are imposed by the basic strategy of the firm itself. In the last few decades, a considerable bibliography has developed covering the histories of large enterprises. Some of these histories are self-serving documents, inspired by the firms themselves; but many are the works of disinterested scholars. Over and over again, these histories impress one central fact on the reader. Like any large bureaucracy, these enterprises develop a central purpose and a collective identity that is distinguishable from that of any country in which they operate. What shapes the behavior of an international oil company above everything else, for instance, is the need to maintain a complex international system that produces, refines, transports, and delivers the product. Exxon, Shell, ENI, and BP operate under this common imperative, though they base themselves in different countries and are responsible to different public authorities. The same could be said of multinational chemical companies or electronic companies or automobile companies. The fundamental needs to exist and to grow normally determine more of the action of these enterprises than do the more subtle ties that link them to any particular territory.

These imperatives operate at two different levels. They inject a certain unity and consistency in the behavior of the affiliates of any given multinational enterprise, as the affiliates respond to the common needs of the enterprise; and they effect the interactions among the leading multinational enterprises that share a given product market, reflecting the common elements of interest among those leaders.

The reasons why the affiliates of any given MNC behave in some interrelated and consistent fashion are, of course, self-evident—a simple consequence of the fact that they respond to a common strategy. However, the reasons why leading MNCs in a given product line are likely to behave in some interrelated fashion are much more complex; to understand why this should be so requires an understanding of some of the characteristics of oligopoly behavior.[18] In many industries where oligopoly prevails, such as oil, aluminum, and basic chemicals, price competition among the leaders can be especially destructive. In such countries, a considerable part of the production costs are fixed without regard to the volume of output, taking the form of plant and of organizational costs. Added production can be undertaken at relatively low marginal cost, and that fact presents a constant temptation for any producer to cut his prices below the full cost of production, in an effort to capture a larger share of the market.

In industries such as these, the leaders have constantly cast about for some means to maintain orderly markets. Efforts of that sort have generally taken the form of tacit cooperation and forebearance, and even of overt agreement. The efforts of the oligopoly leaders to maintain orderly markets and to protect their collective rent have important social implications, and I intend to return to some of them in the pages that follow. For the moment, however, only one point of importance need be made: the interests of the multinational enterprise, individually and collectively, do not correspond very neatly to those of any one nation state. Each enterprise is tied to its own compelling global strategy. Any group of such enterprises has a common interest that derives from their collective leadership in the same industry. The combined effect is to create a pattern of conduct that is not easily understood in terms of the play of interests and forces of the nation states themselves.

DEPENDENCY AND INTERDEPENDENCE
AMONG THE BUSINESS ELITE

In light of the motivations and needs of the multinational enterprise, what can one say about their contribution to situations of dependency and interdependence? More particularly, what is the nature of the interaction that ensues between the multinational enterprises and the cultures of the poor countries in which they operate?

One of the difficulties of generalizing about this interaction is the speed with which it changes. For example, though multinational enterprises may dominate in some branch of business activity for a time, a position of dominance need not last. Branch by branch, multinational enterprises have generally been compelled to share their original dominance with national organizations and even in some cases to surrender the field altogether. By 1960, the plantation companies of foreign companies that had been operating in developing countries through the preceding century had almost disappeared; by that time, too, the foreign-owned electric power companies were just about gone and the remnants of the foreign-owned telephone companies were being pushed off the map.[19] The same trends were visible in manufacturing, though in rather more subtle form. In the older, standardized chemicals and petrochemicals, the huge foreign-owned companies that commanded the field were finding themselves forced to share their positions with other multinational enterprises or with national producers.[20] In office machinery and in consumer durables, in radios, television, and many other products, the same pattern could be discerned.[21]

The reasons for the constant shift in the positions of the multinational enterprises are suggested by numerous studies, whose results bear directly on the questions of dependency and interdependence.

In the developing countries of Latin America, Asia, and North Africa up to World War II, local businessmen could be thought of largely as adjuncts and partners of foreign entrepreneurs.[22] Up to that time, the local businessmen in nontraditional activities in those countries consisted largely of importers and exporters, distributors and suppliers, generally linked in some intimate way to the foreign sector or the expatriate community. If dependency ever accurately described the relation between the local business sector and foreign business interests, it was during that period. At that stage, more often than not, local businessmen and local bankers could be counted on to support the concepts of open markets, free trade, and other familiar principles that coincided with their own business interests.

World War II cut off some local business communities from their overseas sources of supply or from their markets, forcing them into self-reliant patterns of operation. When the war ended, selected sons of the business elite were sent off to the advanced countries to study law, economics, engineering, or business; and when they returned, their own strivings for autonomy seemed stronger then those of their fathers. In a number of countries—including notably Brazil, Mexico, India, Colombia, and Algeria—the distributors and purveyors for the foreign sector began turning to production and distribution on their own. Of course, many of the old partnerships with foreigners persisted, and many new ones were created. But on the whole, one could see the emergence of a tough new breed of local entrepreneur, prepared to make partnerships or do battle with foreign enterprises as their interests required.

Among the new breed, some were simply seeking to improve the terms on which they did business with the foreigners: to get a larger share of a joint venture, to get an assured source of supply, to capture an assured market, or to get a better price. Some, however, hoped to beat the foreigner at his own game and perhaps even to dislodge him altogether, especially in banking, mining, and certain branches of industry. Wherever they thought it useful, they enlisted their governments in the struggle.

The fact that multinational enterprises often succeeded in maintaining and enlarging their overall position in the developing countries during the decades following World War II was not because they managed to prevail in struggles of this sort. Their survival and growth lay mainly in their ability to roll over into other activities as the economies of the developing countries grew more complex and as their needs changed. As multinational enterprises lost ground in some of the older lines, many moved into the newer and more advanced products—from consumer electronics to industrial electronics, from chemicals grown mature to those still in the pilot plant stage, from oil drilling and mining on *terra firma* to oil drilling and mining in the ocean deep. The constant effort of the multinational enterprise was to find some new niche where its strengths could command some special advantage.

Meanwhile, the relationships among the managers of the leading multinational enterprises have also been going through considerable change. Before World War II, if one had been obliged to make large generalizations about the relations among business leaders headquartered in different countries, interdependence would not have been a dominant theme. Numerous contacts existed among the continents, to be sure. However, the contacts tended to be those of barons meeting at the edges of their domains, spying on each other's implements of war, and negotiating over border disputes. That mood was captured in numerous cartel agreements which shaped international trade and investment in leading industries during the prewar period. These agreements were characteristically drawn on geographical lines; the participants parceled out world territories among themselves and laid down conditions under which each might penetrate into the territory of the others.[23] At that stage, personal relations among the business elite across the Atlantic may have been correct, even cordial; but according to the available biographical evidence, they were not very familiar or continuous.

The decade or so after World War II changed all that. In its early phase, U.S.-based enterprises penetrated the markets of the Europeans, establishing permanent bridgeheads in the form of branches and subsidiaries; in a later stage, there was some penetration of Japan, albeit on a limited basis. These foreign implantations of U.S. enterprises took place mainly in the highly concentrated industries, that is, in industries for which heavy research expenditure or large advertising budgets or gargantuan production facilities placed big enterprises at a competitive advantage.[24]

It took a little time for the Europeans and the Japanese to begin reacting to the American advances. By the early 1960s, however, the leading firms based in these areas had begun to absorb the technology, acquire the capital, and develop the organization needed for the riposte. In some cases, the response took the form of new cooperation between the invaders and those that had been threatened, cooperation in the form of partnerships and cross-licensing. In other cases, the answering maneuver consisted of setting up new establishments in the markets of the Americans, both in the United States and in third countries. That response was especially apparent in the industries for which the Americans had no obvious technological lead. In these industries, foreign firms have established themselves in the United States and in other markets that the Americans had dominated, to manufacture products remarkably similar to the mix of the U.S.-based firms.[25]

The thrust and the riposte have had a considerable effect upon the structure of the world's industry. The cross-penetration of enterprises has reduced—reduced, not increased—the degree of concentration in a considerable number of industries in world markets.[26] In standard chemicals, drugs, automobiles, petrochemicals, copper, sulphur, and various other industries, firms of different national origins are more exposed to the consequences of one another's behavior than has ever been the case before. Whether that exposure will lead to more competition or to more collaboration cannot be answered in sweeping generalizations; probably there will be cases of both. Whatever the pattern may be, the degree of interdependence among businessmen with different national bases has greatly increased.

THE EXERCISE OF GOVERNMENTAL POWER

A central theme in most versions of the dependency theory is the need to protect and nourish the power of government in the developing countries. Some versions of the theory assume implicitly or explicitly that the establishment of foreign-owned enterprises inside a developing country weakens that power ipso facto. As far as these versions are concerned, an exploration of the actual consequences of the operations of these enterprises is quite superfluous. Other versions of the dependency concept, however, are more equivocal on this point; in those cases, it is not altogether irrelevant to explore the actual consequences associated with the spread of multinational enterprises.

One of the striking manifestations of the development process in the last few decades has been the growing capacity of governments in the poor areas of the world to exercise their powers as governments. Not long ago, only a few of the national governments in Latin America, Asia, and Africa made any serious claim to the effective exercise of power throughout their jurisdictions. In some countries, loose feudal coalitions blanketed the national territory, coalitions that confined the national government's responsibilities to the capital city and a limited hinterland. In other countries, large areas of national jurisdiction were simply left to fend for themselves. Not uncommonly, firms engaged in mining or in large-scale agriculture were expected—indeed, at times were required—to provide the infrastructure and to perform the functions that ordinarily would be assumed by government.

Remnants of that era still exist, especially in the poorest of the poor countries. But for the most part, national governments in the developing world have been stretching their jurisdictions geographically and strengthening their capabilities functionally. In the process, however, governments have encountered various points of friction with the multinational enterprise which sometimes seemed to threaten the enlarged and deepened role of the governments.

One source of friction arose out of the increased interaction between the national economy and the hitherto secluded enclaves of the big extractive enterprises.[27] In some cases, as governments extended their jurisdictional reach, the firms tried to relieve themselves of their quasi-governmental powers and responsibilities, turning to the governments for the first time to provide hospitals, schools, and roads, to exercise police power, and to administer justice. Ironically, governments were not always willing to take on these tasks, insisting in some cases that foreigners should continue to perform some of these functions.

The opposite sort of case also has occurred. Firms have been unwilling to surrender their quasi-governmental powers and responsibilities, on the assumption that when the government took over, some of those duties would be performed poorly. The irony is that local workers sometimes were on the side of the companies in disputes of this sort, uncertain whether the services promised by the government would be as favorable in cost and quality as the services provided by the companies.

The available data are not good enough to suggest which of these patterns dominated. But that may not matter very much; the fact is that both types of dispute have caused bitterness and friction. And when the enterprise was foreign-owned, as it commonly was, the bitterness usually rubbed off on foreign enterprises as a class.

In the context of the dependency issue, however, jurisdictional irritations of this sort were less important than other issues. Governments in the developing countries increasingly wished to implement a series of national policies in which previously they had not been involved: to replace their imports of manufactured goods with local production; to expand exports; to upgrade the capabilities of the labor force; to increase governmental revenues; and so on. To all of these objectives, foreign-owned enterprises were generally prepared to make a contribution—not necessarily on the terms that the governments sought, but a seeming contribution nonetheless. Foreign enterprises were prepared to mine and export ore—but they often demanded long-term tax exemptions and duty-free import privileges. Foreign enterprises were prepared to produce and distribute chemicals in the local market—but they often sought the government's commitment to keep out others for a term of years. Foreign enterprises could commonly be counted on to introduce training programs for local personnel—but they also resisted the loss of such personnel to other jobs in the country.[28] Where governments could find more favorable ways of achieving their goals, they presumably elected to use them; but certain difficulties stood in the way of making objective and informed choices among the alternatives.

In some countries, the system of incentives and rewards inside the bureaucracy was such that the bureaucracy simply could not consider the alternatives on their cost-and-benefit merits. Explicit ideological positions often determined the choice, without regard to the facts in the individual case. This was true at various times in the history of India, Indonesia, Pakistan, Chile, Egypt, and numerous other countries. In those cases, the incentive-and-reward system usually worked against the foreign-owned enterprises; but there were also cases in which it worked for them. In some governments, key officials assiduously solicited bribes; and where that situation existed, the question of choice depended on the nature of the bidding. In some governments, too, if a well-motivated and well-trained official failed to close some deal with a prospective foreign investor, his hardheadedness was not necessarily viewed as laudatory; instead, there was a risk that he might be regarded as inept or corrupt. In governments such as these, the capacity or willingness of cabinet-level officials to distinguish poor terms from good terms were often underdeveloped.

In the give-and-take between governments and foreign-owned enterprises, the bargaining strength of the enterprises has been evident in the characteristics of some of the deals that actually have been consummated. For instance, in a detailed study conducted by the OECD of some 70 foreign-owned projects in developing countries, all but 10 were found receiving some important special incentive of importance, such as tax concessions or special protection against competition.[29] Just as telling are the patterns of ownership that foreigners managed to create when establishing their subsidiaries. In recent years, as is well known, most developing countries have expressed a clear preference for the avoidance of foreign wholly-owned subsidiaries. Yet, out of 1,027 foreign-controlled manufacturing subsidiaries established since 1959 in developing countries, 550 were wholly owned;[30] this represented a proportion not greatly different from the subsidiaries established before 1959.

The relative bargaining strength of foreign enterprise and national government can be gauged not only by the bargain struck at the time of the original establishment of the enterprise but also in the subsequent interaction between government and enterprise. The problems that have arisen after the establishment of foreign-owned subsidiaries are abundantly documented in numerous studies. From the viewpoint of governments, foreign enterprises often seemed intransigent in the face of some national imperative; from the viewpoint of enterprises, governments commonly violated the basic principles of fairness or the explicit commitments of existing agreements.[31]

The existence of such disputes, taken by themselves, may not bear very heavily on the dependency hypothesis, on the question who depends on whom. But in each dispute some elements of the nationel elite are usually arrayed on the side of the foreign-owned enterprise. The supporters may be local business partners and local suppliers, but they may also be local labor leaders operating in the interests of their own union, or regional public officials operating in defense of their own areas. For example, if the interests of a plant of the Universal Electric Co. in Tucuman, are being imperiled by the demands of a remote bureaucracy in Buenos Aires, then the town fathers and the local labor leaders of Tucuman can probably be counted on to mount a delegation to the capital city. Even inside the national government, the ministry of finance may be arrayed against the ministry of commerce or of industry. To those whose convictions run deep on the basic undesirability of foreign-owned enterprises, divisions of this sort inside countries appear as further proof of the dependency concept.

The concern of the developing countries over internal division and dependency is augmented by some of the problems associated with interdependence. Developing countries, operating through their respective political processes, are being charged over the years with more and more subtle and complex tasks: holding inflation and unemployment in check; bringing up the income of the lagging areas and the lagging sectors; providing a tolerable physical environment; and so on. In a fine twist of historical irony, however, these new obligations have been placed on the shoulders of national governments at the very time when technological factors have tended to reduce the self-sufficiency of individual states. In order to continue to prosper, nation states have been forced to open up their boundaries to the capital, information, and skills that other countries could provide, and have been obliged to look for larger markets elsewhere, while opening up their own markets to others. These measures have added to the exposure of the various countries. Resources from abroad have been needed for national purposes; resources generated in the national economy have been diverted to foreign uses; sources of expansion as well as those of contraction have been transmitted more easily between economies.

One result has been that government officials in many countries no longer look upon their national territory as quite so manageable a unit as was thought to be the case in, say, the early 1960s. The comprehensive national plan, which seemed to have such promise at that time, is no longer regarded very widely as offering a serious approach to the achievement of major national goals.[32] Comprehensive national plans demand that the planner be able to project or to control the foreign sector of the economy. Under this goal, national plans and national planners tended to stress import substitution as a leading strategy and to regard export promotion as a much lower priority. Those priorities have visibly shifted in the past few years. Import substitution is commonly seen today as a limited and fragile strategy, and export promotion as a vital element for growth. Partly as a result, money, skills, and ideas flow across international boundaries in ways that nations find difficult to control. Even when control is easy, nations feel inhibited about cutting off a troublesome flow, since some element of the economy may be benefiting from the flow. Besides, there is always the possibility of retaliation from other nations.

The multinational enterprise plays a part in all of these preoccupations. Sitting astride national boundaries, it is seen as peculiarly able to be both helpful and destructive to the objectives of the countries where its units are located. Decisions on the location of added production facilities and decisions on the investment of liquid funds, for instance, can cut either way. A promise to locate more production in Brazil can be accompanied by a threat to reduce production in Algeria. Decisions of this sort are difficult enough to monitor when they are undertaken by a firm that is unambiguously associated with a single country. When the decisions and the transfers are internal to a multinational enterprise, the ability of the state to observe and to control is likely to be reduced even more.

The problems of government officials in dealing with and monitoring the multinational enterprise are not unlike the problems of labor union leaders in their relation to these enterprises. Like the public officials, the labor leaders look upon the multinational enterprise as a source of potential benefit and a source of potential loss. But labor leaders generally see themselves as negotiating from weakness in determining which potential will be realized. Confronting the representatives of a multinational enterprise in a bargaining situation, the labor leaders see the enterprise as possessing a flexiblity that labor cannot match. The enterprises, it is assumed, can shift their facilities from country to country, whereas labor is largely anchored to its native turf.[33]

The word interdependence implies a two-way flow, a symmetrical situation of exposure and vulnerability. The raw material shortages of the early 1970s have underlined the fact that the concept of interdependence is not wholly out of place in describing the relation of the developing countries to some of the richer nations in which multinational enterprises are based.

No discussion of interdependence, however, can overlook the problem of relative size among the parties. When a stew is concocted from one elephant and one squirrel, it is misleading to suggest that the pachyderm and the rodent are equally represented. The closest contenders to the U.S. position in the non-Communist world command only one-third or one-fourth of the gross national product of the United States. Though many countries have grown more rapidly than the United States in the last decade or two, and though Japan has grown more rapidly than practically any other country, the U.S. economy still dwarfs all the others. For many purposes, it is true, the differences in size are of no particular importance; gross national product is no sure guide to the distribution of Nobel prizes or to the competitive strength of business in international markets. But neither is size an irrelevant consideration.

In the field of international business, the strength of any enterprise is affected by the size of the home market. Though a large home market may be neither necessary nor sufficient to command international markets, it has proved a considerable help in some well-defined types of industry, illustrated by aerospace and computers.[34] In some industries, large-scale government research grants and government purchases provide a lift. In others, the size of the national market allows industries to exploit the economies of scale at home fully before dipping their toes in the more uncertain international waters. In still others, the size of the international market may keep home industries from growing somnolescent; they have to remain alert because they cannot be sure about the quarter from which new competition may appear.

Of all the advantages that go with size, however, the one that is capable of generating the highest level of tension is the political or military power of the home government of the enterprise. The advantages of being able to appeal for support to a big and powerful home government hardly need any elaboration. If the U.S. government decides to support its oil companies in Iraq in the face of that government's hostility, this presumably counts for more than the support that the Netherlands can give to Royal Dutch/Shell.

However, the advantage for an enterprise in being linked to a big country depends on whether the government is convinced that its interests and those of the enterprise coincide. Once that critical qualification is recognized, the advantage bestowed by the size of the United States is not at all clear. Small countries, as a rule, can be counted on to support the one or two multinational giants that may be based in their economies; in any international dispute in which governmental support might matter, the Netherlands can almost surely be counted on to rally to the support of Philips Electric, or Switzerland to the support of Ciba. When the National Iranian Oil Company becomes a multinational enterprise, as is not unlikely over the next decade or so, it will almost certainly be able to count on the unequivocal support of Iran.

From the viewpoint of an American firm, however, U.S. government support is somewhat more problematic, and that problematic quality is not unrelated to the size of the American economy. At the very least, the U.S. government has to consider the interests of other U.S.-based firms. This may sometimes argue for supporting the interests of some imperiled enterprise all the harder, in a special application of the domino theory; but it may also argue for turning a deaf ear and a blind eye to the plight of any single company. If International Petroleum wants the U.S. government's help in dealing with the Peruvian government, as it surely did in the 1960s, America has to weigh the risk of a backlash against other U.S. interests in Peru. If General Motors wants American help to break into the Spanish markets, as it was trying to do in the spring of 1974, the United States has to weigh that plea against the opposition of Ford and Chrysler. Beyond that, there are bilateral questions of military relations, regional questions of inter-American relations, multilateral questions of U.N. relations, and so on, to be taken into account, questions which may be of less complexity in the eyes of a smaller country. Indeed, there may even be times when, in the interest of high politics, the U.S. government may have to take some initiative that places in peril all multinational enterprises based in the United States.[35]

The problematic nature of U.S. government support for multinational enterprises based on U.S. territory is increased by one other factor, much too easily overlooked. As in every other country where multinational enterprises operate, some groups feel helped and others feel hurt by the operations of such enterprises. If the position of the AFL-CIO is to be taken at face value, for instance, it would be eager to have the foreign subsidiaries of U.S. enterprises close their doors. Some members of Congress would also support such a policy. Though such views may not determine the shape of U.S. politics toward multinational enterprises, they inhibit the government at times from actively raising a hand in support of a beleaguered enterprise.

Where does one come out in terms of dependency and interdependence? On a Leninist interpretation of international relations, the answer would be clear. In capitalist countries, the state is the instrument of the system, and the actions of the state are the system's expression. Quarrels may break out among the interests inside the system, but the ultimate unity of these interests is never at issue. Accordingly, the power of the state and the power of the enterprises that express themselves through the state are essentially indistinguishable.[36] If one rejects the Leninist finesse as too simple, as I am strongly inclined to do, then the issues of dependency and interdependence as they relate to the multinational enterprise need more complex definition.

GENERALIZATIONS OF A SORT

The sense of dependency and the concern over interdependency that is commonly reflected in the world's poor countries appear to stem from some fairly basic forces.

One such force is the ineluctable shrinkage of space, which makes contacts across national boundaries more difficult to avoid. This has happened at a time when the tasks imposed on nation states by their internal political processes have grown more ambitious and more complex. In the race between increasing responsibilities and increasing capabilities in the public sector, the agents of the state have sometimes regarded the openness of national boundaries as more a handicap than a help.

That element alone, however, would not be enough to explain the quality of the reaction that is often encountered on such issues, especially when the multinational enterprise is involved as a principal actor. Other elements contribute to the quality of the response.

One is the fact that transnational institutions and processes do not affect alike all the interests inside any national economy. Some proponents of the dependency theory are quite explicit in saying that the capacity of transnational processes to penetrate and fragment national interests is one reason for the strength of their own adverse reaction. Those who hope to build up a sense of national identity and national purpose, leading to national action of one sort or another, find the fragmentation dangerous and destructive. The state socialist in Brazil sees added difficulties in the way of nationalizing the aluminum industry, just as the AFL-CIO sees added difficulties in restricting the outflow of U.S. capital.

Another contributing force is the pervasive sense that the multinational enterprise responds to its own strategic imperatives, which may or may not be consistent with those of any nation state. Some of those imperatives stem from inside the enterprise, a consequence of the basic strategy of the enterprise. Some derive from the need among the leaders of any oligopolistic industry at times to act in a cooperative way in order to protect their common interests. These imperatives may contribute to the achievement of national objectives or they may not. But even when they are helpful, they seem far removed from the needs and aspirations of any country. With nations unable to monitor the activities of most transnational institutions effectively, even those who are not ideologically inclined toward strong national governments may feel uneasy.[37]

That uneasiness is exacerbated by the fact that, even when the information is available, there is no one to speak for mankind. Who will decide when the rate of use of the world's raw materials or the pattern of competition in world markets, for example, are inimical to the world's collective interests? Certainly not the individual nation states or the multinational enterprises. Their cumulative interests are not the same as society's collective interests. And who will adjudicate the cases in which national interests are flatly at loggerheads? Once again, neither the individual states nor the multinational enterprises are in a position to handle such issues in terms of the collective interest.

The intensity of the reaction to the operations of multinational enterprises, however, is probably due to other factors as well, especially when the reaction is found in academic and intellectual circles. Part of the intensity probably reflects the deep-seated tension that exists in many cultures between men of action and men of ideas. Businessmen and military leaders are presumed by intellectuals to be crass and materialistic dolts; intellectuals are presumed by businessmen and the military to be dangerous when let loose in the real world. Businessmen who are also foreigners bear an especially heavy burden, as subtle xenophobia is added to robust contempt.

A special measure of hostility sometimes seems reserved for businessmen from the United States, especially in Latin America. Sometimes that hostility is accompanied by speculation about the nature of U.S. society itself. Despite the complex and contradictory quality of the evidence, the United States is often depicted as hostile or indifferent to the plight of others; a state of dependency or interdependence that involves the United States, therefore, is dangerous for any nation.

When the case against the multinational enterprise is based on views about the nature of the U.S. economy today, it seems to me an exercise in analytical overkill. The concern of intellectuals and political leaders over the operations of U.S.-based multinational enterprises existed long before Watergate, Vietnam, and the invasion of the Dominican Republic. By World War I, these enterprises had been attacked by Austrian diplomats, by Roumanian and Mexican government leaders, and by half a dozen authors in Britain. Besides, concern over multinational enterprises has not been confined to U.S.-based firms. In Indonesia, the main target is the Japanese; in the Cape Verde Islands, the Swedes; in India, practically any foreign interest from a large country. It is a safe assumption that the concern stems from deep-seated factors of the sort that I suggested earlier, rather than from any real or fancied characteristics of the United States.

The underlying problem presented by the growth of the multinational enterprise is the fact that it cannot easily be accommodated or controlled in a global political structure based on the building blocks of nation states. Until some means are found to ensure that the multinational enterprise is accountable to society, it will stir a deep-seated sense of uneasiness in each of the national cultures it confronts.

NOTES

1. Among those associated with the concept of dependency are Fernando Henrique Cardoso, Helio Jaguaribe, Osvaldo Sunkel, Theotonio dos Santos, and Andre Gunder Frank. For a summary of the rather diverse views of the dependency theorists, see Robert A. Packenham, "Latin American Dependency Theories: Strengths and Weaknesses," mimeo, paper prepared for Harvard-M.I.T. Joint Seminar on Political Development, February 6, 1974.

2. For discussions of the concept of interdependence see R. N. Cooper, *The Economics of Interdependence: Economic Policy in the Atlantic Community* (New York: McGraw-Hill, 1968); also E. L. Morse, "Transnational Economic Processes," *International Organization,* vol. 3, no. 3 (Summer 1971): 373-97; and Assar Lindbeck, *The National State in an Internationalized World Economy* (Rio de Janeiro: Conjuncto Universitario Candido Mendes, 1973).

3. A conscious effort to deviate from the assumption is found in J. S. Nye, Jr., and R. O. Keohane, "Transnational Relations and World Politics: An Introduction," in *International Organization,* vol. 3, no. 3 (Summer 1971): 329-50.

4. See for instance W. P. Strassmann, *Technological Change and Economic Development: The Manufacturing Experience of Mexico and Puerto Rico* (Ithaca: Cornell University Press, 1968); W. A. Yeoman, "Selection of Production Processes for the Manufacturing Subsidiaries of U.S. Based Multinational Corporations," unpublished D.B.A. thesis, Harvard Business School, Boston, 1968; R. H. Mason, "The Transfer of Technology and the Factor Proportions Problem: The Philippines and Mexico," *UNITAR Research Report No. 10,* New York, 1972; G. L. Reuber and others, *Private Foreign Investment in Development* (Oxford: Clarendon Press, 1973), p. 195. In some instances, it is clear that more might rationally have been done; in other instances, the case is not so clear; for references to both kinds of situation, see L. T. Wells, Jr., "Economic Man and Engineering Man: Choice of Technology in a Low Wage Country," *Public Policy* (Summer 1973), p. 319-42.

5. An excellent summary appears in Lindbeck, op. cit.

6. General Agreement on Tariffs and Trade, *International Trade 1972* (Geneva: GATT, 1973), p. 1.

7. UN Department of Economic and Social Affairs, *Multinational Corporations in World Development,* New York, 1973, pp. 144-45.

8. General Agreement on Tariffs and Trade, op. cit., p. 1.

9. *Economic Review of World Tourism,* Geneva, 1972, pp. 19-20.

10. Detailed data on the issue of patents have been compiled by the Harvard Multinational Enterprise Study from secondary sources and serve as the basis for these generalizations.

11. J. M. Stopford and L. T. Wells, Jr., *Managing the Multinational Enterprise* (New York: Basic Books, 1972), chap. 5; S. M. Robbins and R. B. Stobaugh, *Money in the Multinational Enterprise: A Study of Financial Policy* (New York: Basic Books, 1973), chap. 3; M. Z. Brooke and H. L. Remmers, *The Strategy of Multinational Enterprise: Organization and Finance* (New York: American Elsevier Publishing, 1970), part I. An indication that economists have finally begun to take the phenomenon into account is found in Kenneth Arrow, *The Limits of Organization* (New York: W. W. Norton and Company, 1974).

12. Studies of the allocation of decision-making functions between parent and subsidiary are rapidly accumulating. As recent illustrations, see Carlos Osmar Bertero, "Drugs and Dependency in Brazil—An Empirical Study of Dependency Theory..." unpublished Ph.D. thesis, Cornell University Graduate School: 1972. See also D. J. C. Forsyth, *U.S. Investment in Scotland* (New York: Praeger, 1972), pp. 233-42; Gerard Garnier, "Pouvoir de Decision des Filiales Quebecoises d'Entreprises Americaines," *Etudes* Internationales, vol. II, no. 1 (March 1971): 11-43; M. Z. Brooke and H. L. Remmers, *The Strategy of Multinational Enterprise,* pp. 64-124.

13. For samples of the growing literature in this field, see D. F. Channon, *The Strategy and Structure of British Enterprise* (Boston: Division of Research, Harvard Business School, 1973); Mason Haire, E. E. Ghiselli, and L. W. Porter, *Managerial Thinking* (New York: John Wiley & Sons, 1966); Michael Yoshino, *Japan's Managerial System* (Cambridge: M.I.T. Press, 1968); also the following unpublished D.B.A. theses, Harvard Business School, 1972: Gareth Pooley-Djas, "Strategy and Structure of French Enterprise"; R. J. Pavan, "Strategy and Structure of Italian Enterprise"; and Heinz Thanheiser, "Strategy and Structure of German Enterprise."

14. John Gennard, *Multinational Corporations and British Labour: A Review of Attitudes and Responses* (London: British-North American Committee, 1972), pp. 8, 21. But another study, covering Scotland, shows more labor strife rather than less; Forsyth, op. cit., pp. 165-72.

15. For example, G. L. Reuber et al., *Foreign Direct Investment in Development* (Oxford: Clarendon Press, 1973), p. 176.

16. C. T. Goodsell, *American Corporations and Peruvian Politics* (Cambridge: Harvard University Press, 1974), p. 181 passim.

17. For a typical assertion, see Jeffrey Harrod, "Multinational Corporations, Trade Unions and Industrial Relations: A Case Study of Jamaica," in Hans Gunter ed., *Transnational Industrial Relations* (London: Macmillan, 1972), pp. 173-94.

18. The subject is developed at some length in Raymond Vernon, *Sovereignty at Bay* (New York: Basic Books, 1971), chaps. 2 and 3. See also F. T. Knickerbocker, *Oligopolistic Reaction and Multinational Enterprise* (Boston: Harvard Business School, 1973), chap. 3.

19. It is instructive to note Lenin's heavy emphasis on investments of these types in his 1916 study. V. I. Lenin, *Imperialism: The Highest State of Capitalism* (Moscow: Progress Publishers, Scientific Socialism Progress edition), pp. 73, passim.

20. See my "Competition Policy Toward Multinational Corporations," *Papers and Proceedings* of the American Economic Association, May 1974, pp. 276-81; also R. B. Stobaugh, "The Product Life Cycle, U.S. Exports and International Investment," unpublished D.B.A. thesis, Harvard Business School, 1968.

21. Though the evidence is quite diffuse and not very rigorous, it is still fairly impressive. Much of it is summarized in Vernon, op. cit., chap. 3.

22. Vernon, *The Dilemma of Mexico's Development* (Cambridge: Harvard University Press, 1963), pp. 39-47, 163-69; Warren Dean, *The Industrialization of Sao Paolo, 1880-1945* (Austin: University of Texas Press, 1969), pp. 125-43; Tomas Filiol, *Social Factors in Economic Development: The Argentine Case* (Cambridge: M.I.T. Press, 1961), pp. 42-47; J. P. McKay, *Pioneers for Profit: Foreign Entrepreneurship and Russian Industrialization 1885-1913* (Chicago: University of Chicago Press, 1970), part I; Michael Kidron, *Foreign Investment in India* (London: Oxford University Press, 1965), pp. 19-26.

23. Ervin Hexner, *International Cartels* (Chapel Hill: University of North Carolina Press, 1945).

24. R. E. Caves, "International Corporations: The Industrial Economics of Foreign Investment," *Economica,* vol. 38, 1971, pp. 1-27; also Vernon, *Sovereignty at Bay,* op. cit., chap. 3.

25. See Stephen Hymer and Robert Rowthorn, "Multinational Corporations and International Oligopoly: The Non-American Challenge," in C. P. Kindleberger, *The International Corporation* (Cambridge: M.I.T. Press, 1970), pp. 57-94. The point will be more fully explored and documented by E. M. Graham in a forthcoming D.B.A. thesis at the Harvard Business School.

26. See Vernon, "Competition Policy Toward Multinational Corporations," op. cit.

27. See, for instance, P. E. Church, "Labor Relations in Mineral and Petroleum Resource Development," in R. F. Mikesell, *Foreign Investment in the Petroleum and Mineral Industries* (Baltimore: The Johns Hopkins Press, 1971), p. 93; W. F. Whyte and A. R. Holmberg, "Human Problems of U.S. Enterprise in Latin America," *Human Organization* (Fall, 1956), part 6, pp. 22-26; Revel Denney, "Oil Town: New Style," *The Lamp* (Fall, 1958), pp. 6-7, 16-17; D. H. Finnie,

Desert Enterprise: The Middle East Oil Industry in its Local Environment (Cambridge: Harvard University Press, 1958), pp. 136-39; and Subbiah Kannappan and E. W. Burgess, *Business Performance Abroad: The Case Study of Aluminum Limited of India* (Washington, D.C.: National Planning Association, 1962), p. 49.

28. OECD, *Pilot Survey on Technical Assistance Extended by Private Enterprises,* Paris, 1967, pp. 22-25, 32-34; G. L. Reuber et al., op. cit., p. 201 passim.

29. G. L. Reuber et al. op. cit., p. 127.

30. Unpublished data from the Harvard Multinational Enterprise Study.

31. Most of the materials on this subject, whether in support of governments or of enterprises, are typically polemical and doctrinaire. For some relatively objective descriptions of the nature of the conflict, see C. F. Diaz-Alejandro, "Direct Investment in Latin America," in C. P. Kindleberger ed., *The International Corporation,* pp. 319-44; Goodsell, *American Corporations and Peruvian Politics,* op. cit. Mira Wilkins, *The Emergence of Multinational Enterprise: American Business Abroad from the Colonial Era to 1914* (Cambridge: Harvard University Press 1970); Mira Wilkins, The *Maturity of Multinational Enterprise* (Cambridge: Harvard University Press, 1974); D. R. Mummery, *The Protection of International Private Investment* (New York: Praeger Special Studies, 1968) esp. chap. 2.

32. For an account of this change in Western Europe, see Vernon ed., *Big Business and the State; Changing Relations in Western Europe* (Cambridge: Harvard University Press, 1974).

33. See for instance, David H. Blake, "Multinational Corporation, International Union and International Collective Bargaining: A Case Study of the Political, Social, and Economic Implications of the 1967 U.A.W.-Chrysler Agreement," in Hans Gunter ed., *Transnational Industrial Relations* (London: MacMillan, 1972) pp. 137-72; Karl Casserini, "The Challenge of Multi-National Corporations and Regional Economic Integration of the Trade Unions, Their Structure and Their International Activities," ibid., pp. 70-93; Duane Kujawa, *International Labor Relations Management in the Automotive Industry: A Comparative Study of Chrysler, Ford and General Motors* (New York: Praeger, 1971): I. A. Litvak and C. J. Maule, "The Union Response to International Corporations," *Industrial Relations,* vol. 11, no. 1 (February 1972); and John Gennard, *Multinational Corporations and British Labour: A Review of Attitudes and Responses,* op. cit.

34. See M. S. Hochmuth, "Aerospace," and Nicolas Jequier, "Computers," in Vernon, *Big Business and the State,* op. cit.

35. One serious scholar contends that the U.S. government's emphasis on land reform in Chile in the early 1960s contributed to undermining the U.S. copper companies' position by alienating conservative interests in Chile; see T. H. Moran, "The Multinational Corporation and Politics of Development: The Case of Copper in Chile," unpublished Ph.D. thesis, Harvard University, 1971.

36. Lenin, *Imperialism, the Highest State of Capitalism,* chap. 7, op. cit.

37. C. F. Diaz-Alejandro presents a well argued if slightly polemical description of such uneasiness in his "North-South Relations: The Economic Component," Economic Growth Center Discussion Paper no. 200, Yale University, April 1974.

3

THE SOCIAL ORGANIZATION
OF DECISION–MAKING IN THE
MULTINATIONAL CORPORATION
Louis Wolf Goodman

The subject of this chapter is how the multinational corporation (MNC) does business in the Third World. Our purpose will be to provide a relatively detailed grounding for the more "macro" perspectives on the role of the multinational corporation offered in the other chapters of this volume.

When the multinational corporation is viewed from the perspective of a Third World nation, the focus is often on the impact of the corporation on that nation.[1] This essay, however, addresses a topic which is antecedent to the study of multinational impact—the constraints which influence corporate managers as their decisions produce this impact. This topic has long been of interest to European and American scholars concerned with the functioning of business[2] and is now of vital concern to scholars observing the role of the multinational in the Third World.[3] Since all Third World nations—even

---

Much of the information in this essay is synthesized from notes of interviews with managers of 27 large U.S.-based MNCs in 1973. These included 3 banks, 6 commodity producers, and 18 manufacturing firms. Initial interviews were carried out in corporate headquarters, and subsequently managers of selected subsidiaries were interviewed in Colombia, Peru, Chile, Brazil, and Mexico. A limited number of interviews with managers of Japanese- and European-based firms were also carried out in Latin America. This research was supported by grants from the Council on Foreign Relations, the Joint Committee on Latin American Studies of the Social Science Research Council and the American Council of Learned Societies, the Carnegie Endowment for International Peace, and Yale University.

relative "isolates" such as China, Cuba, and Tanzania—will continue to deal with multinationals in the coming years, this topic also concerns host country nationals responsible for these "dealings." The object of this essay is to clarify some of the bases of decision-making in multinational corporations as they affect Third World nations in the context of the contemporary world socioeconomic system.

THE FIRM IN AN INTERNATIONAL CONTEXT

The study of the MNC extends the traditional study of the firm to an international context. Initiating and sustaining business operations which sprawl across national borders requires that multinational managers digest information that would rarely cross the desk of a domestic manager. How this information is processed and how corporate goals are serviced have important consequences for citizens of Third World nations. The goals that managers set for their corporations, and the factors which determine whether or not a given corporation chooses to do business in a given nation, must be understood to gauge the impact of the multinational corporation as an instrument of development. This essay will discuss the mixture of goals and investment criteria which are central to the corporate decision-making process. In doing so, it will attempt to shed light on why some firms are actively involved in international business and why others shy away from many apparent opportunities. It will also indicate emerging parameters for international business in Third World nations, and how MNCs are responding to these new rules of the game.

The International Business of the MNC

The MNC activity most frequently discussed in the social scientific literature is direct foreign investment (DFI).[4] However, DFI is only one of a number of business activities carried out by MNCs. In fact, it is more sensible to think of DFI as an integrated package of the range of business operations available to firms. These operations include *importing* and *exporting* raw materials and goods in various stages of manufacture; *licensing agreements* which authorize the use of patented technologies and trademarks; *management contracts,* which provide managerial services and "know-how" for a fee; *service contracts,* which provide for the maintenance and upgrading of plants, equipment, and processes; *equity investment,* entitling the investor to a share of dividends; *capital lending,* wherein the MNC loans funds to the firms in the nation; *marketing contracts,* where products of a country are sold in international markets by an MNC; and even *financial speculation,* where the operations of a corporation in a Third World nation allow the MNC to attempt to take advantage of fluctuations in international money markets.

Knowledge of the variety of MNC operations is important to gain at least three different basic understandings about relationships between multinational corporations and Third World nations:

1. The MNC operations in a given nation never follow a set formula. Each nation has its particular legal, economic, political, and social environment for business. The result is that the activities of a given firm in a given country will be a combination of the different operations listed above. In a few nations, all will be part of the firm's activities. In most, some operations will be carried out by one multinational, others by other multinationals, others by local firms, and others by the host government.

2. Historically, MNCs have been relatively aware of the variety of types of operations which they could carry out in a Third World nation. This history of corporate awareness has meant that when an MNC has decided to work out a business arrangement, it has chosen that arrangement only after considering and rejecting many alternative arrangements.

3. Third World consciousness of the range of alternatives is rapidly rising. Third World nations increasingly are dictating terms to MNCs, deciding for themselves what kinds of business arrangements they want to work out, and limiting the alternatives open to foreign firms.

To make sense of the impact of multinationals on these nations, one must view MNC operations as broadly and flexibly as do MNC managers and Third World government functionaries. Limiting the discussion of multinationals to direct foreign investment and not including importing, exporting, capital lending, management contracts, and so on, results in talking about not much more than the tip of the iceberg.

BUSINESS GOALS OF THE MULTINATIONAL CORPORATION

Many different answers have been posed to the question "What is the firm after—what is its goal?" Answers such as short-term profits, short-term stock market value, dividend value, sales value and volume, long-run survival, stabilizing the firm's environment, minimizing competition, and maximizing managerial discretion have been put forward by a variety of writers.[5] None of these considerations can be shown to be irrelevant, and all are interrelated to some extent. However, the focus of this chapter is corporate decision-making, so the goals discussed should be those which corporate decision makers have in mind as decisions are made.

The two business goals which my research has shown are foremost in the minds of corporate decision makers are: (1) to achieve a satisfactory level of corporate earnings; and (2) to achieve a satisfactory level of managerial (their own) discretion.[6] In attempting to achieve a satisfactory level of discretion, a manager essentially attempts to structure tasks and time commitments to be free to act as he or she deems appropriate in any given circumstance. This freedom is relevant for discussions of all business situations. Managers want to be able to spend necessary time on tasks important to them and not to be constantly plagued by details of relatively unimportant projects. For example, one of the managers I interviewed expressed great frustration at having to spend as much time dealing with the complicated affairs of a relatively small installation on a Caribbean island as he had to devote to much larger, but apparently more easily understandable, investments in Canada. Other managers complained that their discretion was being infringed upon by new regulations on foreign investment by Latin American nations; an equally large number complained of infringements on their freedom of action by their home offices, or by U.S. government regulations. It is possible to argue that achieving satisfactory earnings is simply a necessary condition for having sufficient managerial discretion and that, therefore, satisfying managerial discretion is the decision makers' only goal. However, the issue of earnings levels is so important in the discussion of relationships between corporations and nation states that it must have equal billing with managerial discretion.

These two goals are quite complex in themselves. Our discussion of them will by no means be complete, but the dimensions of the discussion can be seen by the reader thinking out the implications of the following three equations:

$$\text{Earnings} = f\left(\frac{\text{revenues} - \text{costs}}{\text{capital invested}}, \text{market size, future earnings prospects}\right)$$

$$\text{Managerial Discretion} = f\left(\frac{\text{No. choices desired} - \text{No. choices proscribed by others*}}{\text{Managerial time spent on the decision}}\right)$$

$$\text{Action on a Business Opportunity} = f\ \text{Earnings (Managerial Discretion)}$$

The first equation states that when a manager thinks about the earnings resulting from a given business opportunity, he is pleased if revenues exceed costs, if this difference represents a reasonable return on invested capital, if the market is large enough to be of concern, and if earnings in later time periods are similarly adequate. The indeterminate form of the equation leaves open the questions of "How much earnings?", "How large a market?" and so on. These will be treated next when we discuss alternative models of the firm.

*"Others" include other managers, competitors, home or host country regulators.

The second equation indicates that managerial discretion is a function of the amount of time needed to implement an alternative and the amount of freedom of choice the manager estimates he will have in dealing with the contingencies of the alternative. While the first equation indicated that capital is a scarce and desired resource for the firm, this equation indicates that managerial discretion is at least as desired by corporate decision makers. Just as a project is evaluated for the return it will bring to capital invested, so it is evaluated for the return it will bring to the executive time invested in making and implementing the decision, and the freedom of choice open to the implementors.

The third equation indicates that levels of both earnings and managerial discretion are taken into account when action is taken on a business opportunity. An example may further clarify this discussion. Imagine two projects, A and B. Both projects have equal estimated earnings. Project A will require 100 hours of executive time to negotiate and manage, project B 200 hours. Here project A is obviously the referred alternative. However, one could also pose a project C, earning half as much as A or B but only requiring 50 hours of executive time; or a project D, earning twice as much as A or B and requiring 250 hours of executive time. Choosing among A, C, and D would require that the decision makers carefully consider which resource is more scarce for their firm: capital or managerial discretion. Project C would be preferable to A despite its lower earnings, if managerial discretion were scarcer than capital. Project D would be preferred if capital were more scarce than managerial discretion. In any case, the ideal project would be one like project E, where the firm's earnings goal is satisficed with reduction of managerial discretion such as time demands minimized. (The appropriateness of the term "satisficed" will be discussed in the next section, Models of the Firm.) The figure below summarizes these five projects.

Factors Affecting Choice	Projects				
	A	B	C	D	E
Earnings	100	100	50	200	satisficed
Time Demands	100	200	50	250	minimized
Goal Maximization	both moderately	earnings moderately	time	earnings	both perfectly

In this discussion of corporate goals, it is argued that earnings or return on capital can never be taken by itself as a measure of fulfillment of an MNCs goals. Furthermore, a totally distinct phenomenon—managerial discretion—is at least as important an objective for corporate decision makers and is as amenable to quantitative measurement as are earnings.

This discussion. of corporate goals is based in the view of the firm as a satisficer rather than a maximizer. To clarify these views of the firm we now turn to a brief discussion of models of the firm.

MODELS OF THE FIRM

The Perfect Competition Model

The simplest model of the firm depicts the firm as if it were maximizing profits. It competes in perfectly competitive markets. Information is a free good—prices and market conditions are given, as the entrepreneur has perfect information. Firms fail when marginal costs exceed marginal revenue.

This model depicts the firm as an institution with clearly ordered objectives and with the capacity to move toward these objectives as its decision makers dictate. It would seem that such a firm would fail only when a vital market were distorted by political or some other natural phenomenon.

The Satisficing Model

The perfect competition model fails to take into account the complexity of the firm's environment. Information is not a free good. It is virtually impossible for a firm to have perfect knowledge of all or any of the markets in which it is a buyer or seller. This includes knowledge of labor markets. Rather than singlemindedly pursuing the optimal path of profit maximization, a firm develops some satisfactory level of payoff and settles for any outcome which approximates this level.

Satisficing rather than maximizing is characteristic and desirable for large firms such as multinationals for at least two reasons:

1. When firms attempt to maximize in the short run, earnings follow a volatile pattern—high in good years, low in bad. The high earnings of good years raise owners' and stockholders' expectations so that they become easily dissatisfied with managerial performance in lean years.[7] Short-run maximization is therefore dysfunctional for managers, as it results in wild

earnings swings which are beyond the comprehension of stockholders. Such a strategy will only serve to undermine the confidence that others have in these maximizing managers.

2. Information costs increase as the complexity of the firm's organization increases. A large corporation such as a multinational corporation will accept satisficing solutions because of the risks involved with the information costs of seeking optimal solutions. Only when special circumstances arise (such as the pharmaceutical industry's ability to write off huge research and development costs, or the oil industry's ability to use tax payments to cover exploration costs) do departures from crude satisficing take place.

In the satisficing model, goals are set as a function of past performance and estimations of future capacity. New decisions are made to realize earnings goals with minimum sacrifice of managerial discretion. Interviews with MNC managers consistently show that a manager would prefer to have objectives realized and "presented on a silver platter" than to have to agonize over every step of a project, nursing it from hopeful beginning to profit-making end. (Such a preference seems to me to be quite rational and healthy.)

In the next section we will turn to a discussion of variables which influence decision makers' views of the chances of satisficing corporate goals by doing business in a given country. Central to this discussion are the points we have made so far: that corporate managers satisfice rather than maximize goals, and that indicating earnings goals alone is not satisfactory for describing a firm's objectives.

DETERMINANTS OF BUSINESS DECISIONS

At least four entities impinge on the shape of international business decisions:

1. The *firm* making the business decision;
2. The *host country* where the business may take place;
3. The firm's business *competition;*
4. The *home country* in which the firm's international headquarters is located

When one speaks of the social organization of decision-making in the firm, the subject is the patterned interaction within and among these social actors.

The twin goals of revenue satisficing and managerial discretion satisficing are pursued differently by firms with differing characteristics and by firms confronted with different types of competition in home and host countries. In order to focus on the MNC and development, later sections in this chapter will outline how firms are adjusting to changed Third World-host country demands. However, it is first necessary to indicate the characteristics of each of these four social actors.

Characteristics of the Firm

When a manager is judging the advisability of constructing a new factory or exporting a new product to, say, Colombia, he should be conscious of both the amount of risk his firm can absorb at the moment, and how much risk is involved with the problem at hand.

This usually means that the manager first considers whether or not his firm is conducting business there. Continuing *existing business relations* is a prime concern of all MNCs, whether they are in a strong position and can take big risks or whether they are vulnerable and must be cautious. Existing business relations obviously play a part in the e$rnings picture of a company. If existing earnings are affected by new decisions, the net impact on worldwide corporate earnings must be examined. Equally important is the net impact on managerial discretion. A new MNC-host country arrangement may inadvertently force changes in existing arrangements in other parts of the world. When the Andean Pact countries demanded in 1970 in their Regulations for the Treatment of Foreign Capital that 100 percent foreign-owned corporations sell a portion of their equity to host country nationals or the host government, the loudest MNC protests were not simply because of expected earnings reduction (these could be negotiated). At least equally important was the possibility that, if the foreign firms gave in, other host countries would make similar demands, thus precipitating a global change in MNC autonomy vis-a-vis the host countries.[8]

Such changes would not only reduce managerial discretion through formal arrangements but would also reduce discretion by absorbing managerial time in rounds of sensitive negotiations and by making the future of existing arrangements even more difficult to predict.

Whether the multinational has an existing investment in the country in question is of prime importance. It affects not only the local situation but also long-term global revenue and discretion objectives.

Many other variables affect the manager's view of a new opportunity. Whether an MNC manager is cautious regarding a new business decision because of existing business relationships is a function of the *vulnerability of his own position in the company,* his perception of the risk threshold of his company, and the risks he perceives involved with the problem at hand. Furthermore, uncertainty in any of these three areas will provoke further caution among these decision makers. (Risk and uncertainty must be distinguished. Risk describes a situation where a decision maker can assign probabilities to success or failure. Uncertainty describes a situation where the decision maker finds it impossible to evaluate such probabilities. Multinational managers describe business decisions in industrialized countries as normally involving relatively more risk, and business decisions in Third World countries as normally involving relatively more uncertainty. They are much more comfortable coping with risk than with uncertainty.)

It is impossible to list all of the factors which affect the firm's evaluations of *risk thresholds*. Before listing some of the principle determinants, one should know that firms behave very differently when they can absorb much risk and uncertainty (have high risk thresholds) from when they have lower risk thresholds. In times of high risk thresholds, new goals may be important determinants for corporate decision makers. Revenue and discretion satisficing may give way to other considerations. These may range from criteria reflecting abstract theories about corporate expansion developed by particular managers, to personal family considerations of MNC decision makers. In the 1960s, some multinationals expanded without consideration of revenue and discretion satisficing. This expansion was sparked by the theory that the long-term survival of a multinational corporation required covering the globe in its entirety. With the passage of time, many subsidiaries established on this basis have folded.

Risk attached to foreign operations is evaluated very differently in firms which are *heavily dependent on foreign operations* and firms which are only marginally dependent on foreign operations. Firms which depend on foreign operations for large proportions of their sales and profits have already committed themselves to operating outside the country of their corporate headquarters and have usually gained expertise in evaluating foreign business opportunities. Such firms quickly label an opportunity "promising" or "out of the question." Firms with smaller foreign operations are more likely to be indecisive when evaluating new opportunities.

The level of *diversification of foreign products* has a similar impact on evaluation of risk. The more diversified a firm's product lines, the more varied its experience evaluating business opportunities. This experience results in a more crystallized view of new opportunities. Here, as with the case of dependence on foreign operations, it is critical whether these evaluations are made in terms of current world conditions or conditions which prevailed at a past moment of great import in the firm's history.

The *recent history of a firm* also has a great impact on its risk evaluation. MNC managers who perceive their foreign operations as growing in importance will be much more sympathetic to the development of new foreign operations than will managers for whom foreign operations have failed or have not increased in importance. When evaluating the promise of doing business in the Andean Pact in the early 1970s, managers of firms which had entered Brazil in the early 1960s before Brazil's "economic miracle" were much more enthusiastic about prospective Andean business than were firms with little or late experience in Brazil. The former managers minimized or discounted the risk involved in entering new business situations of relative uncertainty.

A firm's *organizational maturity* also has an impact on risk evaluation. Firms which are just beginning to develop international interests are likely to be less centralized in their decision processes when compared with highly internationalized firms. In the former firms, international operations or international division may exist as islands apart from the rest of the firm. When risk evaluations are left exclusively to international managers, enthusiasm for new international business operations usually is higher than when home country or global managers have a dominant hand in decision-making.

Another critical variable has to do with the *nature of high level decision-making in the firm.* Normally, the final decision regarding international business ventures is made by members of a body such as the executive committee of the board of directors. This typically includes the president of the corporation, the executive vice president, a legal counsel, and a comptroller. These people, in turn, are heavily influenced by their one or two closest advisors. Thus, for example, both the president of the corporation and the assistant to the president of the corporation are critical actors in this decision-making process. Firms in which one or more of these critical actors have had recent firsthand business experience in Third World countries behave differently from firms in which none of these actors have had such experience.

This experience must be recent, as business climates in these countries have changed so dramatically in the last ten years that experience predating the mid-1960s may confuse rather than clarify decisional processes. These crucial decision makers may have such experience by virtue of recent promotion from Third World management positions, of recently switching employments from other firms, or of old ties which are continually renewed for short periods. For example, one of the firms most successful in maintaining business relationships and remitting profits during the Allende period in Chile has as assistant to the president an individual who had been in another firm's financial office in the southern cone of South America during the 1950s and who annually renewed his business ties in those countries. He was able to provide this firm with insights for dealing with Chile's problematic business climate which were lacking in other firms. In another firm, managers of subsidiaries were systematically brought into the high level decision process. They were able to provide insights similar to those provided by this assistant to the president.

Risk becomes virtually nonexistent when a firm is perceived to have a monopoly on any good or service which is deemed essential for a host country's economy. Thus, IBM can present a far harder line when exploring new business opportunities than can a firm such as Ralston Purina which must face far more intense food processing *competition* than does IBM in the computer field. Through the 1960s, mining companies experienced minimal risk both because of their control of metal refining technology and their access to world markets for metals. Now that firms in Third World nations have increased access to these technologies and are beginning to learn about marketing of minerals, risk calculations of mining companies have changed.

Another very important consideration is whether the firm *depends on the host country* in question for any one of the factors which makes its business possible. If it depends on Brazil as a market for tractors, for example, or on Hong Kong as a source of labor, or on Mexico as a source of sulphur for downstream manufacturing processes, or on Chile as a source of copper which it sells, unprocessed, the risk of losing this factor will outweigh the risk involved with doing business in a changing business environment.

Characteristics of the Host Country

A firm naturally evaluates *what the host country has to offer* the firm. Markets, raw materials, labor, technology, capital, technical advantages (such as being a tax haven), or any combination thereof determine the initial lure of a country for a corporation. For manufacturing firms, the market is of primary consideration. Although the size of a market is important, of greater importance is the expected growth of a market. Firms do not necessarily want to invest in countries with large populations. They wish to invest in countries where the number of potential buyers is increasing rapidly, thus making it easier to find buyers who do not have established preferences for competitors' products.

Among the other attractions mentioned above, *raw materials* are especially important for firms involved in mining and petroleum production. Lacking access to these products, such firms would go out of business. For such firms, market growth is of little importance at this point in history. Refined petroleum and copper have eager buyers in most parts of the world. Access to raw materials is more problematic. Without crude oil or copper ore, such countries have no product to market. Third World countries which once automatically gave MNCs access to their raw materials are now making such access a privilege which must be paid for dearly.

Labor, technology, and capital are three factors of production which are usually thought of in totally separate terms. If the business transaction in question is dependent on these factors—that is, if it is a direct foreign investment—then corporate planners weigh each and aggregate the capacity of the host country to provide these three commodities when considering a business agreement.

Labor has a number of facets which must be distinguished in order to fathom the process of evaluating business opportunities. The movement of labor-intensive manufacturing plants from the United States and Japan to Taiwan, Hong Kong, and Singapore seems to indicate the importance of minimizing labor costs in manufacturing production. However, the cost of labor is only one aspect of this phenomenon. At least two other labor-related factors must be considered in this calculus: the quality of labor and the docility of labor.

If certain skills are needed in the production process, a firm will prefer making use of a labor force which can easily supply already trained workers than to have to identify and train laborers for its plant. With the world's revolution of rising expectations, labor docility is probably the most important aspect of the labor force for corporate managers. Strikes, especially in the United Kingdom but also in other nations with active labor unions, have caused managers to look for countries with docile labor forces when establishing new facilities. The docility of the labor force has always been reported in business publications evaluating business prospects in Third World countries. Recently, it has also been mentioned more widely such as in advertisements placed in U.S. newspapers by Third World nations hoping to attract new investments.

Managers negotiating a new direct foreign investment (DFI) not only investigate labor union activity in a nation but also determine how local officials deal with labor militancy. In extreme cases, corporations have demanded guarantees of police action against the formation of unions or the arrest of principal union militants as preconditions for establishing a plant in a host country.

Labor quality is usually perceived as of lesser importance to MNC managers in the early stages of an investment. Managers often anticipate that they will be able to train unskilled blue collar workers to operate the facility satisfactorily in a reasonable amount of time. Such projections have met with varying degrees of success. However, successful foreign investments have usually been able to solve such labor problems, and they rely on local labor to carry out all but upper management functions.

Labor quality is also an issue in terms of recruiting management. Management is a kind of labor, albeit highly priced and skilled. For foreign operations, MNC managers try to utilize host country nationals as much as is possible in the management of DFIs. Typically, a DFI has a high proportion of foreign managers during its first years of operations. Thereafter, the number of foreigners is steadily reduced until (ideally) the entire subsidiary is managed by nationals. Most MNCs have come to realize, however, that the success of their business is not based in a manager's nationality but in his management skills and his loyalty to the MNC. A Bolivian or a Belgian can be just as skilled and just as loyal to a U.S.-based MNC such as ITT as can an American. The trend in MNCs is for high level management to become increasingly internationalized without disrupting the basic structure of the firm.

Thus, the cost, quality, and docility of labor are considered by MNC managers when evaluating international business opportunities. However, no one of these facets of labor necessarily has primacy over the others. All are aggregated with the other considerations relevant to the decision process.

The ability of the host country to provide technology and/or capital for a corporation's operations would appear to have little relevance since these are factors that it is normally supposed a MNC contributes to a Third World nation. The corporation is supposed to be the provider of capital and technology to lands where such commodities are scarce. In fact, these commodities are similar to all other factors of production in that a corporation will prefer to carry out its operations in settings where it can minimize the amount of capital it has to risk and also minimize the technological problems it may have to incur.[9]

The surprising degree of multinational reliance on host country *capital* markets has been discussed elsewhere.[10] It should not be surprising that a corporate decision maker would prefer to do business in a host country where local capital is available to him for his business operations rather than import the capital needed and, in the process, reduce the amount of capital available for other operations. If a $20 million plant in, say, Brazil, can be financed with $2 million of the MNCs capital and $18 million in local money, while an identical plant in India requires $15 million in MNC capital, it is immediately clear that, *ceteris paribus,* the Brazilian investment is preferred.

Technology is a two-edged sword. While a corporation would prefer not to do business in a technological wasteland—a host country without the capacity to service, even minimally, a plant or equipment—it also wants to avoid investing in a locale where its techniques may be too readily copied and partners turned into local and international competitors. Thus, MNC managers look for situations with adequate infrastructure but where the maintenance of technological monopolies is relatively assured.

The variety of *technical advantages* which a host country can offer a firm can only be touched upon here. They range from providing a central location for worldwide transshipment (as does Brazil, located at convenient distances from North America, South America, Africa, and Western Europe) to levying no or miniscule corporate taxes. This latter situation—described as a tax haven—is currently provided by such countries as Luxembourg, Panama, Ireland, the Bahamas, Cayman Island, and a host of other nations. By establishing facilities or, in many cases, merely setting up an office in a tax haven, the firm's financial managers markedly increase their managerial discretion.

A number of firms which manufacture goods in Latin America for consumption or additional processing elsewhere, transship through a tax haven (the favorite is Panama). Such transshipment gives the multinational finance office the opportunity to adjust prices so that the bulk of the product's value accrues either to the host country, the tax haven, or the country of destination, depending on which is most advantageous to the corporation. Sometimes this can reduce the worldwide tax burden of the MNC when profits are disproportionately declared in tax havens. However, the requirement by some host nations that books be consolidated on a worldwide basis can reduce this advantage.

Increasing the amount of funds available to multinational managers through such tax breaks is probably not as important as the general flexibility that such arrangements afford the firm's financial managers. This ability to fix the prices at which goods are transferred among MNC subsidiaries (called transfer pricing) allows MNC managers to locate capital within their network of subsidiaries in the manner that most benefits the firm, with little regard for the restrictions set by many Third World nations on the import and export of foreign exchange. When a nation attempts to improve its balance of payments problems by limiting the size of foreign exchange profit remittances sent to other countries, a corporation can circumvent such regulations by adjusting the transfer price of some good it exports or imports to the country in question.

Other technical advantages may include exceptional freedom to import or export goods, freedom from antitrust regulations, monopoly in local markets, or special patent protection.

One of the things which powerfully affects an MNC manager's disposition to do business in a host country is the ease with which the manager feels he and his colleagues will be able to understand the business environment of the host country. This is not something that can be as easily identified as market growth, the availability of raw materials, or a docile labor force. The time needed to master a Third World nation's business environment is as much a function of the experience of the firm and managers in question as it is the characteristics of that business environment.

With the invention of the jet engine, the International Telex System, and the international credit card, the geographical spread of a firm's subsidiaries has diminished as a problem for MNC managers. Telex and telephone networks keep foreign subsidiaries in constant touch with their home office. Travel facilities have so improved that managers can be physically present within a day's time to troubleshoot at any subsidiary within a day's travel from their base at worldwide headquarters.

While the problems of being able to move among a firm's subsidiaries and rapidly transmit information internationally have diminished for MNC managers, a host of problems regarding the content of that information remains. If a firm has never done business in a particular host country, it will experience considerable problems understanding that potential host country's legal system, political realities, geography, consumer market, labor force, and so on. These problems will be multiplied if the firm has never had experience investing in a similar country or if any of these conditions undergoes rapid change in the host country.

Firms, like other organizations and even individuals, are able to operate more effectively if they understand their environment and can predict its future shape. Therefore, *a relatively stable and understandable business environment* is of crucial importance to a manager of a multinational corporation. (We have already argued that changing business environments affect perceptions of managerial discretion on the part of managers, and that this variable and the satisficing of revenue goals are jointly evaluated as managers make business decisions.)

A host country with a rapidly changing business environment different from settings familiar to the firm in question would have to offer unusually attractive market, labor, technical, raw materials, or other advantages to an MNC in order to induce it to invest. In designing a package which would be attractive to MNC managers, the Puerto Rican designers of "Operation Boot Strap" not only set up an arrangement which could easily satisfice revenue goals, but also structured legal arrangements and political arrangements in terms that could be easily understood by mainland U.S. executives. Other Caribbean islands (for example, Jamaica and the Dominican Republic) are not permitted legal arrangements similar to Puerto Rico's United States commonwealth status which allows special earnings advantages. Such countries have not been able to structure, for political and cultural reasons, their political and business situations in terms as closely parallel to the United States as has Puerto Rico. When such nations attempted to create business environments easily understandable to MNC managers, they did so through the autocratic wielding of naked power (for instance, the Trujillo and Balaguer governments in the Dominican Republic). Other Caribbean nations (such as Colombia and Trinidad) have consistently provided foreign firms with high returns. However, none has gained great popularity as a market or a site for investment because of difficulties of imposing U.S. business practices in these locales, and difficulties with MNC managers feeling uncomfortable with their political, legal, and geographic environments.

Especially problematic for Latin American governments is the presumption by many MNC managers that their political situations are in a constant state of upheaval and revolution. Managers with this vision of Third World nations take a dim view of prospects for developing business relationships with them. With political instability may come a whole new set of formal and informal ground rules for business, and the need to develop personal relationships with new decision makers whose cooperation is needed if business is to continue. Mastering these ground rules and gaining the confidence of key decision makers are time-consuming for MNC managers. Furthermore, as mentioned above, MNC managerial time is a scare commodity both from the point of view of the firm—because there is a general scarcity of good international managers and because their time is expensive—and from the point of view of the manager, because the more time he must spend shoring up the basis for existing business relationships, the less time he can devote to expanding and improving the business activities for which he is responsible.

The *role that the host country can play within the global network* of flows of revenue and/or factors of production also constitutes an important characteristic of the host country which is taken into account by MNC managers. In recent years the emphasis of this concern has changed dramatically. From the end of the great depression until the middle 1960s, Third World nation host countries were viewed by raw material companies as providers of raw materials, and by manufacturing concerns as parallel markets to be penetrated one by one. This view was prompted by policies of import substitution adopted by many Third World nations. Up through the first third of the twentieth century, apart from the production of raw materials, most relationships between Third World nations and foreign firms were based in firms exporting manufactured products from industrialized nations and importing them into Third World nations. During the depression of the 1930s, new policies were developed in many Third World nations whereby they attempted to improve their balance of payments situations by substituting goods manufactured in their home countries for these imported products. While much of this production was carried out by domestic firms, a substantial proportion was carried out by subsidiaries of multinationals who established themselves in Third World nations, often in exchange for agreements with host country governments that they would have absolute monopolies on the manufacture and sale of the items they produced in these countries. Thus, the one brand of razor blade sold in many Latin American countries was an American brand; the one brand of many drugs was a Swiss brand; the one brand of automobile tire was an American brand, and so on. Furthermore, where formal monopolistic agreements did not exist it was quite simple to establish difficult barriers to entry. This was achieved simply by establishing high tariffs for goods not physically produced in the host country, or by selling a product whose research and development costs or advertising costs were so high that it was difficult for a potential rival to amass the capital to research or advertise adequately and enter the market as a competitor.

Beginning in the late 1950s, host countries began to reevaluate such arrangements and attempted to increase the benefits that host countries received from these arrangements. Tariffs were lowered and questions posed about research and development costs, the role of advertising, the role of the international Patent system, and other aspects of international business. At the same time, MNCs developed a capacity for dealing with more than one country at a time with greater ease. Multinationals began to think of worldwide subsidiaries as a network of operations coordinated among themselves, more in a fashion of a spider web than following the pattern of a center directly and separately coordinating the activities of each of its subsidiaries. Thus, different subsidiaries could carry out different stages of a production process and ship intermediate goods from country to country until the final product was produced. In this way, raw materials for chemicals could be purchased from Mexico and the United States, processed in the United States into basic materials for pharmaceuticals, and shipped in bulk to Colombia where the bulk was broken down to individual doses to be sold in Colombia and the rest of Latin America. Similarly, iron ore could be purchased in Venezuela and brought to steel mills in Pennsylvania, then shipped to Brazil to be turned into automobile engine blocks which would in turn be shipped to all of Ford Motor Company's Pinto subsidiaries for use in new Pinto cars.

This new capability of large firms was complementary to the new needs of prevailing governments in most Third World nations. Third World nations desired sources of export income without giving up control over their domestic markets to foreign business. This MNC global division of labor provided just that service for Third World nations; it also gave multinational corporations tremendous flexibility in terms of how to locate the components of their productive processes. Hong Kong, Singapore, and Taiwan have been the most notorious Third World nation export platforms for multinational corporations. However, as wages, markets, and availability of raw materials change, these nations become less attractive and other nations become new export platforms. Thailand has become a new export platform in Southeast Asia, and MNC subsidiaries in Brazil and other Latin American countries have begun to assume this role.

The importance of satisficing the revenue goal makes host country characteristics which affect flows of funds extremely important. Laws which limit the amounts of funds which can be repatriated to a multinational's headquarters country, and laws which allow exchange rates to be unpredictable, diminish the attractiveness of a Third World nation as a potential partner in a business relationship. Similarly, dramatic actions such as nationalizations or the possible reevaluation of corporate property dim international business prospects.

However, the large set of MNCs who already have sunk investments in Third World nations have little choice when a host country changes its legislation concerning repatriation, the exchange rate, or valuation of property, or nationalizes an MNC subsidiary. As a result, home countries of prominent investors—the United States, Japan, European Common Market

Countries—have adopted a variety of insurance and tax relief schemes designed to spread the risk involved with these investments.[11] All of these countries have government agencies which provide insurance against losses due to risks such as nationalization, exchange rate fluctuations, and so on Similarly, corporate tax laws allow deductions for losses incurred in overseas investments and give tax credits, against the United States' taxes, for taxes paid abroad. The recent cases of the nationalization of American copper company interests by the Allende government in Chile shows the importance of these hedges against loss, and their importance to the multinational corporations. These cases have also demonstrated to other firms that nationalization may have some benefits which outweigh the benefits of continuing troubled business relations in a host country in which the business climate is growing increasingly hostile. Thus, a number of corporations have welcomed and even forced nationalizations in countries such as Peru, Venezuela, and Chile, realizing that their tax and insurance protection will earn them important short-term credits, and that the elimination of these subsidiaries may have a positive effect on their corporate image and, as a result, on the evaluation of their stock and their ability to buy out other companies through exchanges of stock.

Apart from export platforms, the integration of the global network of an MNC's subsidiaries has other important consequences for the corporation. Plants need no longer be limited in size to the consumption limits of the nation in which the plant is located. For example, Kodak can now sell photographic supplies produced in Mexico not only to the Mexican market but throughout Latin America. This depends on the ability of Kodak to monitor production flows among its subsidiaries, and on tariffs not being raised to make such transactions uneconomic.

The result is increased production efficiency due to economies of scale and, hopefully, both lowered consumer prices and reasonable corporate profits. The global integration of the multinational corporation has been widely discussed. Nevertheless, it is important to underscore the significance that this trend has for Third World nations. The overall impact will be to sharpen business cycles in these nations. The continuation of international business relations will be less based in the needs of the host country and increasingly based in the nature of the role the host country can play in MNCs' global network.

The impact of this on national economic systems will be to shorten and sharpen business cycles. When costs of the factors involved in a firm's production process, and/or perceptions of the nature of the business climate, change, multinational managers' disposition to continue existing business arrangements will also change. Domestic firms will be less likely than MNCs to change their business plans under such circumstances. The impact of multinational corporate attempts constantly to maintain an optimal factor cost mix will deepen depressions and heighten booms in national economies.

Characteristics of the Firm's Competitive Situation

As argued elsewhere in this volume, multinational corporations engage in oligopolistic competition when they are producers, and oligopsonistic competition when they are buyers.[12] A very few firms are the only producers or sellers of a given commodity and, hence, situations of monopolies, although they exist, are relatively rare.

In terms of the problem at hand, oligopolistic competition means that a given firm is aware of what constitutes its competition and how that competition is behaving. In making its own plans, it evaluates both its own position and its competition when deciding which alternative to pursue on its own behalf. Sometimes competition may dissolve into naked collusion, as when corporations such as large electronics firms producing electric turbines, or pharmaceutical companies producing a limited range of drugs, get together either to divide up markets, giving certain firms monopolies in areas of the world, or get together to fix prices at agreed levels.

As far as we know, the overwhelming bulk of business decisions made by corporations toward the Third World are made in the context of oligopolistic competition. The discussion will be limited to that situation.

At different stages of the business decision process, the presence or absence of intense competition will have different impacts on firm decisions. When competition for a given commodity is just beginning, a competitor's interest in that commodity will largely serve as evidence for an MNC decision maker that he too should be interested in that commodity and should evaluate such business prospects. Later on in a decision process when there is more intense competition and many firms are bidding to buy a commodity or to have the right to mine it, to produce it, or to market it, increased interest by a firm's competition will not only spark increased interest in the firm in question but will also affect the type of bargain that it is possible to strike between firms and host countries. This happens simply because, when a host country has a number of offers to choose among instead of just one or two, the process of picking and choosing and evaluating competitive bids will drive the terms of the bargain further and further in the direction favoring the host country.

The commodity in which the firm is interested will also affect the nature of the firm's behavior and its relationship with the host country. If the multinational corporation has a monopoly on the ability to develop, produce, and market the commodity in question, as did many oil companies immediately after World War II and many steel and copper companies until quite recently, a host company wishing to exploit the resources in question has no choice but to deal with one of the firms able to provide such services.[13] The company will accept the offer which it perceives as the most favorable to it. Once the business arrangement is under way, the life of the agreement will be characterized by a constant tug-of-war between the firm and the host country, each attempting to maintain or improve its own terms.[14]

The history of the twentieth century has largely been the history of Third World nations extracting better and better terms in their business agreements with multinational corporations. There have, however, been periods such as that immediately following World War II when terms became more favorable for the firms. Similarly, Third World nations have been dramatically more successful in negotiating with firms dealing with some commodities—such as petroleum and aluminum—and less successful with firms dealing in other commodities, such as computer technology. In recent years, competition has become so intense and the cost of entry of a new firm so reduced in a number of fields that Third World nations have cancelled or dramatically altered existing arrangements with MNCs and have initiated business relations with the original firm's competitors. The terms of oil exploration contracts have been most frequently renegotiated in recent years. In a wide range of industries, limits on profits, terms of ownership, permissible price levels, and many other aspects of business behavior are now routinely renegotiated in many Third World nations as conditions of competition change.

Manufacturing firms usually engage in international business agreements as part of an attempt to increase the size of the market they service. When sales to a given country or region of the world are relatively small, these relations will usually be carried out through the export of goods from the headquarters country and their import to the host country. However, as the flow of goods increases and Third World countries give advantages to firms producing goods domestically, manufacturing firms will set up plants in Third World nations. A firm's overall business strategy and its recent history will determine the strategy it employs for market penetration; these factors will also determine its ability to service and its need to acquire an expanded market. When firms have similar histories and needs, they will begin exporting and/or setting up plants simultaneously. When needs, strategies, and histories vary, firms will make these moves at different points in time. Hence, when a Third World nation is confronted by a set of oligopolistic competitors with similar strategies and histories, they will be more likely to entertain many bids simultaneously and be in a good position to extract relatively favorable terms. When a single firm with a deviant strategy or history embarks alone in an area, it may incur inordinate risks or uncertainty but it will more likely be able to extract terms more favorable than if it were competing with a number of other similar producers.

However, oligopolistic competition may also be characterized by firms reacting more to each other's behavior than to their own internal needs or strategies. Such behavior is usually called the "bandwagon effect," and occurs when competititors follow an industry leader and "get on the bandwagon," making similar business decisions with respect to a host country.[15] When a set of firms is "on the bandwagon," the first firm usually extracts relatively favorable terms which are eroded as competitors make their interests known and strengthen the bargaining position of the Third World nation.

Characteristics of the Firm's Home Country

Characteristics of the firm's home country will also determine how, when, and why the firm looks abroad for business opportunities. Japan is a nation with a minimum of natural resources such as petroleum and iron. The result is that Japanese corporations are heavily involved in guaranteeing supplies of such resources for its nation's manufacturing plants. The explosion of international investment by U.S.-based multinational corporations after World War II was more characterized by a search for new markets than by a search for raw materials. American firms had been involved in raw materials searches since the late nineteenth century. After World War II, manufacturing firms went abroad searching for markets to add to those within the continental United States.

When the cost of a factor of production changes, a firm will search for ways of maintaining a cost which is compatible with its business structure. For example, when labor costs rise as they have in the northern United States or in Japan, firms will search for cheaper and docile labor. Such pressure spurred the migration of U.S. firms from New England to the southern United States and to the Caribbean, and the migration of Japanese firms to Thailand, Taiwan, and other Asian nations.

How a firm searches for international business opportunities is very often linked to its relationship with its home country. Firms which are totally privately owned behave differently from firms which are state owned or have a large component of state ownership. Firms such as Pegaso of Spain and Fiat of Italy are partially owned by their respective governments and have easier access to sources of credit and a greater capacity to spread risk than do firms which are totally in private hands. Similarly, Japanese firms are legally tied to a system which requires such a high credit-to-equity ratio that finding Yen to use in sound international business operations is not a major problem for Japanese multinationals. American firms have far fewer close ties with national credit managers. As a result, they are heavily reliant on the imagination of their bookkeeper to provide a cash flow sufficient to fund both international and domestic business operations.

Providing easy start-up or rescue credit is only one way that a home country may underwrite the risk that a multinational firm may incur. Industrialized nations have developed the systems of investment insurance discussed earlier. The operation of such risk-spreading institutions and the availability of credit are important determinants of firms' international business behavior. Firms with a great capacity for risk-spreading are much more likely to engage in venturesome international business than firms with a lower capacity.

STAGES OF THE DECISION-MAKING PROCESS
IN MULTINATIONAL CORPORATIONS

The process in which the importance of each of these considerations is weighed may be divided into four stages:

1. The initial stage when *general issues* concerning the potential host nation and potential business relationship are being discussed;

2. A stage when *issues specific to the project* under consideration are being discussed;

3. Negotiations that take place after the *project has been approved* by MNC decision makers;

4. Negotiations that take place after the *business relationship is in operation.*

So far, the tone of this discussion has implied a focus on a rational financial officer carefully estimating costs and benefits for his firm to satisfy revenue and managerial discretion goals. However, there are other important decision-making scenarios. These include the manager who built a plant in Tunisia because his daughter married a Tunisian and he wanted to give his son-in-law steady employment, or the manager who began exporting to France because he needed excuses to spend vacation time on the continent and wanted a way to write off transatlantic flights as business expenses.

On one level, these decisions may appear capricious when compared with the profit-satisfying financial analysis. However, they warrant mention both because some decisions are actually made in this fashion and also because they serve as reminders of the importance of focusing on differences among the initiators of a given project, the motivations of these initiators, and the impact that these differences may have on the characteristics of home countries, host countries, and competitors that are taken into account (or not taken into account) in coming to a business decision.

When a project is first suggested, it may be suggested by a variety of sources: the future host country can solicit a business arrangement; the chief executive officer of a firm can make a suggestion; a financial planning officer can launch a plan; similarly, a private entrepreneur, a manager of a local subsidiary, or an official of the home country government can all offer ideas. If the initiator of a project is in a powerful position in the company or is in a position to affect the company powerfully, the project may move to the next stage of the decision process much more smoothly than if it is initiated by a weak actor. Thus, a first step in the examination of stages of the decision process is to identify the initiator of a decision and to analyze his power to affect the eventual outcome.

After a project has been suggested, the evaluation process begins. Only a very small percentage of all projects suggested and evaluated by a firm actually come into being. In the first stages of this evaluation process, broad issues are considered. The company's needs are assessed and the host country is evaluated in terms of the amount of uncertainty and risk involved with a business relationship there. Risk and uncertainty are important to evaluate, not only to gauge probable future profit levels but also to gauge probable future levels of executive time that may have to be spent maintaining the business relations upon which future transactions will be based. First, the evaluators look at the host country's political and social stability so it can gauge whether laws, key host country decision makers, and costs of factors of production will be stable for the life of the investment. The potential market is investigated by manufacturing and service firms; the amount and availability of raw materials is examined by extractive firms.

If this first evaluation concludes that the investment climate is sufficiently understandable, that inordinate managerial time will not be expended over the life of the business arrangement, that profit levels will not be volatile, and that markets and/or raw materials are available in sufficient supply to generate a reasonable absolute return, then the evaluation will enter a new stage in which the focus is on specific characteristics of the project rather than on the general characteristics of the host country and the firm.

Corporate planners make relatively precise estimates of transportation, intermediate processing, and final marketing costs. In the initial stages of evaluations, such estimates are made in relatively precise terms along with explicit "conference intervals" for the estimates. For example, a paperboard company may estimate that it will cost 79 rupees to produce a unit of paperboard in India, but they would also state that this is an estimate and that the cost may be as low as 57 rupees or as high as 118 rupees.

These evaluations move up the corporate ladder, from the evaluation staff to regional or product line managers, to the financial office, to the board of directors and, finally, to the executive committee of the board of directors. In many cases, the precise-sounding estimates seem to take on greater and greater importance as the evaluations rise through the corporate hierarchy; the recognition of possible variation often takes on less importance in the discussion. At every stage, impressive statistics, charts, and discussions are marshalled to make points. Ambiguities and uncertainties which are usually given substantial attention in the earlier, lower-in-the-hierarchy stages of project consideration, are often neglected at this stage. Five possible explanations of the lack of precise evaluation made by high level corporate managers exist: corporate higher-ups may assume that lower level evaluators have already sufficiently dealt with such issues; they may recognize the impossibility of satisfactorily resolving these points; perhaps they are professionally incapable of making such evaluations; they may be too burdened with a large number of decisions to examine each with sufficient care; finally, totally different considerations might possibly be brought to bear at the final stage of the evaluation of the project. Lower level evaluators examine the project on its own terms. Evaluators working for the subsidiary evaluate it in terms of its utility for the subsidiary. The executive committee of the firm's board of directors makes its evaluation from the overall position of the firm, which may or may not be consistent with the interest of the firm's individual subsidiary in the host country in question. When making such an evaluation from its own perspective, it often ignores much of the rationale and data used in building up evaluations from different viewpoints.

After a specific project has been debated within a company and the company decides to go ahead with the establishment of business relationships, negotiations take place between the company and the host country about how the project is to be carried out. This involves settling with relative precision the terms of bringing into being the estimates considered in the firm's prior evaluations. Firms and countries discuss tariff levels, prices of imported and exported goods, the cost of labor, the value assigned to mining rights and to the ore taken from mines, tax levels, collective bargaining procedures, and many other issues, each of which may be crucial to the success of the project.

If these negotiations can be carried out to the satisfaction of the parties involved, then finance capital is raised, productive facilities may be set up, transportation arranged, and labor mobilized.

However, negotiations do not stop with the setting up of a project. Negotiations continue throughout the setting-up process and throughout the life of the project. After the project is "on stream," the terms and conditions of some of the costs negotiated in the first go-round may be changed. New competitors may be willing to settle for lower profit rates, and these may be used by the country to reduce profits of the original firm. Governmental crisis, changes in the labor situation, inflation, and many other considerations may make it necessary to renegotiate the terms of the contract from the host country's side. Similarly, unforeseen costs or global corporate plans may make it necessary for the MNC to initiate a renegotiation.

Such negotiations seem to follow a pattern.[16] A bargaining cycle is set up whereby, before an investment is made, substantial power is in the hands of the potential investor. After money has been committed and capital has been sunk, bargaining power moves in the direction of the host country, as the investor is dependent on the host country to allow an adequate return. The investor is not, however, without power. Unfair practices by the host country will damage future business negotiations with this and other companies.

Similarly, international business relations cannot continue smoothly without the cooperation of the corporations involved. Therefore, the negotiating process and the decisions involved are a continual tug-of-war between the host country and the multinational. Each time the company considers investing new capital, introducing a technological innovation, importing a new product, or changing its marketing structure, advantages accrue to the MNC. After these decisions have been put into practice and the multinational becomes dependent on the host country for their continuation, bargaining power shifts accordingly.

NEW PARAMETERS FOR INTERNATIONAL BUSINESS DECISION-MAKING

The establishment of the Organization of Petroleum Exporting Countries (OPEC) has changed business relationships between Third World countries and multinational corporations. The immediate success of the OPEC countries in dealing with multinational corporations is indeed dramatic, but it is by no means a unique example of Third World countries changing the terms of their relationships with multinational corporations.

In East Africa, in Central America, in Indonesia, in the European Common Market, and in continental South America, nations have been reevaluating their goals and have been attempting to improve their bargaining power vis-a-vis multinationals.[17] Sometimes this has resulted in experimental national legislation. Other times this has taken the form of the establishment of regional blocks of nations, which promote their own development and/or improve their bargaining power with developed nations and MNCs.

This improved bargaining position has resulted in new types of contracts between multinational corporations and Third World nations. Compared with earlier arrangements, recent contracts are more likely to be, in the words of Carlos Diaz-Alejandro, decomposable, reversible, and standoffish.[18]

Contracts are *decomposable* in that separate agreements are specified for separate functions. When a package deal is proffered by an MNC, the components of that deal will be separated in the contract so that each is accepted or rejected on its own terms. In deciding to set up a firm in Ecuador, a watch company had to distinguish among provisions, such as those related to the generation of the finance capital for the factory, those regarding the provision of technology for the factory, those for setting up the productive capacity and the terms involved with managing the plant once it was set in place, and the terms involved with marketing the final product. The advantage of such decomposable contracts is that once a Third World nation has mastered any one part of a package, it can then renegotiate this element and perform this function for itself without destroying the rest of the package and without prematurely destroying the multinational corporation's interest in participating in the project.

Reversible contracts establish procedures that allow either party to back out of the contract if the terms are no longer satisfactory. When contracts are both decomposable and reversible, the chances of resolving host country-MNC disputes increases and the possibility of such disputes overflowing from business to the political arena is diminished.

Standoffishness characterizes relationships between two parties when contact between the parties is restricted to clearly specified exchanges. An idealized example of a standoffish relationship is the "silent trade" between primitive tribes.[19] "Silent trade" occurs when one tribe brings goods which it wants to exchange and leaves them in a clearing or some traditionally agreed-upon locale. The other tribe observes this deposit, collects the goods, and places some of its own goods there in exchange. The first tribe later retrieves the new goods and the trade is completed. By carrying out a number of such exchanges over the years and adjusting the amounts of goods deposited, the two tribes establish norms of fair exchange. This intertribal exchange takes place without face-to-face interaction. "Silent trade" is ideally standoffish in that virtually all of the contact needed for the exchange is directly related only to the exchange. The exchange takes place without political threats, without promises of inter-tribal aid contingent on some aspect of the exchange, and without special privileges being offered to any member of either trading team. Given the history of host countries defending the interests of subsidiaries of multinational corporations based within their borders against the interests of local business, home countries trying to pressure host governments to grant MNC subsidiaries special treatment, and MNCs attempting to influence host country decisions by offering bribes, it is especially important that future MNC-host country relations be standoffish.

Apart from the changed nature of contracts, one can observe many other changes in international business relations. The activities of multinationals have been subjected to increased monitoring by host countries. When a new business relationship is contemplated, government agencies attempt to evaluate all components of this relationship to judge whether entering into it is consistent with national interest. This means that government agencies engage in evaluations of the nature of ownership, technology, capital, price structure, and the other aspects of international business discussed above. This evaluation ideally continues through the entire life of the project, so that the capabilities of the foreign corporations can be adjusted to suit the changing needs of the host country. Disclosure by MNCs is fuller than it has been in past years. Requirements such as registration of capital, specification of ownership, and justification of prices are now within the capabilities of host country evaluators and are being required of multinationals.

Financial constraints are being placed on MNCs. The amount of local credit available to them is limited in many host countries. Pricing controls have been placed on intercorporate transactions and on intracorporate transactions, making transfer pricing more difficult (although not impossible). In some cases, limits have been placed on the amount of profit which may be remitted to the home company. The Andean pact has limited this amount to 14 percent of registered capital in a given year.[20] Furthermore, contracts are being written in which profits may not be remitted in foreign exchange but in kind, such as crude oil by Japanese corporations in Peru, or fruit pulp for fruit juices by Coca-Cola in Mexico. Other contracts have been written in which all foreign exchange leaving the country—either for the purchase of factors of production or for the remission—must be balanced by exports of equal value by the company in question. Thus, Massey Ferguson, in building tractors in Peru, plans to make some parts there which will be exported for use in plants in other nations. This is required so it can have the flexibility to import other products to its Peruvian plant and to remit profits.

Host countries will not now permit the importation of technology by MNCs without review. When a process or machinery is designed for use in a Third World country by a multinational, it must now be registered with an agency of the host country and evaluated for its appropriateness. This prevents the dumping of obsolete technology on Third World nations, the use of untried techniques, and overpricing in technology transfer.

The practice of 100 percent ownership of subsidiaries by multinational corporations is in eclipse. Many Third World nations have specified that sectors of their economy which are vital to national security are excluded from participation by multinationals. Such sectors include public utilities, transportation, insurance, banking, media, and extractive industries. Furthermore, in order to improve local industrial capacity, some countries require local participation in all new ventures within their borders. The theory is that national ownership—either by private sector entrepreneurs or by the state—will result in greater local knowledge and give an impetus to national industrialization. Andean pact nations require the fade-out of existing arrangements, whereby ownership gradually shifts from foreign hands to local hands. Restrictions have been placed on the circumstances under which local firms can be bought out. This prevents multinationals from taking over well-run existing operations and restricts their local participation to setting up new enterprises or rescuing failing ones.

THE MNC RESPONSE TO CHANGING PARAMETERS

There is great variation in the response of MNCs to these changing parameters. Some firms at times appear unaware that the world is changing (although this number shrinks with each passing year). Others see the changes and fight them. Others attempt to adjust their existing operations to take them into account as best they can. Still other firms have developed new strategies of worldwide organization which explicitly include these changes as part of their strategy.

The response of a given firm on a given decision is, of course, determined by a wide variety of factors as was emphasized above. However, the firms of nations which had traditionally dominated international business in a given area of the world have been slower to respond to these changes than have firms of nations with little experience. Thus, U.S. firms cling to the past more tenaciously in Latin America; Japanese firms cling more in Southeast Asia; Europeans hold on in their former colonies in Africa and Asia.

Another variable which determines response is the ability of management to take a differentiated view of the costs and opportunities associated with international business. The managers whose concern is simply the amount of profit remitted directly from a given subsidiary are by and large inflexible. Such managers are behind the times in that they have not acquired the perception of their firm as having a global strategy, and they lack insight into the complexity of corporate goals and how profits are generated.

More flexible managers try to ascertain how a given opportunity fits into its firm's global strategy and can see that access to a market, raw materials, cheap labor, convenient sourcing spots, or financial flexibility, while not producing directly remittable profits in a given host country, may contribute substantially to their firm's worldwide strategy.

Thus, Japanese firms sign mining contracts expecting only minimal profit because raw materials are essential for the continued functioning of Japanese industrial plants. Furthermore, they can make profits on other aspects of mineral transactions, such as financing the investment or transporting the minerals to be refined or sold. Similarly, Eastman Kodak can sell photographic paper in Latin American countries at reasonable prices because their Mexican plant can supply most of this market, and much of the cost associated with the production of these materials has already been absorbed in the establishment of the Mexican plant. Sales to Peru are thus profitable for Kodak despite the fact that profits from these sales are reflected on the books of the Mexican company, not the Peruvian branch.

Six other characteristics of the firm, which have been touched upon in our earlier sections, are also useful clues to corporate responsiveness:

1. The presence of personnel knowledgeable and interested in directing the proposed business relationships. Firms lacking such personnel would be unprepared to respond.

2. The recent history of the firm in international business: the more successful the firm's international business experience and the more similar

this prior experience is to the opportunity in question, the more responsive the firm's managers will be to this opportunity.

3. Changing factor costs: if one of the factors of production of a company (for example, labor, raw materials, capital) has become more costly and the business opportunity represents a chance to obtain this factor at a lower cost, the firm will be more likely to be favorably disposed.

4. Need for diversification: if the firm is experiencing problems either in its existing product lines or in its existing market areas, it has a need to diversify. Its managers will look more favorably on new opportunities than they would if no such need existed.

5. Product life cycle: The product life cycle has been discussed in other chapters in this volume. If the firm produces an item which can be made more cheaply outside the home country than within the home country, it will be favorably disposed to produce this abroad.

6. The bargaining cycle: the responsiveness of the firm will be affected by its relevant bargaining position with respect to the host country, as outlined on pages 86 and 87 of this chapter.

The host country can do at least two things to make its opportunities more attractive: First, it can initiate contact with firms. This can be done by having a prior idea of which projects it wants to promote and asking specific companies to make bids on these projects. In doing so, it can offer guarantees which clarify the costs and benefits involved with a firm entering into such a business relationship. Second, it can attempt to make its business environment more understandable. It is virtually impossible to make frequent government changes or frequent changes in business law understandable to interested MNCs. However, it is possible to explain how one's political system works, the nature of a country's legal system, the availability of natural resources, the country's labor market, how the host country is linked to international transportation systems, and the experiences of other foreign corporations in the host country. If it is made readily apparent to MNC managers that it is easy and advantageous for them to do business in a host country, they will feel that their discretion as managers will not be curtailed through spending inordinate time managing business opportunities in that host country and will, therefore, be more favorably disposed to do business there.

Firms are also influenced by their competition. The oligopolistic reaction, or "bandwagon effect" discussed earlier is one indication of this. Direct competitors take such pains to keep themselves aware of each other's movements that it is reasonable to assume that all are aware when a rival has established a business relationship or is considering doing so. If a firm feels a competitor is threatening to outdistance it, it will attempt corrective action.

Business policy in the firm's home country will also affect its responsiveness to international business opportunities. If the home country has adopted ways of sharing risks with corporations who engage in international business, firms will be much more likely to look abroad for investment. Such risk-sharing devices were also discussed earlier. The enactment of risk-sharing policies is in many respects dependent upon the nation's economic history and current position in the international economic system. A nation undergoing economic expansion is more open to involvement in international business opportunities and the enactment of supportive action than a nation in economic decline; the latter may make it difficult for its firms to move resolutely on an international front while it is attempting to resurrect its economy. In such cases, firms may try to take action without the support of their home countries, and a struggle will result between the transnational actor—the firm—and the home country trying to control it.

CONCLUSION

The roles of multinational corporations in the world economic system change with the times. One thing is clear, however: scholarly understanding of these roles lags far behind the abilities of corporations to adjust to new conditions and to develop new strategies. This essay does not pretend to cover all the factors which must be considered for understanding multinational corporation behavior. However, it has presented a rather extensive list of considerations which are only a small part of the picture. The fact that these considerations are not neatly intertwined, allowing the formulation of an elegant abstract theory of how international business decisions are made, speaks to this point. There are few areas of international business activity where social scientists are sufficiently prepared to generate more than the most primitive and commonsensical hypotheses regarding corporate behavior. Behavior within firms which employ thousands of individuals are as complex as those of cultures normally included in anthropology and ethnographies. If a set of social scientists wider than economists and political scientists were to study these social organizations, the result would yield information both pregnant with potential for social theory and with wider immediate social policy implications.

Building upon literature currently available to social scientists, this chapter has tried to make four general but basic points:

1. The goals of the managers of multinational corporations cannot simply be thought of as profit-maximizing. Rather, they are more

complex—involving both revenue goals and personal discretion goals—and must be viewed in a satisficing rather than a maximizing framework.

2. The range of multinational corporations' decision-making involves a wide variety of business functions and not merely direct foreign investment, as is often implied by the literature.

3. Any study of multinational corporation behavior must take into account all of the relevant actors: the MNC, the home country, the host country, and the MNC's competition.

4. New nationalisms are developing in many formerly docile host countries. These nationalisms may appear hostile to traditional forms of international business, but they do not preclude the establishment of international business relationships which are congenial with national plans.

The most successful MNCs of the future will be those that can take advantage of these new opportunities which are consistent with host country nationalism. Managers guiding these firms will be those who are not blinded by past successes and demand their repetition. Successful MNC managers will and do take a differentiated view of the kinds of benefits which can flow from a given international business relationship, and will work to realize these benefits while taking into account all significant business actors.

Representatives of Third World nations are building an understanding of the functioning of the international socioeconomic system. With this knowledge they will strive to strike bargains which reflect their interests and viewpoints. Multinational managers with a long-term vision will build these perspectives into their plans as they do business in Third World nations.

NOTES

1. Examples of discussions of the impact of multinational corporations on Third World nations include: Fernando Fanjnzylbar, *Estrategia Industrial y Empresas Internacionales: Posicion Relativa de America y Brasil* (Rio de Janeiro: Naciones Unidas, CEPAL, November 1970); Ronald Müller, "The Multi-National Corporation and the Under-Development of the Third World," *Foreign Policy* (December 1973); United Nations, *The Impact of Multi-National Corporations on Development and on International Relations* (New York: United Nations, 1975); Raymond Vernon, *Sovereignty at Bay,* chap. 5 (New York: Basic Books, 1971); Constantine V. Vaitsos, "Interaffiliate Charges by Transnational Corporations and Intercountry Income Distribution," unpublished Ph.D. dissertation, Harvard University, June 1972.

2. Two books which summarize much of this perspective are: Michael Z. Brooke and H. Lee Remmers, *The Strategy of Multinational Enterprise* (London: Longmans, 1970); and John M. Stopford and Louis T. Wells, Jr., *Managing the Multinational Enterprise* (New York: Basic Books, 1972).

3. The following together with works cited in footnote 1, are examples of works which critique existing relationships and help point to ways in which Third World nations and

multinationals can work out new forms of relationships: Carlos F. Diaz-Alejandro, "North-South Relations, The Economic Component," Center Discussion Paper no. 200, Economic Growth Center, Yale University, April 1974; Norman Girvan, "Making the Rules of the Game: Country-Company Agreements in the Bauxite Industry," *Social and Economic Studies,* Institute of Economic Research, University of the West Indies, vol. 20, no. 4 (December 1971); Joyce Katz, "Patentes de invencion, Convenio de Paris y paises de menor grado de desarrollo relativo" (Buenos Aires and New Haven: Instituto Torcuato di Tella and Economic Growth Center, Yale University, 1973); Samuel A. Morley, "What to do about Foreign Direct Investment: A Host Country Perspective," *Studies in Comparative International Development X* (Spring 1975): 45-66.

4. Three widely read works which focus on DFI are: Lawrence G. Franko, *Joint Venture Survival in Multinational Corporations* (New York: Praeger Publishers, 1971); Charles P. Kindleberger ed., *The International Corporation* (Cambridge: The MIT Press, 1970); and Vernon, op. cit.

5. The range of answers to the question, "What is the firm after?" can be seen by reading such works as: Paul A. Baran and Paul M. Sweezy, *Monopoly Capital* (New York: The Monthly Review Press, 1966); Chester I. Bernard, *The Functions of the Executive* (Cambridge: Harvard University Press, 1950); William J. Baumol, *Business Behavior, Value and Growth* (New York: Macmillan, 1959); Richard M. Cyert and James C. March, *A Behavioral Theory of the Firm,* (Englewood Cliffs, N.J.: Prentice-Hall, 1964); Robert A. Gordon, *Business Leadership in the Large Corporation* (Berkeley: University of California Press, 1961); Herbert Simon, *Models of Man* (New York: John Wiley, 1957); Oliver E. Williamson, *The Economics of Discretionary Behavior* (Englewood Cliffs, N.J.: Prentice-Hall, 1964).

6. See Williamson, op. cit., and Yair Aharoni, *The Foreign Investment Decision Process* (Boston: Division of Research, Harvard Business School, 1966), esp. p. 306.

7. John M. Blair, *Economic Concentration* (New York: Harcourt, Brace, Jovanovich, 1972).

8. The importance for the multinational of maintaining control in the face of changing host country policies is discussed in Jack N. Behrman, *Decision Criteria for Foreign Direct Investment in Latin America* (New York: Council for the Americas, 1974).

9. The view that multinational corporations make largely positive contributions to host countries is stated by George Ball in "Cosmocorp: The Importance of Being Stateless," *Columbia Journal of World Business* 2: 1969, 25-30. Critical assessments of the impact of multinationals are made by Richard J. Barnet and Ronald E. Müller in *Global Reach: The Power of Multinational Corporations* (New York: Simon and Schuster, 1975).

10. United Nations, *Multinational Corporations in World Development* (New York, 1973); United States Senate, Committee on Finance, *Implications of Multinational Firms for World Trade and Investment and for U.S. Trade and Labor, Report on Investigation No. 332-69, Under Section 332 of the Tariff Act of 1930* (Washington: Government Printing Office, 1973), p. 427; see Vernon, op. cit., p. 156.

11. The United States government's investment insurance agency—The Overseas Private Investment Corporation (OPIC)—is described in its many inhouse publications. These may be obtained from OPIC, Washington, D.C. 20527. Criticisms (and support) of OPIC can be found in the proceedings of the Foreign Relations Committee of the U.S. Senate's hearings on OPIC in 1973.

12. See the essays by Magdoff, Müller, Ranis, and Vernon. This has also been recently treated by Frederick J. Knickerbocker in *Oligopolistic Reaction and Multi-National Enterprise* (Boston: Division of Research, Harvard Business School, 1973), and Luciano Martins in "The Multinational Corporation, 'National Economies' and Intercapitalist Competition" (Paris: mimeo, 1975).

13. The impact of changing control over technology on the behavior of multinationals is discussed in Raymond Vernon, *Restrictive Business Practices: The Operations of Multinational United States Enterprises in Developing Countries* (New York: United Nations, 1972).

14. A model for the dynamic analysis of foreign investor-host country relations can be found in Theodore H. Moran, *Economic Nationalism and the Politics of International Dependence: The Case of Copper in Chile, 1945-1973* (Princeton: Princeton University Press, 1974).

15. For discussions of the "bandwagon effect" see Aharoni, op. cit., pp. 65-68, and Knickerbocker, op. cit.

16. See Moran, op. cit., for a discussion of the pattern of investor-host country negotiations.

17. The press regularly reports on the activities of OPEC and other attempts to create producers' cartels such as UPEB (banana producers) and CIPEC (copper producers). Information on regional programs in existence before 1970 can be found in Miguel Wionczek, *Economic Cooperation in Latin America, Africa, and Asia: A Handbook of Documents* (Cambridge: The MIT Press, 1969). Various aspects of the Andean Pact are discussed in the essays of *Andean Pact: Definition, Design, and Analysis* (New York: Council of the Americas, 1974).

18. These concepts are more fully developed in Diaz-Alejandro, op. cit.

19. Described in Fritz Moritz Heichelheim, *An Ancient Economic History* (Leiden: A. W. Sijthoff, 1958), vol. I, p. 87.

20. See Article 37, Decision 24 of the Commission of the Acuerdo de Cartagena, Lima, Peru, December 31, 1970.

4

THE MULTINATIONAL CORPORATION AS AN INSTRUMENT OF DEVELOPMENT
Gustav Ranis

The role of the multinational corporation in development has been subjected to one of the highest "heat to light" ratios in the literature of any familiar to this observer. Much comment on the subject can only be called polemical, emanating, on the one hand, from those who believe that any foreign corporate presence in a developing country entails the loss of postcolonial virginity and, on the other, from those who view such presence as a simple augmentation of the LDCs' capacity for doing what it wants to do in a smooth neoclassical context. The remaining literature usually occupies intermediate high ground by listing the pros and cons, often as not concluding that the net weight of the argument "depends" on the particular circumstances of the case.

It is, of course, an open question whether anyone can do better than provide such a listing, that is, ferret out what is generalizable about this important and growing phenomenon, at least with respect to its economic impact on the development process.* There is general agreement—if on little else—that the multinational corporation is relatively new, relatively

---

*I hasten to add that although the conference for which this chapter was developed used "political considerations" as its subtitle—and although I readily acknowledge the pervasive political economy setting within which the subject must be viewed—I find myself, perhaps predictably for a "bourgeois economist," unable to incorporate these dimensions to my satisfaction.

The author wishes to acknowledge the very helpful comments of Louis Wolf Goodman.

important, and that it has been growing by such leaps and bounds in the postwar era that it seemed at one time to threaten shortly to gobble up virtually all the world's GNP. Even if that prospect is no longer threatening, the phenomenon clearly cannot be ignored, in terms of its increasingly large role not only in the field of foreign investment but also in international trade. One's perceptions of what it does or does not contribute to development, or what it may or may not contribute in the future, are thus not in the category of precious points for scholastic debate but of rather major importance for the citizenry of both the rich and the poor countries. The drama has at least two leading actors: the MNC (multinational corporation) and the LDCG (less developed country government); and two supporting actors: the DCG (developed country government) and the LDCI (less developed country industrialists). As to the benevolence or malevolence of the instrument from the vantage point of these various concerned parties, there is virtually no agreement and as yet therefore no general political consensus as to where policies affecting the multinational corporation should be heading.

This paper takes the basic position that the role of the multinational corporation in development cannot be assessed independently of time and place, but that such assessment must be related to the particular phase of a developing country's life cycle, as well as to the type (for example, size and resource endowment) of the LDC in question. Secondly, this paper emphasizes the point that the MNC is not by any means a monolithic organizational concept but itself a shorthand for a heterogeneous set of organizational forms ranging from wholly-owned subsidiaries, at one extreme, through various kinds of joint ventures, to licensing and management contracts, on the other. Thus a more helpful, that is, generalizable, interpretation of "it depends," may be, to our mind, one which differentiates among LDCs in terms of both historical and typological dimensions and differentiates among various possible organizational manifestations of the MNC.

While we are quite agnostic on whether it is, in fact, possible to treat this phenomenon in a scientific antiseptic fashion, we nevertheless feel that one has an obligation to try. Resorting to caricatures or mystiques is not particularly helpful in this effort. The MNC did not just happen—there are deep-seated reasons for its existence, persistence, and growth, as well as for the always controversial nature of its report card. We must try to understand these reasons not in terms of some isolated, if fascinating, phenomenon but in relation to what has been happening in the developing world over the past quarter century of attempted transition from colonialism to economic maturity.

The phase a particular LDC finds itself in as well as its size, endowment, and so forth, will, we believe, dictate a differential analysis of the causes, the impact, and, most importantly, the particular organizational manifestation of

MNC activity. Put another way, the MNC is comprised of a bundle of activities including variable proportions of capital, technology, management, training, entrepreneurship, and information. The prominence of different components calls for different organizational structures and consequences. Exploration of these relationships in a more "disaggregated" sense is, we believe, likely to be more fruitful than the customary assessment of the role of "the" MNC in "the" LDC.

The second part of this chapter briefly sketches in what we conceive to be the main contours of the typical LDC transition process and relates it to the changing motivation, organizational content, and impact of the MNC in an idealized sense. The third part deals with the many real world deviations from that idealized historical path and attempts to relate such deviations to some of the current controversy surrounding the MNC phenomenon. The final section presents some modest suggestions concerning the additional light this type of analysis may shed on future policy options facing the various concerned parties.

THE IDEALIZED ROLE OF THE MNC
IN AN HISTORICAL CONTEXT

Kuznets has aptly defined the development problem as one of transition between a long epoch of agrarian stagnation and a long epoch of modern growth.[1] Such a transition, history tells us, may last anywhere from 30 to 50 years and is likely to be composed of a number of subphases during which the development characteristics of the society undergo marked change. In the preindependence or *colonial epoch,* developing countries were characterized by the essentially enclave nature of their production and trade pattern, that is, the coexistence of an export-oriented cash crop sector and a large, relatively stagnant, food-producing agricultural hinterland. Proceeds from this land-based export activity were deployed to finance the consumption needs of the workers and entrepreneurs engaged in the enclave, with the rest either reinvested in the further expansion of the export-oriented enclave—or reinvested abroad, as dictated mainly by the commercial and political interests of the mother country. Once LDC governments had achieved political independence after World War II—earlier in Latin America—they almost invariably attempted to intervene in order to redirect these traditional colonial patterns of production and trade. This redirection is known as the *import substitution subphase* of transition in which LDCGs aim at gaining full control of their critical raw material export earnings through exchange controls and reallocating them towards domestic industrial and overhead expansion. It usually includes substantial government deficit financing accompanied by inflation and increasingly overvalued exchange rates, quantitative import restrictions, and the rationing of other critical materials. In fact, this regime may be characterized as still fuelled by traditional land-intensive exports, but with both foreign exchange and domestic saving now channeled towards the growing industrial sector and a new protected industrial entrepreneurial class. In this subphase the brute act of saving and of redirecting the flow of both new foreign and domestic investment is crucial. It is in this period also when the fine points of appropriate technology choice or even of appropriate output mix choice take a back seat to the exploration of the domestic market, while entrepreneurs are given a chance of learning-by-doing under the cover of protection, with distorted relative prices assuring them of substantial windfall profits.

Let us now turn to the MNC in the context of such a transition from dependent colonial to independent import substitution growth. The old colonial flow of investment to the overseas territories represented a type of long-term movement of capital, management, and entrepreneurship which can be viewed as a forerunner of the MNC.

British foreign lending before 1913, for instance, was primarily portfolio rather than direct, with most of the investment going to the relatively more advanced regions like the United States or relatively more secure places like U.K. colonies. Regions not fitting either of these categories, for example, Latin America (with the exception of Argentina), received relatively less in toto, of which a relatively higher proportion apparently was in the form of equity.[2] Thus even the form of capital flows differed depending on the country of destination and on its overall state of economic and entrepreneurial preparedness. In the postindependence, post-World War II era, the political control which used to be associated with the colonial type of long-run capital movement was, of course, no longer acceptable—neither was the almost exclusive concentration on raw materials and extractive activity which characterized it. Instead, during import substitution investment is channeled mainly into the industrial sector of the LDC, with the main contribution of the MNC one of adding to industrial savings, capital accumulation, and management capacity. At this point in time, when the market, the role of relative prices, efficiency, and so forth have been put aside, at least temporarily, in order to ensure as rapid a rate of industrial growth as possible, foreign capital and management can provide an important assist. This is usually a period when technology choice generally consists mainly in the act of turn-key borrowing from the "shelf" of advanced country technology. Thus the fact that the MNC is very likely to be biased in the same direction has been no cause for special alarm. In this period, the watchword is getting the job done as quickly as possible, with relatively little concern for efficiency—certainly not at international prices.

Pursuing our idealized scenario, the coming of foreign capital, either of the portfolio variety or (more likely where risks are high, intervention difficult, and domestic managerial capacity low) in the form of equity, can thus be expected to play an important role in this phase. The rationale for the wholly-owned subsidiary is undoubtedly stronger at this particular time in the history of a typical LDC than at any other. If the proper conditions can be established attaching to such dimensions as the excessive use of domestic loan capital, the provision of training and upgrading of local management and labor, the avoidance of certain designated areas where domestic managerial and entrepreneurial capacity already exist, plus an *ex ante* agreed-upon time frame for gradual disinvestment or transformation, the contribution of this particular form of MNC presence may be viewed as potentially mutually beneficial. It constitutes the contemporary manifestation of the long-term movement of international capital and management skills in the "right" direction.* Help with what the LDC needs most at this stage, that is, a contribution to the brute act of saving, of getting things done, of managing a relatively new type of activity, can be provided by the wholly-owned subsidiary in this idealized setting.

We do not wish to engage here in the protracted and rather sterile debate on the merits and demerits of the import substitution subphase itself. Faithful to our historical perspective, we will simply assert that we do believe that the infant entrepreneurial/infant industry argument has merit at a point in time, and that much of the criticisms along the Little-Scitovsky-Scott lines[3] is properly directed towards the issues of how much, how long, and what kind of import substitution packages make sense.[4] If the regime is sufficiently flexible, and the vested interests which typically grow up under it not excessively strong, we would expect, after some time, a transition towards a more open and export-oriented subphase of growth to be effected. We do know that this is bound to happen sooner or later because primary or consumer goods import substitution will run out of steam, either because the industrial sector no longer has sufficient markets domestically to keep going and/or because the ability of the agricultural and cash crop export sectors to keep fuelling an often highly inefficient industrialization process without any help from industrial exports becomes ever more questionable.

It should, of course, be readily admitted that many LDCs try to persevere with import substitution, moving from the primary (consumer goods) to the secondary (capital goods and raw materials processing) type. But this becomes an ever more costly process and can be sustained in the longer run only by countries with a reliably favorable natural resources base—and even here problems of increasing unemployment and a worsening distribution of

---

*Needless to add, a logical accompaniment of such factor mobility would be access of unskilled labor into the advanced countries.

income may well force a halt at some point. This struggle between the "necessities" of a changing resource endowment, sociopolitical pressures, and the reluctance of the new industrial class and the civil service to give up their windfall profits and power is another, very interesting—but separate—story.[5]

If these obstacles are successfully overcome, the system is likely to move from its land or raw material fuelled import substitution subphase to an unskilled labor based *export substitution subphase*. The latter is characterized by the capacity of the now more experienced domestic entrepreneurs to combine with the country's abundant supply of cheap labor and begin to look outward, away from the limited domestic market, and toward expandable export markets for labor intensive industrial goods. The industrial sector can now be expected to begin to help fuel its own further growth on a sustained basis, while the economy's entire production and trade pattern swings closer to the lines dictated by resource endowment and efficiency considerations. This change in the system's underlying abilities must, of course, be reflected in accommodating changes in the LDCG's policy package, that is, a gradual move from direct controls and distorted prices towards indirect controls and more realistic relative factor and commodity prices. Devaluation, import liberalization, interest rate reform, the dismantling of other licensing systems, and so on, are all part and parcel of such changes in the policy package as we have witnessed in a number—though still small—of developing countries.

While no endowment or indeed policy changes are likely to be abrupt, what we are contemplating here is the gradual shift from a forced march pattern of import substitution to the more flexible ballet-style advance of export orientation along comparative advantage lines. Consequently, in this more efficiency oriented labor-intensive production and growth phase, the idealized role of the MNC may also be viewed as subject to important change. For, at this point in the life cycle of an economy in transition, the role of appropriate technology and output mixes in penetrating international markets becomes much more important. One can now conceive of a benign and productive combination between the advantages of the MNC, with its global scan of markets and technology, and the growing domestic expertise based on the specificity and pecularities of the local resource endowment and institutional factors. In this period, the MNC presence in the organizational form of joint ventures seems to make increasing sense. As indigenous entrepreneurial and management capacities have by now gradually matured and as, with the diminution of windfall profits, the premium on efficiency increases, there is increasing scope for a functional symbiotic association between foreign and domestic capital as well as talent.[6] Under generally more competitive conditions there is an increasing need for coming up with the right amalgam of imported and adaptive technologies and output mixes to ensure the continued outward-looking expansion of the industrial sector.

Finally, after a period of sustained export diversification, with industrial sector labor absorption proceeding at a rate far ahead of population (and labor force) growth, the LDC will ultimately approach the end of its labor surplus condition and the beginnings of the epoch of mature growth. One would now expect joint ventures increasingly to give way to licensing and management contracts as the "final" manifestation of the MNC presence in the interplay among advanced countries—along with the movement of portfolio capital in response to international differences in the rate of return. We would expect such interactions to be a continuing, flexible feature of the international movement of capital, accompanying a global division of labor with respect to both final and intermediate products.

If we accept, even in rough outline, this idealized, if undoubtedly somewhat naive, two-track picture of the gradual phasing of growth regimes within the developing country, along with the gradual phasing of what constitutes the optimal expression of an MNC presence, the outlines of a changing, mutually beneficial relationship can be discerned. The emphasis gradually shifts from the pure generation of saving and getting the management job done to one of efficiency and entrepreneurial flexibility; from the simple transfer of technology and tastes perfected in different contexts, to the search for imaginative indigenous technology and output mixes; from the simple capital-intensive add-on to the import substitution enclave, to the labor intensive partnership with substantial spillover effects.

In all these efforts, the additional possibility presented by a foreign MNC presence is, of course, just that, an additional potential advantage *if* the above idealized script is not entirely discarded. The real world, we all know, is likely to be many steps removed from such an ideal. The basic suggestion of this paper, therefore, is not to claim that "all is for the best in this best of all possible worlds" but to indicate—by contrasting the real world with such an ideal—that much of the pervasive misunderstanding on the role of the MNC in development may be related to the fact that some or all of the major parties involved too often choose to ignore the historical context and thus the changing nature of any potential mutually beneficial interdependence between the MNC and the LDC. If, for one reason or another, one party or another attempts—as they do—to move against these underlying realities, for example, to rearrange the sequence, or to prevent the sequence from playing itself out, global welfare benefits decline and frictions rise as to their distribution. We intend to illustrate this point and to pursue the resultant inevitable generation of substantial conflicts in the next section.

DEPARTURES FROM THE EVOLUTIONARY IDEAL

If we read the record of the past quarter of a century correctly, substantial real world obstacles exist to any such idealized or "normal" phasing of a changing relationship between the LDC and MNC. On the side of the MNCs there has been a clear reluctance to move from the wholly-owned subsidiary to the joint venture, licensing, and so on, as host LDC entrepreneurial capacity matures and pure saving assumes a lesser importance. On the part of the LDCGs there is often a desire to retain import substitution controls long after their rationale has lost its force but, as the MNC mystique declines, large MNC profits are noted, and nationalistic resentments increase, often together with attempts to change bargains struck with the foreign investor. This is likely to be due to a mutual misunderstanding of the predictable dynamics of the relationship over time. The bargains struck initially during early import substitution are almost bound to guarantee the MNC an extremely high rate of return, based in substantial part on the public grant of monopoly power, which it is later understandably loath to surrender. The LDC for its part, often wants the MNC presence at that point for reasons of prestige, bandwagon effects, or security, almost regardless of the terms—and often at terms much in excess of what it would take to attract it. Witness not only the protection and market-power granted through licensing and other controls but also the lavish tax holiday and other fiscal favors customarily bestowed. Moreover, regardless of one's judgment about the relative benefits accruing to the two parties as a result of a particular foreign investment at this point in time, there should be general agreement that the advantages to the recipient LDC will decline over time and those to the investing MNC increase over time—in the absence of any change in the nature of the contract.

An example of the reversal of the natural sequence which is sometimes attempted is for the MNC to view the joint venture not as a (later) instrument for accommodating to the growing local entrepreneurial, management, and research expertise but to utilize it (earlier) to try to circumvent LDC government controls increasingly aimed—in response to growing domestic pressures—at foreign capital, as import substitution proceeds. Such tendencies are more likely if the product line is fairly broad and diversified, trademarks and patents can be used to gain control over the domestic market, and there is relatively little risk of loss of "real," that is, appropriable, technology via local partners—or of disagreement with them on transfer pricing or other noncompetitive practices. Similarly, with respect to the relative importance over time of research, development, and engineering, we often see an attempt to support research, often very basic, during import substitution within both the public and private sectors of the LDC—almost invariably leading to a substantial wastage of resources—instead of de-emphasizing such activity until much later—and even then, placing more faith in engineering improvements emerging at the factory floor and repair shop level rather than the large breakthroughs of the corporate lab variety. We know that the licensing of technical processes is often used by the MNC, for example, in India,[7] as a device not really to transfer technology among

relatively coequal partners but to gain certain market-sharing advantages or
evade the exchange controls and, by the cooperating domestic firm, to be able
to enlist the help of the foreigners in convincing the "controls bureaucracy" to
issue certain vital slips of paper. The entire arena of so-called technology
transfer is thus often misused by both parties—one party claiming that it is
transferring knowledge when it is, in fact, only utilizing such devices to gain or
maintain a monopoly or trademark advantage; the other, claiming it is
receiving knowledge when, in fact, it requires the mystique of the MNC
hookup to consolidate its own hold within the import substitution hothouse.
Thus we encounter certain code words and payments for services other than
those stipulated, with the main loser the LDC consumer and the development
objective generally. Patents, licensing, and technical collaboration
agreements "before their time," that is, before there can be some reasonable
equality in the technological partnership and some services for the payments
rendered, have given rise to considerable controversy.[8]

Even with respect to the transfer of capital, pure and simple, this reversal
of the idealized sequence is frequently encountered. During import
substitution when domestic interest rates are usually kept artificially low (part
of the effort aimed at favoring local industry), it is the MNC which receives
favored treatment when local capital is rationed. Thus the wholly owned
subsidiary may be more than 50 percent financed by subsidized local capital
with only 25 percent representing new equity flows. During the more
competitive, export oriented subphase, in contrast, when the contribution to
brute saving is less crucial, higher interest rates within the LDC may induce
the MNC to bring in a relatively larger share of new investment capital from
the outside.

We may thus observe a marked lack of sensitivity on the part of the MNC
to the changing capacities and needs of the LDC as it attempts its transition to
modern growth through various historical subphases, and an equal lack of
sensitivity on the part of the LDC as to how it can really maximize the benefits
and minimize the costs of this foreign presence at different points in its life
cycle. In fact, all the actors are likely to be guilty of causing major departures
from the ideal. There are good underlying reasons for such "deviant"
behavior. *First,* the MNC, whose profits are initially based mainly on market
imperfections, may find itself naturally unwilling to shift voluntarily from
windfall to earned profits as required by the nature of the phasing. *Second,* the
LDC government which often "blows hot and cold" with respect to its
regulatory attitude on foreign enterprise, may refuse to try to differentiate
among the various organizational manifestations of the MNC in any
consistent fashion—and end up either welcoming all parts of the MNC bundle
or rejecting all. (It may thus be obtaining the worst of both worlds, in
extension of the well-known shibboleth that a consistent, if tough, policy vis-
a-vis the MNC would be much preferred by foreign investors to one that is

better "on average" but fluctuating and unpredictable.) *Third,* the private LDC investor who initially almost unthinkingly welcomes the presence of large foreign companies to help him "test the waters" and provide political support for government policies favoring the industrial class often later turns on the MNC when he finds himself unable to compete effectively with foreigners who have favored access to capital markets, bureaucrats, and so on. *Fourth,* the governments of developed countries seeking to support the actions of their own investors abroad—which they claim are also in the interest of the LDCs—often do so without any perception of changes in the landscape and the consequent need for change in the nature of the potentially symbiotic relationship. Often, the policy approaches that of "right or wrong, this is my MNC." Aid is tied to the host country treatment of MNCs in the form of Hickenlooper and Gonzales amendments; and manifestations of modern extraterritoriality extend as far as the application of antitrust and Trading with the Enemy acts to U.S. subsidiaries abroad (as in the celebrated recent case of Argentine motor sales to Cuba).

Little wonder that we sense the current rising tide of dissatisfaction and friction but have thus far had little success in disentangling the meaning of "symbiotic coexistence" in this particular sphere of global interdependence. Blame is placed by any one of the actors or the other without any real consideration of the meaning and substance of any ideal (or at least "better") relationship at any particular point in time, or of what elements of flexibility could be built in as a safeguard for the (inevitable) change in the underlying conditions. The all too frequent interventions by all parties in any such idealized phasing which may be postulated can be placed at the doorstep either of a basic misreading of history or a basic misunderstanding of the requirements of long term coexistence, or—if one prefers—a malevolent conspiracy among colluding vested interest groups who, laboring under a short-time horizon, are endeavoring to "get rich quick" by defrauding the LDC public. While it is always most difficult to determine motivation, we shall assume here—for the sake of argument—that the LDCGs taken as a whole are well intentioned and desirous of striking the best bargain for their societies and that most MNCs are not interested in a hit and run strategy but rather in realizing long-term profit goals. If they don't succeed, it is not because we accept the inevitability of conflict under an idealized phasing on both sides but because there is misunderstanding and miscalculation. In order to give this (admittedly vulnerable) argument a little more concreteness, let us look at a couple of points of controversy to see if they can be related to interventions with what we have called the ideal phasing of the relationship.

The role of the MNC in providing scarce capital is one. Those who accept the straight neoclassical line would argue that the MNC is basically an example of a long-run capital movement from capital rich to capital poor regions and don't understand why there should be any question in terms of both global welfare enchancement and benefits to the host LDC. On the other hand, we have seen that MNCs often actually don't bring in very much capital, frequently only 25 percent of the investment is in the form of foreign equity, with 50 percent or more made up of loans obtained at favored rates in the local money markets. In the early import substitution phase, when savings are still the most scarce item, a wholly-owned subsidiary should, therefore, be asked to bring in most of its capital from abroad, either in loan or, more likely, equity form. But once the particular domestic shortage which can be alleviated through the MNC presence shifts from capital towards entrepreneurship and information (especially in the realm of intermediate goods markets and global technology scanning capacity), the LDCG's concern should shift accordingly.

In addition, there is the much repeated, and undoubtedly correct, accusation that the MNC, especially in its wholly-owned subsidiary manifestation, has unprecedented power, unchallenged by either the LDCG or DCG, to show its profits where it pleases by allocating its overhead, setting transfer prices, moving currencies about, and so on. On the other hand, many of these so-called abuses, serious as they may be, spring from the environment created by the LDCG in its desire to avoid foreign competition and provide special access to credit, investment guarantees, tax advantages, and "the quiet life" for its industrial entrepreneurs generally. Whether or not LDC governments create such hothouse environments, attract MNCs and then blame them for continuing to prosper in the shape of the increasingly disliked subsidiary—even after the logic has passed—or whether the MNC influences the LDCG both to adopt these policies initially and then to refuse to turn down the temperature later may not really be the important question. Undoubtedly some of both is correct and the result is the same: an intervention in the capacity for a natural transition from import to export substitution on the part of the LDCG and in the pattern of transition from a wholly-owned subsidiary to the more flexible joint venture, licensing, and management contract manifestations of the MNC.

A closer look at the area of technology transfer and technology choice may serve to illustrate the point further. Let us differentiate, at the outset, between the various components of what normally goes under the name of "technology." First of all, there is existing knowledge about different processes or different ways of producing a given commodity in different endowment situations—and ways and means of devising new ones. (This is what the economist usually has in mind.) Second, there is existing knowledge about different types and qualities of goods—and ways and means of devising new ones (this is what the businessman usually has in mind). Finally, there is the distinction to be drawn between the "actual" transfer of technology—of either kind—from rich to poor countries, and the "fictitious" transfer, for instance, via patents, trademarks, and the like, as a device to preserve oligopoly power and/or avoid exchange controls. To put it quite bluntly, much of the discourse on the role of the MNC in technology transfer has been thoroughly confusing because these very different dimensions have not been analyzed separately and, most important from the point of view of this paper, report cards have been issued on the basis of only a very partial view of the performance and without regard to the historical context.

Specifically, MNCs are, for example, often taken to task for selling overpriced patented "know-how" to their subsidiaries or licensees, the main purpose of the transaction being to restrict entry to both domestic or other MNC competition while increasing the domestic demand for "overspecified" or luxury goods (soft drinks and toothpaste are frequent examples). There undoubtedly is a tendency for MNCs to be less active in this regard when the "technology" transferred is less appropriable, for example, focused on techniques as opposed to quality variation. Yet does that mean that the famous Veblenite "advantage of the late-comer" in borrowing from the international shelf of technology is but a fairy tale—possibly commissioned in some corporate board room in New York or London?

We really do not think so; these advantages are real but often eclipsed by even larger advantages based on other-than technology characteristics. As long as the LDC finds itself in the heavily monopolistic era of import substitution growth it will try to transfer "technology" of the Pepsodent (or product differentiation) type when what the LDC really needs is capital and management. It will try to obtain a thoroughgoing emulation of the international (previously imported) good (such as Coca-Cola and drip-dry shirts) when adaptive goods (such as Green Spot and bush shirts) would serve better, that is, prove cheaper while producing the same amount of consumer utility. Later on, once a more competitive and export oriented environment obtains, the government of the LDC should realistically welcome the inflow of information and technique and product-oriented technology change to ensure the successful and sustained participation of her industrial sector in world markets. In fact, it often does not try to draw this distinction and hardens its attitude—on the basis of its now greater entrepreneurial confidence and/or stronger nationalistic attitudes—just at the time when it could derive larger benefits. The MNC, for its part, as has been shown by the experience of Japan, will not necessarily "cut and run" when forced to concentrate on "real" technology transfers but will instead accept lower (earned) levels of profit in place of higher (unearned) levels of monopoly rents. But it is also, and quite understandably, perfectly willing to continue playing the import substitution game, even if now directed (via export subsidies, tax concessions, and the like) towards the more favored export markets. One need only remind the reader that negative value added can be as negative when contributed in production for export (and by foreigners) as in import substitution.

The product cycle presumes to tell us something about the changing motivations of the MNC as it first explores its own domestic DC markets, then exports, then moves defensively to produce abroad and, finally, seeks to export from its LDC base. While no necessary synchronization exists between this sequence for any particular product line and the natural evolution of the resource endowment, the policy package in any given LDC, or the particular organizational manifestation of the MNC, we would expect to find relatively more of the wholly-owned subsidiary type of MNC in India and relatively more joint ventures and licensing arrangements in Taiwan. This assumes that the admittedly substantial departures from the evolutionary ideal are distributed more or less equitably across countries. In this way, our view can be subjected to some rough and ready tests not only longitudinally, that is, by examining postwar LDCs in transition, or the longer historical experience of Japan, but also cross-sectionally, for instance, by contrasting contemporary LDCs in different phases of development.

We have not attempted any such tests in the context of this paper—which is intended only as suggestive of possible new directions of analysis. Nevertheless, in addition to the somewhat loose and episodal discussion concerning the contemporary LDCs, a word on the Japanese historical case which does not, at first blush, seem to fit the case terribly well, may be in order. Japan, it should be emphasized, experienced a relatively unique early transition period. On the one hand, it was relatively neglected, even after the seclusion period ended, by foreign colonial powers who were busily occupied elsewhere; on the other, the unequal treaty provisions of the Meiji period forced Japan into a relatively mild (that is, low protection) version of the import substitution subphase. This meant the virtual absence of the colonial type of investment in overheads while in industry proper subsidies and extensive technical assistance to domestic investors or direct government ownership replaced the creation of a heavily protected hothouse beckoning to foreign as well as domestic enterprise. Nevertheless the wholly-owned subsidiary form of foreign investment was used in an era where Japanese experience and entrepreneurial capacity was as yet deemed insufficient, for example, in international trade, banking, and shipping until the turn of the century. The predominance of foreign firms in these areas was reduced after 1900 when a more outward or trade oriented policy coincided with greater interest on the part of foreign companies in joint ventures (then called "joint companies") with the increasingly formidable Zaibatsu groups, in such industries as electrical engineering, rubber products, metals, and linoleum, culminating in a substantial expansion during the 1920s and 1930s. As we would expect, technical assistance, patent and licensing arrangements became more prominent thereafter. Thus the Japanese case may be said to represent a "mild" version of the idealized sequence with both the subphases of transition and the changes in the MNC presence muted by the twin forces of early (and consistent) Japanese government resistance and early lack of interest on the part of the Western world.[9]

The way in which technological change is itself generated is subject to a similar and, of course, related cycle. If we distinguish not only between R and D (research and development) but add also E (engineering) and I (information), we can perhaps arrive at some general statements about what constitutes an ideal sequence in a particular product area. Basic R and D would presumably be carried on at the outset in the home labs of the MNC, that is, during the LDCs' import substitution subphase, with scarcely any technology-related activity taking place abroad.* Facing a relatively low volume LDC domestic market, the main objective of the MNC would be to gain assured access with the help of transplanted turn-key technology, restricted model choice (and as little foreign capital input as possible). During this phase, MNC subsidiaries very often even carry outright prohibitions against exports to reassure rivals on market share stability. Once the host country's infrastructure and entrepreneurial capacity has progressed to permit a move toward substantial industrial export orientation, the MNC can be seen to take an increasing interest in the possibility of new product design specifications and the use of a more labor intensive technology. As the MNC's profit source abroad is forced to shift from production and sale in the home market to export sales, expenditures on R and D and E become important for the first time. Conventional corporate laboratory R and D may, however, still have a much lower value than the small modifications in technology and product design which are more likely to emanate from the machine shops and assembly lines of the LDC plant. The accumulating evidence indicates[10] that most of these consist of labor using adaptations peripheral to the machine or core process proper, including mainly handling, packaging, storing, and so on. However, there are also examples of machine speedups supplemented by greater (manual) quality control and more intensive machine maintenance, and the upgrading of a lower quality raw material into a standard quality intermediate product (in cotton yarn and plywood production, for instance) via the application of "more labor." In addition, the willingness to sacrifice minute gradations in quality, for example, yarn counts, can often yield large benefits in additional factor substitution potential. Such nonspectacular but nevertheless highly important rearrangements of the production line (adaptive technology) or nonspectacular adjustments in quality (adaptive goods) are the consequence largely of plant engineering changes (E) rather than R and D—though "adaptive research" emanating from the workshops is

---

*Globally more than 95 percent of MNC "official" R and D expenditures are made at home.

just as appropriate a label. Interview-based episodal evidence indicates that it often takes considerable time and energy to persuade the mother company that such modifications are possible without unintended sacrifice of the sacred cow of an internationally advertised product quality.

At the end of the sequence running from E to adaptive R and D (opposite from the DC sequence), that is, once the LDC is well into its export oriented development phase, the case for supporting overseas R and D becomes stronger. Leaving aside such arguments as the attraction of lower legal control standards on research (for example, in pharmaceuticals), we are focusing only on the enhanced possibility for a mutually advantageous real content interpenetration of know-how among now relatively more equal partners tied together via a nexus of cross-licensing and patents. That this world does not often exist in DC-LDC relations—it does within Western Europe, between Europe and the United States, and, to some extent, between the United States and Japan—does not alter its increasing realism as we look to the future.

It is interesting to note that even LDCs still deeply ensconced in their import substitution subphase (as most are) may open up a selected portion of their industrial sectors to export substitution—via the so-called export processing zone device. Here MNCs working with subsidiaries or local partners abroad often begin by placing assembly operations abroad in special zones out of the reach of LDC tariff and other controls. Raw materials are imported from abroad, value added is mainly labor, and the product is reexported. This device, along with such provisions as (in the case of the United States) Sections 806.30 and 807.00 of the Tariff Code, which permit reentry duties to be levied on only the value added abroad, enables the MNC to take advantage of the LDC's cheap unskilled labor supplies. The growing phenomenon of international subcontracting by process, for example, in electronics, textiles, leather goods, gloves, and so on, has been growing by leaps and bounds over the past decade. It now constitutes more than one-sixth of total U.S. imports from LDCs. Even more to the point is that what initially starts as a simple process of taking advantage of cheaper labor abroad usually becomes, after some time, a source of labor-using technology change. Once the logjam on the preservation of quality standards is broken, additional LDC processing levels, forward and backward from the initial emphasis on assembly, are likely to be added. One rather convincing demonstration of the contrast of the role of E, D, and R (in that order) between a more competitive export-oriented and a less competitive domestic-oriented industrial environment is provided by comparing technologies in use in the same industry in the same country at the same time. To cite but one example, MNC brassiere manufacturers in the Mexican border industries produce much more labor intensively than those serving the still protected domestic market. Once forced to abandon the "quiet life" of windfall profits and satisficing entrepreneurial behavior, MNCs—like their local counterparts—will "scratch around" to find technological alternatives; they could eventually—for instance, in the Mexican case cited, if given permission—"export" competitively into their own domestic market and thus reverse the normal Linder sequence of international trade.[11]

The rejection of export processing zones by some labor surplus LDCs and their generally bad press, even where they have been booming along successfully, is somewhat puzzling and presents another example of interventions in our natural sequence, that is, the beginnings of export orientation patterns in a generally still protectionist system. Surely these are enclaves with relatively small technological spillover effects, but just as surely they are not exploiting irreplaceable natural resources but "exploiting," or rather absorbing, otherwise unemployed and thus forever "wasted" human resources.

As the LDC nears economic maturity, access to information (I) is exposed as an increasingly important source of MNC profits as other components of MNC superiority fall away. Especially in the particularly imperfect markets for intermediate goods and in the global search for appropriate technology the common assumption of freely available information is most suspect—even in the later more competitive phase of development. Thus a natural evolution sees the MNC initially with little interest in transferring technology to the LDC, then moving to the encouragement of E, finally R and D—reversing its normal behavior in the DC sequence. The joint venture, LDC licensee or independent producer will then become increasingly concerned with I, access to information on both technology and design alternatives and markets. Imitation or adaptation elsewhere of the Japanese trading company organizational form—which permits access to an essentially highly imperfect international market by smaller independent domestic producers (now also being attempted in Brazil) could help assure a better distribution of the profits—with due regard to only the legitimate functions of effectively utilized patents, licenses, and so on. It could also permit greater scope for joint ventures between smaller MNCs and these smaller domestic firms. Where "real" economies of scale are exaggerated and dwarfed by artificial economies of larger size (and market power), such combinations are likely to be very effective, especially in penetrating foreign markets.

POLICY OPTIONS

Where then does this idealized evolutionary view of the potential for productive coexistence—plus a description of the very substantial real world deviations from it—lead us with respect to the future? While one is hesitant to make any predictions, it can be asserted with some confidence that the reality is becoming uglier and that LDCs and MNCs currently find themselves on something of a collision path as the result of the cumulative effects of too many "interventions" by all the parties. There seems to be a general tendency towards confrontation in the relations between the rich and the poor in areas which matter to the rich (as on critical raw materials) and towards not-so-benign neglect where they don't (as on foreign aid). Neocolonial fears currently fuelling a new populism in many LDCs are, moreover, interacting with a defensive economic nationalism in a developed world perplexed by its own current plethora of seemingly insoluble problems. The spiral seems to point downward and could well lead to autarky (and anarchy) in international economic relations.

On the other hand, we also perceive an opportunity in the midst of the current upheaval. With so many moorings loose and so many once comfortable assumptions under reexamination, it is reasonable to believe that this is also a good time for a reexamination of the potential developmental role of the MNC. This is likely to be true whether or not our own notions concerning the anatomy of an ideal and dynamically changing relationship among the four main actors are accepted. Since we are necessarily somewhat partial to what has gone before, however, we shall, in this section, attempt to derive some conclusions for policy based on our own analysis of the issues.

First and foremost, we would argue for an unbundling of the MNC into its component parts and a much more explicit examination as to just what is being transferred and what is being paid for and at what rate at each stage of the development process.[12] Most misunderstandings arise because of the mystique of the powerful, footloose MNC, bargaining with the poor, optionless LDCG, the latter thus being pressured to buy what is essentially a "pig in a poke." The capital, technology, management, and entrepreneurship components of any deal should be spelled out as fully as possible and each component priced out. Screening procedures which exist in virtually every LDC, especially during the import substitution subphase, should concentrate more on disaggregation and full disclosure, thus permitting comparative shopping and other than all or nothing acceptances or rejections. Fade-out and divestiture agreements can similarly be negotiated much more intelligently *ab initio* in the light of some historical perspective which might provide, for example, for a transition from the wholly owned subsidiary to the joint venture form after ten years, and possibly further reassessments in the direction of licensing or management contracts thereafter.

We must, of course, contend with the argument that "it is unlikely that multinational firms will ever be willing to repeat the Japanese experience elsewhere because, from their point of view, they helped create formidable competition to themselves for very meager returns."[13] Clearly, if offered more at every stage they will seek more. If, however, there is a clear and anticipated transition from one function (and one bundle) to another within a particular LDC, competitive pressures among the MNCs should assert themselves to dictate a willingness to accept reasonable rates of return. In this we would be safer in relying on the MNCs' long-run profit objectives rather than on some public spirited impulse.[14] Negotiations should recognize that it is mutually better to plan on living together under changing rules than to attempt to deny the declining value of some major MNC components over time and thus inviting expropriation or other retaliatory action. The burden of proof would have to be on the side of those, for example, Vernon, who claim to see, as indeed may sometimes be the case, a general tendency for a broadening and deepening relative role for the MNC over time.

LDCG screening procedures governing MNC presence should thus be modified in the direction of greater automaticity, greater predictability and more built-in flexibility over time. Such procedures should reflect a recognition that some of the excesses of the MNC, ranging from transfer pricing to the payment of unduly high wages, to the inappropriateness of the technology selected, to the underutilization of patents and the overutilization of domestic credit and export prohibition clauses, are not unrelated to the policy environment created by the LDCGs for all industry. The MNC can be most effectively forced to put its energies into building better mousetraps, and using adaptive (labor-intensive) technologies in doing so, if it is forced to give up the "quiet life" of the satisficing monopolist as the transition to a more liberal policy regime is effected. MNCs are quite capable of coming up with appropriate technology and output ideas when there are pressures to "scratch around" further, witness the above cited experience in the export processing zones and the labor-intensive multipurpose Ford and GM vehicles, using simple sheet metal, jigs and fixtures, currently being produced in Southeast Asia.[15]

Some of the windfall profits created through protection, subsidization, and so on, are necessary to compensate entrepreneurs for undue risks during early import substitution. Even "old" MNC subsidiaries have learning and institutional problems to overcome. There are advantages, however, even then, in working for some harmonization among neighboring LDCs to avoid being played off one against the other, on the one hand, and granting concessions far in excess of what is required to effect the move, on the other. Moreover, where the major "advantage" of the MNC is trademark recognition in a low technology area, with domestic producers threatened by displacement and domestic consumers by demonstration effects, screening procedures should restrict entry. Removal of the veil of secrecy and full disclosure requirements thereafter would constitute a giant step in the direction of avoiding unnecessary frictions. Much of the present problem is one of perception and mutual suspicion causing secular love/hate rather than arm's length relationships.

Much can and should also be done by the DCG's individually and collectively to facilitate the evolution of a natural and mutually beneficial sequence. Most important perhaps is a sustained effort to move away from the image of a knee-jerk DC reaction in favor of its MNC citizens abroad—right or wrong. Hickenlooper and Gonzales amendments are viewed as only slightly modernized versions of gunboat diplomacy; they are equally ineffective. The United States has made no major effort in recent years to get rid of these and other well-encrusted barnacles on the vintage 1961 aid legislation. The extension of domestic antitrust and Trading With the Enemy legislation and other forms of extraterritoriality to U.S. MNCs abroad represents, in general, an ineffective and highly offensive instrument. Similarly, the administrative practice of public sector aid tying sets an unfortunate example for intra-MNC movements of capital, both adversely affecting the LDC's choice of technology.

Closely related is the issue of OPIC-type government investment guarantees. There would seem to be little reason to provide MNCs quasiautomatically with DCG-subsidized specific or extended risk guarantees on the basis of financial criteria only. Any MNC investment thus guaranteed by the DCG carries with it the implied blessing of the rich country; it is incumbent on the DCG to reassure itself that no unfair trade practices, exclusive market demands, export prohibition clauses or other objectionable procedures are being contemplated before any guaranty is extended.

Finally, DCGs should be ready to support LDC efforts to move out of import substitution and into export-oriented growth phases. The most important contribution here is by not slamming the door (via higher tariffs, quotas and threatened quotas) in the face of the successful LDCs. More "aid" spent at home, that is, in the DCs' domestic markets in the form of effective adjustment assistance, would be of great help for any sustained export-oriented strategy by a substantial number of transitioning LDCs. Moreover, it is often substantially easier to overcome both vested interests and honest doubts concerning an impending import liberalization within the LDC, if temporary aid ballooning is possible to "protect" exchange reserves and public revenues during the transition. On the technical assistance side, donors should generally view with favor LDCG efforts to beef up their own legal and economic staffs in order to deal more effectively—and on a more equal footing—with their large and powerful MNC counterparts. International assistance with research on adaptive industrial technology (see the analogies to rice and wheat research), as well as in providing greater access to markets and information to all parties (large and small firms, domestic and MNCs) on an equitable basis, would also be of considerable help.

Internationally, the intended and actual application of the Paris Convention on Patents (1893) certainly needs to be reviewed if wholesale LDC defections are to be avoided. Whether a fair conduct code governing

MNC-LDCG relations along the lines of the recent Kindleberger proposal will do much good at this particular point in time is questionable;[16] but it is clear that unless we move in such a direction as a longer term goal, Krause's analogy between the MNC internationally and its domestic counterpart within an expanding United States common market will continue to limp rather badly.[17]

The world thus still finds itself a long way from George Ball's cosmocorp or Harry Johnson's uniglobe. In fact, there are some current danger signals that, at least in the short term, we may be moving in precisely the opposite direction, that of increasingly autarkic warring parties both as between the rich and the poor and as between Europe and the United States and even as between the least developed and the less developed countries.

Yet, we believe there is reason for hope. For one, the real interdependence of "spaceship earth," long a part of establishment rhetoric, is being recognized as never before in the wake of the oil crisis; and even though the lesson has been an expensive one, there is increasing realization of the need for an approach to symmetry in international economic relations if future breakdowns are to be avoided. In this context, greater understanding of the differential contribution the MNC can make to development in different phases of the growth process can help, both in curbing the excessive appetite for quick profits and the excessive annoyance with red tape on the part of corporate managers, and the excessive fear, on the part of the LDCs, of corporate excesses or big power, neocolonial machinations. The best basis for harnessing the additional resources and talents that are there, it seems to us, is full knowledge of what is and what is not in any particular MNC bundle and what is and what is not helpful—and at what price—at each stage of the development process. We are not at all sure that our attempt to unbundle, disaggregate, and insert a time dimension has gotten to the heart of the matter—certain psychological and political dimensions are clearly left to one side—. We do believe, however, that we have to search in this general direction if the global maximization principles of economic interdependence are to be reconcilable with differing distributional claims in an imperfectly competitive real world.

NOTES

1. S. Kuznets, *Modern Economic Growth, Rate, Structure and Spread* (New Haven: Yale University Press, 1966).

2. The above information from Brinley Thomas "The Historical Record of International Capital Movements to 1913," in *Capital Movements and Economic Development: Proceedings of a Conference held by the International Economic Association,* ed. John A. Adler and Paul W. Kuznets (New York: St. Martin's Press, 1967).

3. I. Little, T. Scitovsky, and M. Scott, *Industry and Trade in Some Developing Countries—A Comparative Study* (Oxford: Oxford University Press, 1970).

4. For a fuller explanation, see the author's "Relative Prices in Planning for Economic Development," in *International Comparisons of Prices and Output,* D. J. Daly ed., *(National Bureau of Economic Research),* 1972, as well as the report of the discussion with P. Eckstein, R. Ruggles, and W. Stolper.

5. See, for example, I. Little, T. Scitovsky, M. Scott, op. cit.; J. C. H. Fei and G. Ranis, "Development in Open Dualistic Economies," *Journal of Development Studies,* forthcoming; A. L. Hirschman, "The Political Economy of Import-Substituting Industrialization in Latin America," *Journal of Development Studies,* vol. 82 (February 1968): 1-32.

6. We, in fact, find the percentage of wholly owned multinational projects declining by about 10 percent between 1939 and 1967, UN *Multinational Corporations in World Development* (New York: UN Publications, 1973), p. 156.

7. V. N. Balasubramanyam, *International Transfer of Technology to India* (New York: Praeger, 1973).

8. Vaitsos, for example, "Patents Revisited: Their Function in Developing Countries," *Journal of Development Studies* (October, 1972), concluded that "in the real world of multiple patent ownership by large corporations, the main functions of patents is not to encourage inventive activity but to aid profit maximization through minimization of competitive forces." Premature patenting is often simply a prelude to the acquisition of local firms. Machlup, "Patents," *International Encyclopaedia of the Social Sciences,* vol. II, believes that mainly DCG pressures and mistaken prestige motives account for LDC membership in the international patent convention.

9. See also G. C. Allen and A. G. Donnithorne, *Western Enterprise in Far Eastern Economic Development: China and Japan* (London: Allen and Unwin, Ltd., 1962), and Edwin P. Reubens, "Foreign Capital and Domestic Development in Japan," in S. Kuznets ed., *Economic Growth: Brazil, India and Japan* (Durham, N.C.: Duke University Press, 1955), pp. 179-228.

10. See H. Pack, "Employment and Productivity in Kenyan Manufacturing," Economic Growth Center Discussion Paper, February 1974; G. Ranis, "Industrial Sector Labor Absorption," in *Economic Development and Cultural Change,* March 1973; and W. P. Strassman, *Technological Change and Economic Development* (Ithaca: Cornell University Press, 1968).

11. S. Burenstam Linder, *An Essay on Trade and Transformation* (New York: John Wiley, 1961).

12. See also Carlos F. Diaz-Alejandro, "North-South Relations: The Economic Component," Growth Center Discussion Paper no. 200, April 1974.

13. Larry Krause, "The International Economic System and the Multi-national Corporation," *Annals of the American Academy of Political And Social Science* (September 1972): 99.

14. As Henry Ford II was quoted in a 1974 issue of *The Wall Street Journal,* "A corporation can serve society only if it is profitable. And it can [*stay*] profitable only if it is responsive to the [changing] needs ... of the society in which it operates." (Emphasis added.)

15. Ford executive William O. Bourke, "Basic Vehicle for South-East Asia," noted in *Technology and Economics in International Development,* AID Seminar, May, 1972, p. 75: "simplicity is often harder to achieve than sophistication". It can be achieved when the motive is there, however. The adaptive (labor-intensive) case should be distinguished from the so-called complementation programs, that is, to produce a conventional vehicle by siting different processes in different countries, which has been less successful.

16. See C. P. Kindleberger and P. Goldberg, "Toward a GATT for Investment: A Proposal for the Supervision of the International Corporation," *Law and Policies in International Business* (Summer 1970), as well as the Code of Conduct referred to in the 1972 report by UN/

ECOSOC, "The Impact of Multinational Corporations on the Development Process and on International Relations."

17. Kindleberger and Goldberg, op. cit.

5

THE MULTINATIONAL SPREAD OF JAPANESE FIRMS AND ASIAN NEIGHBORS' REACTIONS
Yoshihiro Tsurumi

Events between August 15, 1971, when President Nixon of the United States forced Japan to revalue the yen, and mid-January 1974, when Prime Minister Tanaka of Japan became the target of anti-Japanese demonstrations in Thailand, in the Phillipines and, most clearly, in Indonesia repeatedly forced Japan to reconsider the three basic pillars upon which Japan's rapid economic growth of post-World War II had been planned.

The "Nixon Shock" of August 15, 1971, destroyed the first premise that the rest of the world, notably the United States, would continue to purchase increasing amounts of manufactured goods from Japan thus enabling Japan to keep accumulating foreign exchange reserves. The oil embargo enforced by the Arab countries against Japan in October, 1973, destroyed the second premise upon which Japan had built her industrial and commercial structures since the end of the Second World War. Put extremely, Japan's economic growth strategy was predicated on the assumption that her increasing needs for such vital natural resources as oil and industrial raw materials could be perpetually met in the world commodity markets. With the frustration of these two basic premises, industrial and governmental circles in Japan took refuge in the new and third premise that Japan's direct investments abroad for captive sources of natural resources and her increasing penetration into overseas markets for manufactured goods would provide her basic economic security. It was this third premise that crumpled severely in the wake of many

The research for this paper was financed by the Ford Foundation grant to the Multinational Enterprise Project of Harvard Business School. The project was coordinated by Professor Raymond Vernon.

Table 1

**Accumulated U.S. and Japanese Direct
Investments in Asia
(millions of U.S. dollars)**

Host Country	U.S. 1971	Japan 1971	Japan 1973
Ceylon	N.A.	2	3
Taiwan	133	85	110
Hong Kong	286	139	180
India	329	12	15
Indonesia	512	241	311
S. Korea	277	33	256
Malaysia		50	121
Singapore	307	33	150
Pakistan	96	5	6
Philippines	719	74	110
Thailand	124	91	200
Others	266	14	15
Total	3,049	779	1,477

Source: The U.S. data for 1971 were obtained from *Survey of Current Business.* The Japanese data for 1971 are estimated by Yoshihiro Tsurumi from *Tokei Geppo,* June 1972 (Toyo Keizai: Tokyo), pp. 4-5, 8. The 1971 data appeared previously in Donald R. Sherk, *Foreign Investments in Asia: Cooperation and Conflict Between the U.S. and Japan,* Federal Reserve Bank of San Francisco, (October 1973), p. 24. The 1973 data were estimated on the basis of the information gathered through the fieldwork of the author in 1973.

anti-Japanese, anti-Tanaka demonstrations by other Asians in mid-January, 1974. What were the Asian host countries trying to tell Tanaka? Why were Japanese investments resented so thoroughly in Asia?

Table 1 compares U.S. and Japanese investments in Asia as of the end of 1971. The U.S. investments in Asia were about four times as large as those of Japan. In every country, Japanese investments were less than the U.S. investments. While the 1973 data for the United States were not available, I estimated through fieldwork that except for Korea and Thailand, the United States was the largest investor in 1973. Why, then, is Japan likely to be singled out for hostility by the host country? Besides the wartime memory of Japan, is there anything inherent in Japanese investments that make them more vulnerable to political attacks?

THE VIEWPOINTS OF THE DEVELOPING COUNTRIES

Just as in the case of a manufacturing firm, the industrial growth of a country requires such factors as (1) investment capital, (2) foreign exchange, (3) manufacturing technologies, (4) export market contacts, and (5) managerial skills. Historically, various countries have chosen a number of ways to obtain and augment these five necessary factors for their industrial developments. At least up until 1973 when the Canadian Parliament passed the Foreign Investment Review Act designed to regulate further efforts of foreign investments and created the Canadian Development Corporation designed in part to buy back selectively foreign assets in Canada, this country had encouraged the inflows of foreign direct investments as the expedient way to obtain the conglomerate package of the five necessary factors for Canada's economic development.

On the other hand, the Japanese approach provides the extreme opposite example from the Canadian approach. Since the mid-nineteenth century, and especially since the 1870s when Japan consciously chose to industrialize her economy, she has endeavored to augment for herself the five necessary factors for her economic growth. Foreign borrowing and foreign direct investment were, for the most part, consistently avoided. This conscious strategy of Japan may be characterized as the industrial growth through improvement of "human capital." Therefore, it was no accident that Japan instituted compulsory elementary school education at public expenses in 1873, nineteen years earlier than the British efforts to provide public education for school age children.[1] The investment capital was squeezed out of the domestic economy by holding down the level of consumption. Manufacturing technologies were brought into Japan by the Japanese who went abroad on the mission of "search and bring back" as well as by foreign engineers and teachers who were hired for a terminal contract. At the same time, the political leaders effected such institutional reforms as development of modern legal systems, opening of the parliament and introduction of business corporations in order to facilitate industrial growth. After 1950, Japan consciously exploited technical licensing agreements with foreign companies in order to bridge the technological gap between, say, the United States and Japan. By then, Japan had accumulated sufficiently sophisticated manufacturing and scientific experience to exploit profitably licensed technologies.

However, today, in the mid-1970s, the developing nations tend to adopt an approach to industrial developments somewhere between the Canadian and Japanese models but often closer to the former than the latter. This is partly because the international demonstration effects lead their nationals to aspire impatiently to the material living standard of the advanced nations and make the governments of the developing nations reluctant to hold down the level of national consumption in order to squeeze savings. Accordingly, as a matter of expediency, a foreign direct investment is counted on as the conglomerate package that provides readily the five necessary factors for industrial growth; namely, investment capital, foreign exchange, manufacturing technology, export market contacts, and management skills. The resultant dilemma of the developing nations of today is how much and how long should they pay the price of the political and psychological burden of depending on foreign private firms in exchange for intended benefits of the five factors necessary for their industrial development. Foreign direct investments are perceived more as the necessary evil that needs to be tolerated so long as their intended benefits exceed perceived cost to their host country. Why, then, did the Japanese investments in Asia come to be perceived by the host countries as increasingly intolerable costs?

JAPANESE DIRECT INVESTMENT ABROAD

Of late, Japanese direct investments abroad have increased. The Bank of Japan reported that by the end of the month of March 1972, the cumulative amounts of authorized direct foreign investments by Japanese firms reached U.S. $4.5 billion. Table 2 summarizes the Japanese direct investments by area and by investor-industry. Table 3 shows the number of Japanese subsidiaries abroad by area and by activity. Upon the basis of my own fieldwork in and outside Japan, I estimate that the actual level of assets controlled by Japanese investments is generally at least twice the level of direct investments

TABLE 2

Japanese Direct Investments Abroad: Amounts Authorized by the Bank of Japan
As of March 31, 1972
(in one million U.S. dollars)

Investor / Area	North America	Latin America	Asia	Middle East	Europe	Africa	Oceania	Total
Resource-oriented Investments	407.1	173.6	402.8	363.2	7.0	79.6	293.6	1,726.9
Agriculture	4.6	8.2	49.8	—	0.5	—	5.6	68.7
Fishery	2.5	8.2	15.0	0.7	0.1	7.6	5.2	38.8
Timbers & Pulps	208.0	0.2	17.0	—	—	—	36.8	262.0
Mining	192.0	157.0	321.0	363.0	6.4	72.0	246.0	1,357.4
Market-oriented Investments	719.4	532.4	613.4	7.7	710.5	33.7	94.8	2,711.6
Manufacturing	61.1	333.7	444.9	5.6	57.7	25.9	64.7	993.6
Foods	8.5	11.0	36.4	—	6.5	3.5	15.0	80.9
Textile	7.0	67.2	161.1	—	1.2	17.2	0.9	254.6
Chemicals	11.5	8.2	36.0	—	18.2	1.4	1.0	76.3
Metals	1.1	98.0	40.4	—	9.0	2.5	37.3	188.3
Machinery	10.4	45.0	20.0	1.0	14.4	—	0.5	91.3
Electric & Electronics	3.3	23.7	65.0	1.8	1.4	0.8	2.6	98.6
Transportation Equipment	15.0	74.6	14.0	1.0	4.2	—	6.8	115.6
Others	4.3	6.0	72.0	1.8	2.8	0.5	0.6	88.0
Services	658.3	198.3	168.2	2.1	652.8	7.8	30.1	1,718.0
Construction	7.3	26.8	5.8	0.6	0.6	—	—	40.5
Commerce[1]	413.0	21.5	29.4	1.5	44.4	0.8	14.4	524.1
Banking and Insurance	142.0	80.4	72.0	—	67.8	0.3	12.6	376.6
Others[2]	96.0	70.0	61.0	—	540.0[3]	6.7	3.1	776.8
Total Amounts	1,126.5	706.0	1,015.9	370.9	717.5	113.3	388.4	4,438.5
Percent	25.3	15.9	22.9	8.3	16.2	2.6	8.8	100

[1]Direct Investments mainly by trading companies for their sales subsidiaries. Their relatively large investments in North America reflect the active exporting trades of Japan to the area.

[2]Entertainments, travel agencies, hotels and real estate developments dominate this category.

[3]This includes a sizable investment that Hotel Okura of Tokyo made in Amsterdam for its first European venture.

Source: The Ministry of International Trade and Industry, *Nihon Kigyono Kokusaiieki Tenkai* (Tokyo, 1973), Appendix pp. 2-3.

authorized by the Bank of Japan.* Accordingly, the direct investments abroad by Japanese firms can be estimated to have reached $9 billion by the third quarter of 1973, even after allowing for the average start-up lag of eighteen months for a typical Japanese investment abroad. At mid-1974, the Japanese direct investments abroad were increasing at an annual rate of U.S. $800 million to 1 billion. By late 1974, the cumulative level of assets controlled by Japanese firms surpassed U.S. $10 billion.

Of the general observations one can make about the profile of Japanese investments abroad, two characteristics are worth noting. First, about 40 percent of the total investments are of so-called "natural resource-oriented" types, while the remaining 60 percent are of the "market-oriented" types. The latter are designed either for deeper penetration of overseas markets for manufactured goods or for such on-site services as banking and construction to accommodate Japanese ventures abroad. Of 4,899 investment projects authorized by the Bank of Japan by the end of March 1972, approximately 90 percent are of the market-oriented types. In addition, of the manufacturing subsidiaries abroad, about 80 percent are concentrated in developing countries in Asia and Latin America, whose technological and income levels are still materially lower than those of Japan. These two manifestations of Japanese multinational firms provide a clue to the specific political plight that Japanese MNCs will increasingly encounter in Asia and other developing areas.

MANUFACTURING SUBSIDIARIES
OF JAPANESE MULTINATIONALS

In order to compare the multinational spreads of Japanese manufacturing activities with those of U.S.- and European-based manufacturing activities, Tables 4 and 5 have been compiled. From Table 4 one can observe that compared with the United States and the United Kingdom, both continental Europe and Japan have stepped up their manufacturing ventures abroad since the mid-1960s, and that in the case of Japan alone there were few manufacturing ventures abroad before 1960. Indeed, it was only toward the end of the 1960s that Japanese manufacturing

---

*This difference accounts for: (1) funds borrowed outside Japan for the financing of both current and fixed assets of Japanese ventures; and (2) loans and equity capitals subsequently used by Japanese investors, including the retained earnings plowed back into their subsidiaries.

TABLE 3

**The Number of Overseas Subsidiaries of Nontrading Firms of Japan
By Area and Activity
As of the End of 1972**

Activity	North America	Europe	Asia	Latin America	Middle East/Africa	Oceania, S. Africa/ Dominions	Total Number
Resource-seeking	35	6	87	33	24	51	236
percent	15.0	2.5	36.8	14.0	10.1	21.6	100
Manufacturing	50	40	974	130	56	29	1,279
percent	3.9	3.0	76.2	10.2	4.4	2.3	100
Sales	413	185	180	41	9	38	866
percent	47.7	21.4	20.8	4.7	1.0	4.4	100
Others*	103	24	107	25	12	11	282
percent	36.5	8.4	38.0	8.7	4.2	4.2	100

*Travel agencies, hotels, entertainments, and some agricultural and fishing projects fall in this category.

Source: Yoshihiro Tsurumi, *Multinational Expansion of Japanese Firms* (forthcoming), Multinational Enterprise Project Series of Harvard Business School. The data was gathered in Japan mainly through the author's fieldwork in 1972.

TABLE 4

**Number of Manufacturing Subsidiaries
Established by Separate Country-based Enterprises**

	Nationality of Parent Firms			
	U.S.	U.K.	Continental Europe	Japan
Pre-1914	122	60	167	0
1914-1919	71	27	51	0
1920-1929	299	118	249	1
1930-1938	315	99	112	3
1939-1945	172	34	44	40
1946-1952	386	202	129	2
1953-1955	283	55	117	5
1956-1958	439	94	131	14
1959-1961	901	333	232	93
1962-1964	959	319	229	160
1965-1967	889	459	532	235
1968-1970	N.A.	729	1,032	532

Source: For the data of U.S.-, U.K.-, and continental Europe-based manu-facturing subsidiaries, Vaupel and Curhan, *The World's Multinational Enterprises,* Division of Research, Harvard Business School, 1973. Japanese data were compiled from *Kigyobetsu Kaigai Toshi* (Tokyo: Kaigai Chosa Kyokai, 1972).

ventures abroad approached those of other industrialized nations, at least in terms of the number of her overseas subsidiaries established anew.

Table 5 reveals that the relative concentration of Japanese manufacturing subsidiaries in Asia, Oceania, and Latin America does not change much (see Table 3), even when the observation samples are limited to those of Japanese firms sufficiently large enough to make *Fortune* magazine's list of the 200 largest non-U.S. firms in 1970.

Compared with Japan-based multinational firms, U.K.- and European-based multinationals have succeeded in building up manufacturing investments in advanced nations including the United States, thus finding themselves as of 1972 somewhere between the profiles of U.S.- and Japanese-based multinational manufacturing activities. Now, is this comparative profile of Japanese manufacturing activities abroad the result of political and economic factors that are uniquely pressuring Japanese firms to go abroad? If so, is this profile changing at all toward the mid-1970s?

CHANGING PATTERNS OF JAPANESE MANUFACTURING ACTIVITIES ABROAD

An extensive field survey of Japanese manufacturing activities which I have conducted since 1971 leads me to catalogue their development patterns chronologically in the following stages:

Stage 1 (Ad hoc "trial and error" activities—up to 1970): The overseas manufacturing activities of Japanese firms had been, up until 1970, in response to import substitution moves by the developing countries in Asia. The survey of 385 Japanese manufacturing subsidiaries abroad conducted by the Ministry of International Trade and Industry (MITI) for the first quarter of 1971 corroborates my own findings. This survey revealed that regardless of the type of investing industry, such export market-oriented considerations as (1) continuing exports from Japan, (2) defending local markets, and (3) developing local markets explain 96 percent of the cases of Japanese overseas manufacturing activities, with the greatest of these considerations being the defense of previously established export markets.[2] During the 1960s, the developing countries' restrictions on imports of light goods and/or the prospects of local competition from indigenous manufacturers triggered the emigration of standard, labor-intensive (low skill content) products from Japan into the neighboring countries in Asia and, to a lesser extent, into Mexico and Brazil. Typical manufactured products involved were footwear, apparel, cotton and synthetic cloth, print and dye items, simple tools,

TABLE 5

**Relative Geographical Concentration of Manufacturing
Subsidiaries of Large U.S., U.K., European, and Japanese Firms[1]
As of January 1, 1971
(percent)**

| Parent Firm's Nationality | Location of Manufacturing Subsidy | | | | | Total Number of Subsidiaries |
	North America	Europe	Latin America	Asia and Oceania	Africa and Middle East	
U.S.A. (as of Jan. 1, 1968)	13.0	39.0	27.0	15.0	6.5	4246
Japan	4.8	3.3	18.0	65.0	8.6	479[2]
U.K.	13.0	29.0	6.1	27.0	25.0	2265
Germany	9.9	53.0	18.0	9.8	9.8	788
France	7.1	51.0	17.0	6.1	19.0	425
Italy	6.2	45.0	33.0	5.4	10.0	129
Belgium and Luxemburg	21.0	62.0	4.8	1.5	11.0	272
The Netherlands	23.0	54.0	8.5	8.7	5.4	425
Sweden	4.2	68.0	14.0	9.0	4.2	167
Switzerland	10.0	64.0	14.0	7.9	4.1	393

[1]The sample of this table is limited to those manufacturing subsidiaries which were established by parent firms sufficiently large enough to be included in *Fortune* magazine's list of the 200 Largest Non-U.S. Firms, in 1970, and *Fortune's* 400 Largest U.S. firms in 1967.

[2]This number is markedly smaller than that of Japan's column of Table 4. This is because, unlike the U.S.- and Europe-based multinational firms, the majority of Japanese multinational firms are too small to be recorded by *Fortune's* list.

Source: Vaupel and Curhan, op. cit., p. 122.

galvanized iron sheets, iron bars, drawn plastic mouldings, drugs, paper boxes and cartons, soap, transistor radio assemblies, dry batteries, electric fans, fertilizer, and a limited knock-down assembly of automobiles, agricultural machinery, and compact refrigerators.

Stage 2 (Toward conscious realignments of multinational operations—from around 1971 to the mid-1970s): Towards the end of Stage 1, an increasing number of Japanese investing parent firms began to integrate separate subsidiaries producing related products within the same country. These moves were aimed at improved production efficiency in the subsidiaries, and they were often triggered by parent firms that had recognized the strategic values of efficient "offshore" production bases—the bases located outside Japan in developing nations from which to supply overseas markets like Japan, America, and Europe.

Increasing awareness of Japanese firms' need for "offshore" production facilities has been stimulated by three main factors. The first is the combined result of the revaluations of the yen in 1971 and 1973, the rising wages in Japan which persistently outstripped the productivity gains after 1965 and, particularly, acute labor shortages in a young labor force. Offshore production areas, then, became attractive for the production of mature products with a high labor content because of their ready supply of abundant labor at lower wage cost than in Japan. Often, the host governments, eager to develop some "instant" exporting industries to absorb a rising number of urban unemployed, would attract Japanese manufacturers with income tax concessions, donations of plant sites, and import duty exemptions on necessary imports. When those government subsidies were combined with the investing firms' ready access to world markets and their manufacturing competence, these subsidies were often sufficient for Japanese firms to overcome the relative disadvantages of high cost operations. This is why Japanese firms can export their products made in developing nations even when indigenous firms are prohibited from doing so by high costs and risks involved in developing international marketing abilities.

The second factor stimulating Japanese offshore productions stems from the fact that even for those Japanese-made products which still compete favorably in the markets of the advanced nations, Japanese manufacturers are finding it increasingly difficult to expand their production capacities in Japan. New plant sites are simply not available in Japan for many manufacturers. As a result, when products are in high demand in Japan and abroad, firms are being forced to relocate abroad those portions of their total production processes which are relatively labor-intensive or are technologically simple. Japanese plants are then restructured either to work on semifinished products imported from their overseas plant, or to produce semifinished products for assembling in the overseas subsidiaries. For those products whose production cannot be conveniently broken down into parts, incremental-type production is carried out in plants located close to the overseas markets. In the natural resource-oriented fields, Japanese concerns for environmental quality on the one hand, and the resource-producing countries' demands for increased onsite processing on the other, are contributing to the emigration from Japan of the processing facilities for natural resources.

The third factor is that the conscious defensive strategies of the Japanese firms, especially those operating in electronics fields, were leading them to move to places where notable American electronics firms such as Motorola, RCA, Zenith, Fairchild, and Texas Instruments set up their own offshore production facilities in Taiwan, Korea, Singapore, and elsewhere in order to combat Japanese-made imports to the U.S. market. Their Japanese competitors also moved in there so as not to be outsupplied by their competitors in the world markets.

Stage 3 (Direct investments in Europe and the United States from the mid-1970s onward): Initially, as the host countries in Asia in particular react increasingly against Japanese dominance in their consumer goods industries serving local markets, Japanese parent firms will seek investment opportunities in the more advanced countries. These advanced nations will be inclined to accept Japanese investments in exchange for their own firms' investments in Japan. Secondly, a number of Japanese firms have come to realize that when combined with the revaluations of the yen in 1971 and 1973, increased protectionist moves in America and Europe against Japanese imports make it not only economically but also politically wise to open manufacturing operations in the United States and Europe. After allowing for transportation costs and tariffs, a number of Japanese technology-intensive products can be efficiently manufactured in America and Europe. Furthermore, after spring 1974, when Japanese wages were increased by 30 percent from the level of 1973, high wage costs and high costs of plant sites in Japan have made it profitable even for such labor-intensive products as ready-to-wear clothing to be produced in the United States and exported to Japan. The United States has become another offshore plant site for Japan.

Finally, an increasing number of Japanese firms will find it strategically crucial to operate manufacturing facilities in America and Europe in order to monitor their competitors' moves. In view of the fact that an increasing number of U.S.-and European-based parent firms will shortly commence manufacturing operations in Japan, or will increase their exports to the Japanese market, Japanese firms competing with these American and European firms abroad will meet their competitors' moves by maneuvering into the home markets of the competitors.[3] By meshing their economic territory with those of their potential competitors, both inside and outside Japan, the Japanese firms hope to discourage disruptive competition from others. This strategy of "hostage exchange" will be observed increasingly among mature oligopolies of the world.*

JAPANESE OLIGOPOLISTIC INDUSTRIAL STRUCTURE AND OVERSEAS INVESTMENTS— FOLLOW THE LEADER PHENOMENON

The tantalizing question that remains to be answered is whether or not Japanese direct investments reveal behavior unique to Japanese corporate culture. Table 6 was compiled in an attempt to shed light on this question. It should be noted particularly, with regard to Table 6, that the Japanese parent firms having more than ten overseas manufacturing facilities as of January 1, 1971, are dominated by synthetic fiber firms, with their domestic subsidiaries of weaving and dyeing operations, steel firms with the technology for galvanized iron sheets, and electronics and electric firms that are producing such consumer goods as dry batteries for transistor radios and electric fans. These observations indicate that a high number of overseas subsidiaries arise when these firms open up overseas manufacturing operations in place of their former exporting operations. In marked contrast are the "main line business" recorded in column (1), namely Sharp (desk top calculators), Sony (color T.V. sets and audio equipment), Fujitsu (computers), and two shipbuilding firms, which have relatively few overseas manufacturing operations. In 1971, these latter firms commanded sufficient technological advantage, production efficiency, and export market acceptance of brand names in their mainline products to allow them to continue an export supremacy strategy from their manufacturing bases in Japan.

In addition, one can make three observations about Table 6 by exercising common knowledge of Japanese industrial structures. These are: (1) that the synthetic fiber industry is characterized in the maturing oligopolistic environment by fierce competition among seven firms, including Toray, Teijin

---

*As an example of this "hostage exchange," Dutch Shell's move into sales networks in the U.S. in the 1920s was triggered by earlier moves by Standard Oil of the United States into the territories in Europe formerly held by Dutch Shell. The latest move by Michelin (a French automobile tire firm) into Canada, in 1970, and then into the United States, in 1973, makes sense when it is viewed as Michelin's attempt to move into the United States and Canadian territory of Goodyear and Firestone, which had been disrupting Michelin's markets in Europe. A Japanese tire company was contemplating in 1974 the purchase of a tire company in the United States so that its renegotiation position with Goodyear might be improved when its licensing agreement with Goodyear expired in 1975.

TABLE 6

Classification of Large Japanese Multinational Firms by Parent Firm's Export to Sales Ratio and by Products of Their Manufacturing Subsidiaries

As of January 1, 1971

Export to Sales Ratio of Parent Firm	Number of Overseas Manufacturing Subsidiaries			
	(1) 0	(2) 1-8	(3) 10-15	(4) 16 and up
Above Average of the Sample (ratio 0.210)	Hitachi Ship Bldg. (SB) Mitsui Ship Bldg. (SB) Sharp (EA) Sharp (EA) Sony (E)	Honda (A-KD) Bridgestone (BT) Sumitomo Metals (G) Toyokogyo (A-KD) Kawasaki (A-KD) IHI (SE) NEC (E) NKK (G) Nissan (A-KD)	Kobe Steel (G) Shin Nihon Steel (G) Kawasaki Steel (G) Toyoto (T) Unitika (T) Mitsubishi Heavy Industry (A-KD, IM) Sanyo (E)	Toray (T) Teijin (T) Kanebo (T) Toyota (A-KD)
Below Average of the Sample (ratio 0.210)	Fujitsu (EC) Kirin Beer Ube Chemicals Cement	Asahi Chemicals (T) Snow Brand Milk	Mitsubishi Rayon (T) Sekisui Chemicals (P) Takeda (D)	Hitachi (E) Matsushitu (E) Toshiba (E)

Note: (A-KD) denotes knock-down assembly of autos and motorcycles; (BT) bicycle tires and auto tires; (D) drugs; (E) electric and electronic firms producing abroad electric fans, transistor radios, dry batteries, vacuum tubes, monochrome T.V. set assemblies; (EA) a computer manufacturer; (G) steel manufacturers setting up plants for galvanized sheets and pipes abroad; (P) pcc pipes; (T) synthetic textile firms that have plants of yarn spinning, weaving and dyeing.

Large Japanese firms are those firms which made the 1970 list of the 200 largest non-U.S. firms in *Fortune Magazine.*

Source: Data Bank of the Multinational Enterprise Project, Harvard Business School.

and Kanebo (column 1-4), who vie for leadership in the industry; (2) that in the electronic appliances field, the four leading firms, Hitachi, Matsushita, Toshiba (column 2-4) and Sanyo (column 1-3), are competing with one another at home and abroad; and (3) that the four Japanese steel firms also possess attributes of mature oligopolies. The fact that all these oligopolistic firms in Japan had, by 1971, demonstrated strong propensities to spread their respective manufacturing activities to neighboring Asian countries suggests that the classic theory of oligopolistic competitive behavior of firms would explain the motivation, timing, and plant location of their overseas direct investments.[4]

So long as these oligopolistic firms were pursuing old strategies of competing in domestic and export markets supplied only from domestic sources, they knew one another very well and were able to play a game of market share maximization in a familiar environment. However, if, for the reasons stated in Stage 1 or, in particular, Stage 2, one of them opens a manufacturing base outside Japan, its competitors back home are strongly motivated to follow the leader to avoid the chance of being outsupplied in the market by a competitor who has acquired potentially better manufacturing sources for certain of its products. The best strategy for minimizing uncertainty in the competitive environment at home and abroad is for the oligopolistic followers to open a similar supply source right next door to the leader's plant, the very next day, they hope. Until all possible overseas supply bases are exploited, industrial firms under oligopolistic pressures will attempt to be first in a new place abroad, thus triggering followers' countermoves and renewed attempts by leaders to rush to yet another new place. Nowhere today is this competitive rush to open overseas manufacturing plants by Japanese oligopolies demonstrated more vividly than in Korea, Taiwan, and the United States in the electronics field, or in Indonesia in the fields of synthetic fiber and galvanized iron sheet production. The latest moves into Brazil by various Japanese manufacturers can also be explained by the fierce propensity of Japanese firms to compete among themselves.

Vertical Integration of Firms and Their Propensity to Invest Abroad

In the case of large synthetic fiber firms and large steel firms, it is also important to recognize that in their domestic plants these firms produce only such intermediate products as synthetic yarn or iron sheets, slabs and rods. Why, then, when abroad, are these firms actively involved in such manufacturing operations as weaving, dyeing, wire drawing, or iron sheet galvanizing? The answer is that many large-scale producers of intermediate products in Japan had long been developing their affiliated firm groups in

FIGURE 1

**The De Facto Vertical Integration of a Large
Japanese Manufacturer of Synthetic Yarn and
Nonintegrated Counterpart in the United States**

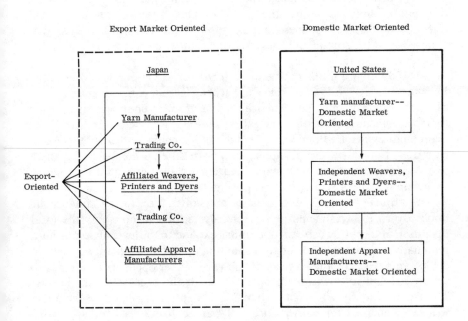

Note: In the case of five large Japanese steel manufacturers, each has developed its own downstream affiliations with small- to medium-sized companies producing galvanized iron sheets, wires, and ferro-concrete bars. Japanese trading companies are involved also in the vertically integrated operations of steel and iron industries as the distributors of products at home and abroad.

order to market their products downstream all the way to the retail distribution of the final products. This was necessary for large-scale producers of intermediate products to keep expanding free of market restraints. These *de facto* vertical integrations of large-scale producers of intermediate goods often include trading companies that carry out for manufacturers physical distribution both at home and abroad. This typical form of vertical integration of a large Japanese manufacturer of intermediate goods has long exposed it to the stimuli and pressures of export markets through the allied conduit called trading firms.

The difference in the degree of *de facto* vertical integration and in the built-in sensitivity to overseas markets between large Japanese manufacturers of intermediate goods and American and European counterparts appears important in answering the intriguing question why such synthetic fiber manufacturers as DuPont and ICI did not or could not enter the Asian countries. For illustrative purposes, the above difference between Japanese and American synthetic yarn manufacturers is shown in Figure 1. Japanese yarn manufacturers' sensitivity to export markets and their economic interest in their affiliated weavers, dyers, and printers often force them to finance the initial overseas investments of weavers, dyers, and printers. As the local operation of these downstream operations expand to the level of permitting a minimally economical scale of yarn spinning operations, a plant capacity of 20,000 spindles, say, the large synthetic yarn maker opens its own plant to supply its captive downstream operation with the necessary yarn locally. There is no way for a foreign yarn maker to exploit, for example, Japanese weavers' demands for yarns, since a Japanese firm exists to supply this demand. This vertically integrated approach to overseas manufacturing activities appears to be the most salient characteristic of Japanese manufacturers of intermediate goods.

Transfer of Process-related Technologies Abroad and Behavior of Japanese Firms

In the preceding sections we mainly evaluated the economic factors in Japan which are encouraging Japanese manufacturers to seek overseas production sites. Once a Japanese firm decides to set up a manufacturing subsidiary abroad, is there anything in Japanese manufacturing technology that produces a distinct modus operandi for these manufacturing firms abroad?

Since the 1870s, when Japan began to industrialize, she has succeeded in overcoming her shortage of manufacturing skills and experience and has rapidly caught up with the "advanced" nations. This has been achieved mainly through the "division of labor" among many individuals and firms in Japan. Rather than waiting for a single man or firm to master a breadth of manufacturing skill and experience necessary for certain industrial tasks, a firm or a group of firms in Japan has organized its employees and corporate members to allow one person or one firm to perform essentially a single function. In order to compensate for shortage of skilled workers in Japan, production processes imported from the West were often broken down to a series of standard and simpler operations that were to be linked up again by a group of operators specializing in respective operating skills.[5] Because Japanese wage rates were distinctly lower than those of the industrialized nations in the West, even this kind of division of labor involving many people has brought about economical and rapid assimilation of diverse manufacturing technologies in Japan. This "group" approach of linking diverse divisions of labor among firms and individuals adapts to the Japanese temperament culturally as well. The Japanese valued group cooperation rather than individualistic behavior.* Among a group of firms, one would specialize in domestic and overseas distribution and another would specialize in the manufacture of various products. Thus, the Japanese notion of a manufacturer—a "meka" in Japanese—is distinctly narrower than, say, that of its U.S. counterpart. Usually, in Japan, with the possible exceptions of pharmaceutical and cosmetic products and electric and electronic appliances, financing and marketing functions beyond rudimentary inhouse services or liaison activities have been performed by banks and trading firms, respectively.

The division of labors of Japanese firms that have organized a hierarchy of many affiliate member firms for rapid industrialization have produced two distinct characteristics of Japanese overseas manufacturing subsidiaries, especially in developing nations. First, of 1,280 Japanese manufacturing subsidiaries established abroad before mid-1972, about 40 percent were joint ventures between two or three Japanese firms. Trading firms of Japan have been involved in about 30 percent of overseas manufacturing subsidiaries because trading firms often acted as the organizers of the overseas ventures. Since each Japanese investing parent firm in a joint venture tends to send at least one of "its own" men on site, the number of Japanese expatriate managers in overseas subsidiaries with more than two Japanese parent firms tends to exceed the number of Japanese expatriate managers in an overseas subsidiary of a single parent.

---

*It is estimated that in the 1870s, that over 40 percent of Japan's population were literate persons, as a result of a widespread educational effort during the Tokogawa feudalities period.

TABLE 7

The Number of Japanese Expatriates per Manufacturing Subsidiary by Product Group in Indonesia As of the First Quarter of 1973

Product Group[1]	Modal number of the Japanese expatriates (all categories)[2]
I. *Simple Products* Instant noodles, charcoal makings, sawmills, plastic sandals, plastic films and bags, dry batteries, leather products, furniture, cigarette filters, bicycle assembly.	2 - 3
II. *Less Simple Products* Galvanized iron sheets, steel and iron pipes and structures, drugs, cosmetics, diesel engine assembly, fishing nets, monosodium glutamate (MSG), stretch nylon yarns, electronics and electric appliances, modern printing operations.	7 - 8

1. A more rigorous test of the complexity of manufacturing processes involved can be used, such as better recording of the number of production processes involved and the required degree of machine operation, etc. But the field observations of these product groups and of the required degree of product quality control in the process are adequate for the purpose of this paper.

2. The difference in this modal value does not significantly change even if a few simpler products in Group II, such as assembly of small stationary diesel engines, were reclassified into Group I.

Source: Yoshihiro Tsurumi, *Japanese Direct Investments in Indonesia: Toward New Indonesian Policies of Foreign Direct Investment,* October 1973, Development Advisory Service, Harvard University.

Also, individual engineers and skilled technicians of Japanese firms tend to have a narrower breadth of skill and expertise than those of other firms from other nations, due to the extreme specialization characteristics of Japanese companies. For example, a typical journeyman machinist of Japan can often perform only specialized jobs on his machine, a lathe, say, while his American counterpart can perform multijobs on a number of machines from lathe to milling machines. As a result, in order to provide the minimally requisite skills for an overseas manufacturing subsidiary, the parent firm often finds it necessary to send in a team of engineers and technicians rather than one or two engineers possessing a wider breadth of expertise.

For example, as shown in Table 7, I have ascertained in spring 1973 in Indonesia the evidence that the difference in the complexity of product and process technologies used by manufacturing subsidiaries may well influence the extent of Japanese presence in overseas subsidiaries. The products involved are classified into two categories on the basis of the level of complexity of manufacturing technology required for successful production. Integrated textile mills are excluded from the sample, but the very fact of their inclusion would merely reinforce the conclusion: even a slight difference in the degree of complexity in manufacturing technology affects the number of Japanese expatriates present in the foreign subsidiary.

A rigorous international comparison of the number of expatriate managers by product groups is still lacking. However, in pharmaceuticals in which both Japanese and non-Japanese (Asian and European) multinationals are operating in Indonesia, I have confirmed that for a comparable size of operation, Japanese subsidiaries had in 1973 three to four expatriate managers for non-Japanese firms. This was the case when only one single parent firm was involved as the Japanese investor. This difference in the number of expatriate managers was also observable for commercial banking operations. In Thailand and in Indonesia, Japanese banks operating locally had at least twice as many Japanese expatriate managers (five to eight) as other foreign banks (three to four).

ASIAN NEIGHBORS' REACTIONS TO VULNERABLE JAPANESE INVESTMENTS

As was discussed earlier, from any developing country's point of view, a foreign direct investment is perceived ambivalently not only as the conglomerate package that provides ready capital, technology, and export market contacts for instant industrialization or exporting bases within the host country but also as the political and psychological burdens of depending on foreign private firms.

Certain "dead hands of history" often influence a host country's perception of the foreign investments of certain nations. In this regard, the Japanese presence in Asia tends to be linked with the past dealings Japan has had with her Asian neighbors. From East Asia to Southeast Asia, memories still linger of Japan's crude attempts to establish the "Great Asia Co-prosperity Sphere" during World War II. In particular, Japan's relations with Korea are still marred by Korea's memories of Japanese colonization of Korea on one hand and by Japanese selective amnesia of the same period on the other. As a result, when the expected economic benefits from Japanese direct investments are not too visible to the "man on the street," one has only to dredge up memories of the militarist Japan of pre-1945 in order to find a target at which to vent a multitude of political and economic frustration of one's own country and to raise the specter of Japanese economic imperialism.

Although the developing nations expect to exploit multinational firms for their industrial development, MNCs regard as their private property the five factors of industrial growth: investment capital, foreign exchanges, manufacturing technologies, export market contacts, and management skills. From the viewpoint of the MNCs, these property rights are only to be used as bargaining weapons vis-a-vis outside groups including the host government. The dilemma of the multinational firm is, therefore, how to run a viable business subsidiary and at the same time meet the demands of the host government. The latter tends to regard the package of five necessary factors held by multinational firms as the public resources that will be made available for the governmental needs.

Under these circumstances, foreign investors cannot choose to be liked by the host countries. All that they can hope to achieve is to influence the grounds for dislike by the host countries. In the case of Japanese investors, however, even this leeway appears limited.

Public Visibility of Japanese Subsidiaries

When compared with U.S. investments, three characteristics of Japanese investments in Asia need to be noted. Although at the end of 1971 the United States leads Japan in terms of total investments, Japan has thus far established the larger number of subsidiaries. Furthermore, when narrowed to the manufacturing industries, Japanese subsidiaries are most concentrated in consumer products of light goods and in simple industrial products. Earlier, Tables 6 and 7 depicted these characteristics. The combined results make the Japanese presence far more publicly visible than that of any other foreign investor. The mere fact that the extensive Japanese investments are concentrated in consumer-oriented goods requires Japanese investors to advertise their products. The keen competition among Japanese investors tends to lead to saturation advertisements, which in turn create a public impression of a greater dominance of Japanese products and investments than is actually the case. Thus, "foreign" investments that tend to be disliked anyway are often equated in the mind of the "man on the street" with Japanese investments. In addition to Japanese goods manufactured locally, host countries' imports from Japan have persistently exceeded their exports to Japan. Thus, Japanese subsidiaries are also viewed as the causes of the trade deficits of the host countries and made targets of public protest.

The other particular vulnerability of Japanese manufacturing subsidiaries may be gleaned from the initial reasons for their overseas migrations. As we saw earlier in this chapter, the bulk of Japanese manufacturing subsidiaries was created by domestic firms to defend their historical export markets, and they were oriented mainly to the domestic markets of the host countries. When this domestic market orientation is coupled with the fact that Japanese manufacturing subsidiaries are concentrated in the least technology-intensive product areas, it becomes clear that Japanese investors were often set in direct competition against indigenous industrialists and merchants who had been left out of the joint ventures between Japanese investors and indigenous partners. As greater numbers of indigenous industrialists move into more product areas covered by Japanese manufacturing subsidiaries, the economic benefits to the host country of allowing Japanese (foreign) manufacturing operations in their countries will be increasingly questioned.

THE OWNERSHIP PATTERNS
OF JAPANESE SUBSIDIARIES ABROAD

Myth and Reality

One popular myth still prevails among many observers of Japanese investments abroad and concerns the apparent greater propensity for Japanese vs. other nationality's firms to settle for a minority position in their joint ventures abroad. Since local participation in foreign investments is politically popular with host governments, Japanese past records of sharing in plant ownership with local partners tends to be singled out as the saving grace in an otherwise unpopular trend. Will the Japanese attitude toward the ownership of overseas investments remain unchanged?

It is shown in Table 8 that of the large multinational firms of various and sundry nations, Japanese firms were distinctive in having settled for the

TABLE 8

Ownership of Overseas Subsidiaries by
Nationality of Large Parent Firms
As of January 1, 1971
(percent)

Parent's Nationality	Parent's Ownership of Subsidiaries					
	95-100	94-51	50	49-26	25-5	Total
France	38	23	9	18	12	100
W. Germany	56	22	9	10	5	100
Italy	65	13	5	12	4	100
Belgium-Luxembourg	52	21	6	10	13	100
Netherlands	65	18	7	7	2	100
Sweden	80	9	4	5	3	100
Switzerland	62	25	6	5	3	100
Canada	68	12	7	10	3	100
Japan	27	8	7	25	33	100
Average of Non-U.S. Firms	53	18	7	12	10	100
U.S.*	71	20		9		100

*The U.S. data were as of January 1, 1968.

Source: Vaupel and Curhan, op. cit.

minority positions in their subsidiaries abroad. Table 9 reveals similar trends in Japanese investment patterns. Using as a basis for study 3,031 subsidiaries that had been established by both large and small parent firms of Japan, the subsidiary ownership patterns are shown in which the investments were made. Since over two-thirds of subsidiaries in North America and Europe are sales subsidiaries, majority ownership by Japanese parent firms predominates in this area. In contrast, in Asia, where about 80 percent of the Japanese subsidiaries are engaged in manufacturing activities, in Latin America, where 65 percent of subsidiaries are engaged in manufacturing activities and in the Middle East and Africa, and the British Dominions and Oceania, where 72

TABLE 9

**Japanese Parent Firms' Ownership of Overseas
Subsidiaries of Invested Area
As at end of 1972
(percent)**

Invested Area	Ownership of Subsidiaries					
	Over 51	50	49-26	25-11	below 10	Total
Asia	41	17	32	7	3	100
Canada/U.S.	87	6	3	3	1	100
Europe	74	11	9	4	2	100
Latin America	68	11	14	4	3	100
Middle East and Africa	41	17	22	17	3	100
British Dominions and Oceania	58	17	14	9	3	100

Source: Compiled by Yoshihiro Tsurumi on the basis of field research in and outside Japan and on the basis of *Kigyobetsu Kaigai Toshi of 1972* (Tokyo: Keizai Chosa Kyokai, 1973).

percent and 50 percent of the subsidiaries are engaged in manufacturing activities respectively, one can directly observe that the Japanese have tended to settle for minority patterns of ownership. These findings appear to support the popular myth that, unlike other advanced nations, Japan does not insist on the majority ownership of her overseas manufacturing subsidiaries.

However, my field research uncovered the real economic factors that motivated Japanese firms to accept a minority position in their manufacturing subsidiaries abroad. Japanese firms often had to jump over protective tariff walls when establishing manufacturing operations overseas before entry was completely closed to them by the host governments. For the entering Japanese firms this often meant the commencement of a minimum scale of simple manufacturing operation in a joint venture with the local partner, who would have formerly been the firm's import agent. Rather than insisting on a majority ownership of a subsidiary that might well fail, the Japanese parent investor attempted to spread the risks by involving in the venture other Japanese partners and more than two local partners.

The Japanese group approach to overseas investments, as discussed earlier in this chapter, contributed to the multiparty ventures abroad, which would reduce the possibility of one firm controlling more than 50 percent. Besides, the local market orientation of the Japanese manufacturing subsidiaries that did not bring in sophisticated technologies gave the local partner greater bargaining strength in demanding a sizable, even majority, ownership. Even when the local partner did not pay for its share of capital either in kind (plant sites, and so forth), or in cash, the Japanese parent firm extended loans to him. As a result, the Japanese investments mentioned at the beginning of this chapter produced many atomistically scattered subsidiaries in which most typically two to three Japanese investors held among themselves less than 50 percent ownership of the subsidiary.

By the mid-1970s this was changing. As Japanese firms move into investments of the Stage 2 type, they have increasingly succeeded in obtaining majority control of their manufacturing subsidiaries. For example, in Indonesia, to which Japanese investments have been rushing since 1970, all the foreign Japanese subsidiaries at least started out as majority-owned firms of Japanese parents.

According to my own survey, two considerations lead Japanese firms pursuing the strategies of Stage 2 to insist on majority ownership of their subsidiaries abroad. They are: (1) to maintain uniform sales strategies and avoid confusions of export market demarcations; (2) to influence the production plans and products of overseas manufacturing subsidiaries. All told, the Japanese firms' positions as minority owners of their overseas subsidiaries were the result of investors' trial-and-error behavior during Stage 1 of investment. From now on, like their U.S.-based counterparts, Japanese investors will also attempt to secure effective controls of their overseas subsidiaries and to link them more closely with their headquarters in Japan. These moves by Japanese firms will run against the opposing moves by the Asian host countries seeking greater control over the directions of foreign subsidiaries on their territory.

Headquarter-Subsidiary Communication and Exclusion of Local Nationals

It was shown in this chapter that the process-related production technologies of Japan and the narrow breadth of skills possessed by Japanese engineers and managers led Japanese firms to send in teams of instructors, especially for their start-up operations. These situations, unique to Japanese firms, contribute to the popular view that Japanese firms keep more expatriates than American or European counterparts. In addition, the styles and procedures of decision-making in Japanese parent firms require key posts of their overseas subsidiaries to be manned by persons who have grown thoroughly familiar in Japan with the often implied and informal communication patterns peculiar to each specific firm in Japan.

The so-called "bottom-up" procedure of *Ringi style* decision-making requires not only vertical but also lateral communication among multiple echelons of corporate organizations.[6] This means that for any key decision concerning, say, the production operations of the overseas subsidiary, not only the production manager but also the managers of finance, sales, and all other functions need to keep in touch with their counterparts at their headquarters offices and plants in Japan. In the milieu of a Japanese corporate culture, any requests and messages from outposts such as overseas subsidiaries tend to be processed and compiled in accordance with the amounts of implicit credits and favors the overseas managers have in the past built up with the key persons in the Japanese parent firm who will receive and screen these messages. Unless these key persons see to it that all bases are properly touched and are persuaded to accommodate equally all requests from their overseas subsidiaries, the overseas subsidiaries will remain helpless. In an organic institution such as the Japanese corporate system, no key decision will be made without taking pains to let all the relevant subunits within the firm readjust themselves to adequately accommodate all the issues that overseas subsidiaries inject into headquarters offices. The more sympathetic the recipients of overseas requests are to problems peculiar to their overseas subsidiaries, the more receptive they will be to requests from abroad. This means that all the managers of the overseas subsidiaries, regardless of their functions, need to keep their counterparts in Japan informed of the business developments in the overseas subsidiaries. The requisite communications networks are too fine for handling by a single person such as the president of the overseas subsidiary.

During the fieldwork that I conducted among the manufacturing subsidiaries of Japan in 1972 and again in 1973, I kept running into middle management members of Japanese subsidiaries abroad, who regularly write "personal" reports to "their men" back home. These reports were designed to substitute for the intimate face-to-face communication possible at home. The nature of these reports was such that the drafting of these reports could not possibly have been delegated even to other Japanese expatriates from the same corporation. Without an intuitive feel for *what* to tell *whom,* and *when*—that can only be developed by an intense sharing of corporate values and experience—delicate and intimate trading of information and favors through letters would be impossible for the overseas subsidiaries. Accordingly, for the time being, unless the present multilateral base-touching between individuals in Japan and abroad is changed drastically, Japanese subsidiaries abroad will not be able to bring even the most able local nationals into meaningful communicator roles with their headquarters offices and plants back in Japan. Thus far, many Japanese firms have resisted a drastic change in the communication patterns between headquarters and overseas subsidiaries, mainly because effective communicators serving as "gatekeepers"[7] between Japan and overseas have not yet been developed.

CONCLUSION: DILEMMA OF JAPANESE SUBSIDIARIES IN A HOSTILE ENVIRONMENT

Japanese direct investments abroad are now confronted with many difficulties. A number of manufacturing subsidiaries that are producing least technology-intensive products for local markets of the developing nations will either be forced to close down or divest themselves to local partners. One immediate response to these threats of divestiture has been to turn an overseas manufacturing subsidiary into an exporting base or to upgrade the products to more technology-intensive products for local markets of the developing nations. However, this would compound the problems of transfer of manufacturing technologies and managerial skills from Japanese parents to local firms. A team approach by Japanese parent firms to these problems has given rise to the criticism that Japanese dominate subsidiary operations and keep out local nationals from key decision-making positions.

Their products, process technologies, and the communication patterns between headquarters and subsidiaries have thus far locked Japanese subsidiaries into politically vulnerable positions. To make matters worse, Japanese corporations that are used to almost "collusive" relationships between government and business in Japan have, innocently perhaps, endeavored to reproduce similar relationships abroad. As a result, a number of them have come to be identified too closely with the regime in power.

In addition to the public visibility of Japanese subsidiaries, the close identification of Japanese subsidiaries with the government in power makes them a convenient surrogate target against which the public's suppressed anger against oppressions or corruptions of the current government can be vented. For instance, from spring to fall of 1973, it was widely publicized in Korea that of all foreign subsidiaries, Japanese subsidiaries had the lowest wage level.* This was singularly interpreted as evidence that Japanese firms were exploiting Korean laborers. The survey failed to account for the fact that all Japanese subsidiaries were joint ventures with Koreans, and that many of them were established by so-called medium-to-small Japanese firms, often owned and operated by Koreans residing in Japan. Although these Japanese subsidiaries pay higher wages than comparable small-to-medium firms of Korea, these subsidiaries were matched against American subsidiaries of such large firms as Fairchild, Gulf, and Motorola. The survey did not mention that the wage levels and working conditions of subsidiaries of large Japanese firms such as Hitachi, Toshiba, Sanyo, and NEC were often better than those of their American counterparts in Korea.

Similar campaigns to reinforce public prejudices against Japanese firms have been repeated throughout Asia. When you check the chronology of the sudden appearances of public criticism of Japanese investments by the leading local newspapers, you can observe one distinct pattern. In Korea, Thailand, and Indonesia, local newspapers—often under the government censorships—began to criticize Japanese investments when Japan appeared to overtake America as the leading foreign investor. In Thailand, this happened from 1971 to 1972. In Korea, from the end of 1972 to mid-1973, Japan overtook America. Accordingly, Korean public criticism of Japanese businessmen and subsidiaries was openly stepped up during 1973.[8] In Indonesia, from spring of 1973 to January of 1974, a fear of Japanese domination of the country suddenly appeared.

The analyses of the nature of the public criticisms of these different host countries point out one common theme: that is that Japanese (foreign) investments are not aiding the economic and social developments of the host country. The host country fears most dependency on one foreign country, particularly on Japan. Checked against the expected roles serving as the

---

*During July and August 1973, in Korea, I was reminded of these facts by leading national newspapers *Dong-A Daily* and *Chosun Daily,* which carried them repeatedly on the basis of the data released by the Korean government.

benevolent change agents of developing economies, no private foreign investment could satisfy the host country. Japanese investments have simply illuminated the dilemma of private firms pursuing their private goals while the public spectators expected to see different behaviors.

In such countries as Korea, the Philippines, and even in Singapore where the adverse memories of the militarist Japan still lingers, the host countries often expected Japanese firms to be more sensitive to their needs than their Western counterparts. As a retribution for the wartime destruction or atrocities committed by the Imperial Forces of Japan, these host countries expected Japanese firms to be less privately profit-motivated than their Western counterparts. On the other hand, the Japanese firms, who did not feel responsible for the actions of the militarist regime of Japan, failed to meet the unstated but strong expectations of the host countries. In other Asian countries where the wartime memory of the Japanese Imperial Army is less harsh, Japanese investors were expected to be more "Asian," and hence, more sensitive to local needs of their Asian neighbors than their Western counterparts. These expectations were also betrayed. Their delusion breeds hostility toward Japanese firms.

NOTES

1. It is interesting to note that after 1949, the People's Republic of China consciously adopted a growth strategy which resembled the early Japanese approach. See John Gurley, "Capitalist and Maoist Economic Development," *The Bulletin of Concerned Asian Scholars,* vol. 2, no. 3 (April-July, 1970): 34-50.

2. The Ministry of International Trade and Industry, *Survey of Overseas Investments* (November 1972), Tokyo.

3. For more detailed accounts of Japanese multinational firms' moves in both developing and developed countries, see Yoshihiro Tsurumi, "Japanese Multinational Firms," *Journal of World Trade Law* (January-February, 1973): 74-90; and Yoshihiro Tsurumi, "The Strategic Framework for Japanese Investments in the United States," *The Columbia Journal of World Business* (Winter, 1973): 19-25.

4. This phenomenon is called, "follow the leader." In the case of the large U.S. firms, a follow-the-leader example is seen to trigger the timing of the followers' overseas investments. See F. Knickerbocker, *Oligopolistic Reactions and Multinational Enterprises* (Division of Research, Harvard Business School: 1972).

5. This kind of technological adaptation was also found in the U.S. manufacturing industries of the nineteenth century when the United States was relatively skill-scarce compared with her source of imported manufacturing technologies from the United Kingdom. See H. J. Habakkuk, *American and British Technology in the Nineteenth Century* (Cambridge: Cambridge University Press, 1967). During my field investigation in 1973 in Indonesia, I observed similar adaptive efforts in two of Japan's assembly plants of electronic and electric appliances in order to overcome acute shortages of skilled workers in Indonesia.

6. M. Y. Yoshino, *The Japanese Managerial System* (M.I.T. Press, 1969), pp. 204, 254-62. In *Ringi style,* it is often the middle managements or even lower echelons that initiate the strategic decisions and seek the legislative approvals of top management.

7. Thomas Allen, "Roles in Technical Communication Networks" in Nelson and Pollack ed., *Communication among Scientists and Engineers* (Lexington, Mass.: Heath Lexington Books, 1970), pp. 191-208.

8. The analyses of two leading Korean newspapers, *Dong-A Daily* and *Cho-sun Daily,* for the period of 1972-73, were carried out by my research assistants in Korea, Mr. Yoon and Ms. Ryn.

OTHER REFERENCES

Kim, Jong-hyon. "Kan-nichi Keizai Kyoryoku no Hyoka" ("Evaluation of Korea-Japan Economic Cooperation"), *Asia Koron* (August 1973), Seoul.

Nakane, Chie. *Tekiono Jyoken (Conditions of Adaptation),* Tokyo: Kodansha, 1972.

———. *Japanese Society.* (Berkeley: University of California Press, 1972).

Reuber, Grant. *Private Foreign Investment in Development.* Oxford: Clarendon Press, 1973.

Sivarakra, Sulak. "A Thai Image of Japan," *Bulletin,* no. 25 (April 1970). The International House of Japan, Tokyo.

Stopford, J., and Wells, L. *Managing the Multinational Enterprise.* New York: Basic Books, 1972.

Tsurumi, Yoshihiro. "Nihon Kigyo no Takokusekika eno Jyoken," ("On Multinationalization of Japanese Firms"), *Toyo Keizai Quarterly* (July 1973).

Vernon, Raymond. "Saints and Sinners in Foreign Investment," *Harvard Business Review* (May-June, 1963).

———. "Problems and Policies of Competition and Monopoly Power," *American Economic Review Papers and Proceedings* (May 1974).

Wells, Louis T. "Economic Man and Engineering Man: Choice of Technology in a Low-Wage Country," *Public Policy,* vol. 21, no. 3 (Summer 1973).

Yoshino, Michael. "Organization and Decision Making in Emerging Japanese Multinational Enterprises," in Ezra Vogel ed., *Decision Making in Large Japanese Organizations.* Berkeley: University of California Press, 1973.

6

THE MULTINATIONAL CORPORATION AND WORLD TRADE: THE CASE OF THE DEVELOPED ECONOMIES
Walter Goldstein

In the last twenty-five years, the multinational corporation (MNC) has become one of the critical institutions of power in the world's political economy. In the economically developed structures and the wealthy markets of the "advanced" industrial states, it has established a network of affiliate companies to deploy its financial resources and its manufacturing strength. Today, 200 of the largest MNCs report a sales turnover of $1 billion or more each year; and their foreign subsidiaries are to be found in anywhere from 20 to 120 "host" economies around the globe. It is the argument of this essay that the MNCs have acquired an unprecedented, if still unrecognized, influence. Their authority over the economic mechanisms of "post industrial" society is already considerable. If their power should increase in the future, as now seems probable, the MNC will challenge the autonomy and the viability of the Western nation state.

The MNC has performed in a markedly different manner in the socialist bloc or among the Third World nations from in the mass consumption societies of the West. In the capitalist state, the MNC has come to be accepted as a powerful though footloose agent of economic growth. Its ability to determine political and industrial modes of development has not been seriously constrained; its deflection of international trade flows has not provoked sharp protest. In the Western economic system, the MNC has learned how best to take advantage of the complex structures and the international markets devised by finance capitalism. By helping to promote the spread of transnational investment and industry in the developed world, it has advanced its own wealth as well as the productive capacity of competing nation states. It has been widey trusted in the past, but its present successes might yet lead to an undermining of its future credibility.

It is difficult to measure the influence or the strength that has been acquired by the MNC. Conditions vary widely among national economic structures and industrial sectors. Many sectors or regions have been deeply penetrated by the MNC but others have been ignored. Aggregate data has been gathered to gauge the MNCs' performance in manufacturing or service industries or in the Euro-dollar markets through which finance capital moves in enormous flows. But not enough is known about the influence that the MNC wields in political or trade conflicts. Though preliminary studies have been published by the United Nations, the U.S. government and various academic groups, it is necessary to begin with a word of caution.[1] It is still too early to provide a definitive answer to the question posed in this analysis: How far has the MNC influenced the development strategies of industrialized states and the international trade upon which they depend?

A first attempt at an answer can be made by categorizing the national economies and the sectors of international trade in which the MNCs have concentrated their productive and investment power. This enquiry will begin by asking why the MNC has performed so profitably in the most challenging of markets; and why it has achieved so rapid a rate of growth and expansion in recent years? A second question must then be asked: Has much of the regulatory or planning authority of developed nation states been surrendered to the transnational management of the MNC? Once these questions have been resolved—however tentatively—the central issue can be raised: How far will the development strategies of industrial states and their competition in international trade be determined by the spreading networks of the MNC?

THE MNC AND THE OECD ECONOMY

The highly industrialized economies of the world can be readily identified. They belong to the 'rich nations club' known as the Organization for Economic Cooperation and Development (OECD). They command nearly 75 percent of the world's purchasing power and marketing opportunities in international trade. The twenty-four members of the club are located in North America, Western Europe, Japan, and Australia. All of them maintain a 'free market' economy; and all of them are committed, as far as they are able, to limit government intervention in the operation of a capitalist economy. None of them have adopted the centralized planning procedures found in socialist societies. None of them have expropriated or nationalized alien assets in the manner practised by the improverished or military regimes of the less developed countries (LDCs).

In order to maintain affluent living standards, the twenty-four rich nations have had to compete for the world's challenging but lucrative export markets. Their economic might and political powers have been gauged by their ability to secure ample sources of credit, to enhance the productivity of labor or capital, and to enrich their value-added manufacturing exports. The OECD economies have provided two-thirds, if not more, of the financial resources and of the market opportunities capitalized by the MNC. The remaining one-third has come from the one hundred poorer nations of the socialist nations of the LDC bloc. It is regrettable, but callously irrelevant, that the overwhelming majority of the planet's population live in these latter, unattractive markets. The industrial policies and the economic expectations of these two blocs are utterly dissimlar from those prevailing in the OECD nations. Poor and socialist countries are suspicious of the MNC and attempt to police its subsidiaries. They are excluded from this analysis because they do not allow the MNC a free rein in molding their development strategies. Their response to and control over the MNC must therefore be investigated within a different set of parameters.

The copious literature on multinational business reveals that certain characteristics are unique to the MNC, no matter whether it is American, European, or Japanese in parent origin. The salient characteristics can be briefly summarized.

1. The fundamental decisions of the MNC are globally and organically controlled by the home headquarters, even though its local subsidiary operations are thoroughly decentralized.[2]

2. The investments and affiliate operations of the MNC are concentrated in only a few industrial sectors. They are not found in the primary product or in the labor-intensive sectors of developed economies. They congregate thickly where capital or expensive technologies are required in large aggregations. Thus MNCs play a prominent role in those value-added industries that contribute a disproportionate strength to the growth capabilities and to the competitive standing of a developed economy.[3]

3. The most profitable MNCs have penetrated into those industries that are subject to 'monopoly competition' or to oligopoly controls. These include capital-intensive industries (for example, automobiles, petrochemicals, and oil); science-based industries (such as computers, electronics, and nuclear engineering); and giant chains in the service sector (for instance, hotels, banking, and food processing). Each of these industries relies upon an oligopoly equilibrium. Thus: entry into their markets is arbitrarily limited; or prices are effectively stabilized and administered by a few leading firms; or the size of the firm and its product differentiation expand to meet the marketing requirements of imperfect competition.[4]

4. Organizational "size" is essential to the global expansion of the MNC in its production planning at home and in its strategic plannings overseas. The multiproduct companies that play a mammoth role in the home market are

TABLE 1

MNC Overseas Business

Company (*Fortune* 500 Ranking of 1974)	Foreign Net Income percent of		Foreign Sales percent of	
	Total	($000)	Total	($000)
Addressograph Multi-graph (300)	216.0	9,603	33.0	161,880
USM (285)	114.0	13,137	50.2	264,770
Standard Oil of California (11)	78.1	658,834	54.4	4,226,224
Ferro (488)	77.8	12,277	50.9	130,349
International Harvester (22)	75.1	85,842	27.9	1,170,200
Gulf Oil (10)	71.8	574,000	54.1	4,552,000
Continental Oil (21)	66.0	160,500	N.A.*	N.A.
Mobil Oil (7)	65.8	574,000	67.6	7,491,635
Exxon (2)	65.7	1,606,000	N.A.	N.A.
Texaco (6)	64.9	838,000	N.A.	N.A.
Marathon Oil (104)	62.5	89,600	35.7	563,000
Libby, McNeill and Libby (331)	62.0	5,550	36.0	158,279
Gillette (158)	61.2	53,051	48.8	519,876
CPC International (81)	60.8	45,890	54.4	1,018,000
Otis Elevator (165)	59.8	24,127	58.8	591,664
Pfizer (132)	59.7	72,000	51.9	666,500
Coca-Cola (69)	59.0	126,838	44.0	943,795
Hoover (283)	58.6	19,368	67.9	363,000
Dow Chemical (38)	57.6	158,727	45.8	1,405,400
Uniroyal (72)	57.3	27,000	30.1	626,204
AMP (343)	57.2	26,019	N.A.*	N.A.
American Standard (108	56.7	22,448	46.9	718,000
International Business Machines (8)	54.1	852,537	46.8	5,142,536
International Telephone and Telegraph (9)	52.0	272,475	52.0	5,295,178
Signode (410)	51.8	11,284	36.1	123,413

*N.A.-not available.

Note: Percentages exceeding one hundred are indicated for the first two companies that performed strongly because they had to write off unusual domestic losses; nevertheless, both earn more than 50 percent of their profits abroad in any normal year. The oil companies performed well because U.S. price controls reduced their earnings at home but not overseas—thus creating a grave political controversy. Better profit margins overseas encouraged the vigorous expansion of all 25 companies; but the U.S. Treasury is now looking into the possibility that disproportionate allocations of corporate overhead, interest expense, and R and D costs were employed to lighten U.S. tax liabilities for the parent firm. The weakness of the dollar in the mid-1970s also put foreign earnings in a favorable light, especially for those companies that pre-emptively unloaded the cash balances they held in weaker currencies (such as the lira, the pound, and the dollar) before the slump of 1973.

Source: "Gillette Swings a Mighty Blade," *Fortune* (November 1974), p. 175.

those that also exert the largest influence in host economies abroad. The firms that lead *Fortune* magazine's listing of the top 500 corporations in America are the same as those (with a few remarkable exceptions) that set the pace in many of the strategic growth sectors of European industry.[5]

The significance of these characteristics can be measured in a listing published in the November 1974 issue of *Fortune*. An analysis of the top 500 U.S. industrial corporations revealed that at least 25 of the largest firms (rank ordered in the lefthand column by their total 1973 sales) earn more than half of their after-tax profits from overseas production. All the companies are of giant size, especially in the oil industry. All have established a global control capability to coordinate their affiliates' strategic planning as well as an oligopoly mode of product differentiation and marketing. A listing of European or Japanese MNCs would demonstrate a similar reliance upon foreign rather than home production to swell their overall sales and earnings.

It has become fashionable in the academic literature to debunk the comparisons between the GNP of nation states and the sales turnover of global MNCs. Though there is some merit to the debunking exercise, the fact remains that the headquarter managers of the MNC can reallocate an unprecedented amount of industrial wealth and productive capacity. In December 1974, one of the leading business journals of Europe, *Vision,* not a radical expose, pointed out that 54 of the largest 100 economic units in the world were companies and 46 were nation states. In an era when national prowess is measured in nuclear missiles and per capita GNP, it was significant to the business editors that 26 of the companies were American, 22 European, and 6 Japanese.

Some years ago an alarm about the accelerating growth of the MNC was raised by M. Servan-Schreiber. He predicted, in *Le Defi Americain,* that:

> Fifteen years from now it is quite possible that the world's third greatest industrial power, just after the United States and Russia, will not be Europe, but *American industry in Europe.* Already, in the ninth year [1967] of the Common Market, this European market is basically American in organization.[6]

Though his prediction and alarm were never seriously regarded, the fact remains that the list of American MNC affiliates established in the key markets of Europe is awesome in dimension and in profitability. American industry did not stage a massive takeover of Europe but it did score some notable successes. IBM and Honeywell gained a larger share of the European computer market than *all* of their European rivals (for example, the British ICL, the French CII, Philips in Holland, and Siemens in Germany) combined. The eight "major" oil companies, five of which are American, exercised a distribution and price leadership over local "independents" or "national" oil companies (such as Veba in Germany, ENI in Italy, or ELF-Erap in France) until the OPEC boycott and cartel mechanism deflected the flow of Europe's oil supplies in October 1973. In the chemical industries, DuPont, Dow, and Union Carbide had to counter strong competition from the European multinationals (Imperial Chemical Industries [ICI] Bayer, or Rhone-Poulenc, for instance). They managed to preserve their oligopoly position, however, by creating a maze of joint ventures and cross-licensing agreements; this allowed the MNCs to control the production and marketing of manmade fibers, pharmaceuticals, and naptha or ethylene derivatives. The giant auto affiliates of GM and Ford in Britain and Germany integrated vertically into France and the Low Countries, thus creating hardships for such nonmultinationals as Citroen and British Leyland Motors (BLMC). U.S. electronics companies—such as ITT, Fairchild, Motorola, Texas Instruments—seized a major share of the European market for microcircuits, components and electronic equipment, and their grip has yet to be broken loose.

Even more notable were the successes scored by American MNCs in the service sectors of the European economy. Hilton, Sheraton, Avis, McKinsey, and J. Walter Thompson established themselves in every major city. Morgan Guaranty Trust Bank, Chase Manhattan, First National City, and the Bank of America opened several hundred branches and revolutionized the procedures of investment and retail banking. They came to dominate the $170 billion flow of the Euro-dollar market and the transaction of short-term credit by accumulating gigantic sums in local deposits and in recycled Arab oil dollars. They also created transnational consortia of banks to move amounts of finance capital—variously estimated between $150 and $200 billion—larger than the GNP of Great Britain. Much of this money was channelled through the offshore subterfuges and tax havens that are indispensable to the free mobility of contemporary capital.[7]

Another perspective of the rapid growth of the MNC and of the vital role that it performs in the OECD system can be gained by analyzing the experience of Sweden. Though Sweden provides a home base for a relatively small number of MNCs—255 of the 7,276 parent and 1,159 of the 27,300 MNC affiliate companies listed in the U.N. Report—it maintains a striking profile of activity.[8] 83.4 percent of Swedish affiliates are located in developed economies and they generated manufacturing sales in 1971 that almost equalled the value of Sweden's export trade. In 1970, these affiliates abroad employed the equivalent of 20 percent of the home work force (a ratio that was matched by overseas American MNCs in comparison to the U.S. manufacturing work strength at home). Most of the Swedish production abroad occurred in electrical and nonelectrical machinery and in the chemical industries; in the decade of the 1960s they recorded a growth of 300 percent. The ratio of gross profit to annual sales or to fixed assets was strikingly higher in the manufacturing operations outside rather than inside Sweden. (This overseas profitability ratio is also matched by the MNC reporting of U.S. parent companies.) It is obvious that Sweden's economic growth and foreign trade would have developed in a very different direction if its largest companies had not invested in expanding their operations abroad. Whether the development was beneficial to the nation's work force or to the welfare of the domestic population is difficult to determine. So, too, is a political question: were the investment decisions subject at any stage to the public knowledge or control of a democratic electorate?

The political issues raised by the MNC are highly complex. Neon symbols and advertising across the great cities of Europe project the intrusive wealth of the giant MNCs. Yet the political resentment generated by these alien interests has never reached the peaks of hostility that Marxist and radical critics had once predicted. Ten years ago, President de Gaulle had denounced the technological and monetary imperialism of America; and Prime Minister Wilson had warned against Britain becoming "a helot to the sophisticated apparatus of American business." Despite the stern resolutions adopted by parties and labor unions on the Left, the European Economic Community (EEC) did little to stop the border-crossing expansion of American and European MNCs. The most committed of the Socialist unions and Left groups attacked the profit-seeking growth of the MNC, urging that the ITT-CIA links in Chile would reappear in Bonn or Paris and that monopoly MNCs would exploit the economic frailties of the capitalist system. Prior to the inflationary upheaval and the recession of 1974, however, the Social Democrats in Germany, the liberal governments in Canada, and the Labour regimes in Britain and Scandinavia made few efforts to prevent the wave of MNC takeovers and affiliate implantations that spread into their strategic growth industries. Only the business-oriented governments of France and Japan took serious steps to curb the dynamic intrusion of foreign MNCs.[9] (Parties on the Left have been severely critical of the MNC and have occasionally threatened—in a gentle manner—to nationalize their property. However, no government has dared take forceful action and neither have the trade unions.)

It was not surprising that the MNC settled its many affiliates in the OECD economies with so little fuss. In many, though by no means all, cases productivity has improved and strikes have decreased at plants taken over by foreign MNCs. New production processes and locations were opened up by the incoming MNCs; and many of them made valuable contributions to the finance or technology-intensive sectors of the host economies that they had penetrated. Rather than building cartel positions and Coca-colonizing the fragmented markets of Europe, of which they were accused, they helped spin-off new technologies, management systems, and sophisticated products through their offshore subsidiaries. In doing so, they generated new sources of capital, they accelerated the transfer of complex knowledge and boosted the export performance of many competing economies. Prior to the destabilizing of the international monetary system in 1971, and despite the hostile rhetoric in circulation, the MNC was generally welcome as a stimulant to growth. It is only in recent years that it has been perceived as a severe threat to the political autonomy of an advanced, mass consumption economy.

Corporate leaders and business journals have argued with even greater stridency that the MNC should be seen as a benevolent innovation—or as an exemplary "engine of progress." Prominent executives, politicians, and professors of business have roundly denied that it is launched upon a collision course with the sovereign authority of the nation state. They insist that the behavior, the motivation, and the rewards of the MNC managers are largely beyond reproach. As they put it, the "cosmocorp" is the most successful, secular international organization in recorded history; and it, alone, promises to bring a "business peace" to a politically divided world. As loyal citizens of an "indivisible republic of merchants," the MNCs will harmonize the struggle between American or German banks, the Japanese *zaibatsu* or the OPEC oil sheiks. They will establish a code of "good citizenship" to guide the good sense of the MNC managers and to accelerate strife-free economic growth. In lobbying against the Burke-Hartke bill before the U.S. Senate, a group of leading MNCs—modestly known as the Emergency Committee on American Trade—insisted that their profits and expansion were not dependent upon a forced export of jobs, investment capital, and patented technology. Their interest in enlarging the profits of the parent company and the market position of their overseas affiliates was simply to accelerate the free thrust and the welfare consequences of world trade. In doing so they would arrest the encroaching protectionism of tariffs, quotas, subsidies, and trade wars that was likely to ruin the commerce between nations.[10]

Useful studies have been made of such long-established MNCs as International Harvester, Ford, Singer, and Westinghouse.[11] They have detailed the factor-mobility or the oligopoly advantages that the MNC pursued in competitive markets. By taking advantage of tariff barriers, differential interest rates, variable factor costs, and fluctuating currency exchange rates the global MNC has learned how to overcome competition abroad while defending its home base against the penetration strategies of rival MNCs. Gillette, Michelin, or Volvo became global companies by relocating key production or assembly units abroad in order to open up markets that would otherwise have remained closed to them. Zenith, Rollei Camera, and Hitachi found their risk-taking rewarded when their new plant in Taiwan, Seoul, and Singapore recruited assembly-line labor at 10 cents an hour to manufacture the labor-intensive components of cameras or electronic appliances for expensive markets in which 10 cents can no longer buy a telephone call. The savings generated by these global relocations have greatly improved the profit ratios reported by the MNC. In most industries, the

MNCs reported consistently higher earning than non-MNC competitors. In the British energy industries, for example, Royal-Dutch Shell increased its profit margins between 1972 and 1973 by 159 percent and BP by 332 percent, while the nationalized coal and steel industries reported severe losses. ICI also enlarged its earnings by 100 percent, largely from overseas operations.

More importantly, it has been argued the MNCs have enhanced the world's stock of wealth by scrupulously fulfilling the laws of comparative advantage and all possible economies of scale. In the terms favored by business economists, the MNC has helped secure the "international equalization of factor costs." Thus, German automobile, Dutch electronics, or Swiss watch companies have built "export platforms" in the cheap wage economies of India, Spain, or Brazil. Hoechst Chemicals and ICI have amortized their expensive R and D at home by acquiring $1 billion worth of distillation or cracking plants in North America. Olivetti and Corn Products have taken profits in Canada or Belgium, or wherever taxes were low, and borrowed money from sister affiliates where interest rates were cheap or credit was available. A wise use of transfer pricing allowed Royal-Dutch Shell to move cash balances from profitable to tight money markets; while raising its new money from Euro-dollar funds, BP bought its way into the U.S. market—in a costly acquisition of the Sohio chain—in order to diversify its geographical reach. By standardizing product lines and integrating vertically and horizontally, Unilever and British-American Tobacco enlarged both their foreign operations and their share of world markets. Westinghouse and GE utilized their formidable lead in turbine technology and nuclear engineering to stabilize prices and supply schedules; their activity forced many of the OECD governments to modify their national plans for the nuclear generation of electric power. Given the "technostructure" management and the conglomerate interests of the MNC, these techniques of production and market control helped promote its extraordinary growth and profit.

The annual growth and profit figures achieved by American MNCs were highly impressive, but no more so than those attained by European or Japanese firms. Increasing by 9 percent annually, the book value of American investment overseas totalled $107 billion in 1973. This produced estimated annual sales of $250 billion (or five times the worth of all U.S. exports) and net earnings of $15 billion; thus a 17.3 percent return on direct investments was earned by majority- or wholly-owned affiliates abroad. Identifiable U.S. corporate transactions added a net $9 billion to the U.S. balance of payments in 1972, the last year before the OPEC upheaval. The net outflow of capital from the United States was only $3.4 billion but $4.5 billion in earnings was retained for reinvestment abroad; this was required to expand the MNCs' operations and to decrease their parent company's tax burden.

The Department of Commerce confirmed that American firms abroad had earned $15 billion in 1972. $10.4 billion of this $15 billion was repatriated in royalties, fees, dividends, interest, and earnings. Other countries, however, claimed that this was a "surplus rent" or an imperialist extraction of their wealth, and complaints were lodged with the UN and OECD. After 1972, of course, the pattern of investment inflows and outflows was abruptly reversed. The OPEC oil earnings of $65 billion a year brought an imbalance of payments to all of the developed countries and further devaluations of the reserve currencies of world trade provoked inflationary consequences. Had the MNCs not continued on their pattern of expansion during this fiscal storm, great waves of panic might have swept through the system of floating exchange rates and unbalanced national budgets.[12]

THE IMPACT OF THE MNC

The influence wielded by the MNC over the development plans of the richer economies has varied greatly. In the science-based industries that depend upon large, international markets it has been extensive. In the service sectors, mass-produced manufactures, oil, and banking, the MNC has exerted itself strenuously. Only in retailing, labor-intensive and highly protected (or subsidized industries has the influence of the MNC been weak or politically blocked. A report issued in 1973 by the EEC revealed that MNCs had taken a major, if not a predominant, role in the computer, automobile, hydrocarbon plastics, food, and electrical engineering industries. Action was proposed to try to control the expansion of the MNCs—but in an inconclusive manner. None of the measures proposed were severe; and none of them has been adopted.[13] Though several nations have taken a few timid steps along the lines of the measures proposed, the EEC has not dared to challenge—with the exception of a few antitrust rulings—either the capitalist axioms upon which the MNC depends or the national sovereignty to which member nations cling.

The 200 MNCs that generate $1 billion or more in annual turnover are such recent arrivals on the world scene that it is difficult to gauge the full measure of their strength. Global enterprises such as Volkswagen and Toyota, Akzo, Petrofina, Dunlop-Pirelli, Unilever, Barclays Bank, and the Banque Nationale de Paris, Nestle, Siemens, Hitachi, and Pilkington Glass have spun-off numerous subsidiaries and interlocking ventures. Along with other MNCs they now account for one-eighth of all international trade flows, but it is estimated that by 1980 they will control one-quarter. As it is, the value of their production overseas already surpasses the total profit earned in world trade. The European business journal, *Vision,* frequently ranks the asset size, the profit ratios, or the sales turnover of leading MNCs. In the October 1974 issue, the ranking of the 50 most profitable companies in Europe revealed that practically all of the entrants were MNC parents or affiliates—such as Dow Chemical Europe, Rank Xerox, or the IBMs of Holland, Britain, Sweden,

Germany, and France. The December issue showed that the MNCs also dominated the lists of the largest employers and production sources in each country and they ranked among Europe's 50 largest banks.)[14]

Mobile and powerful, the MNC can threaten, if it so chooses, to undermine the regulatory controls and the economic autonomy of the nation state. The nine EEC nations and the U.S. government have long recognized this capability. However, they found during the winter petroleum crisis of 1973 that they could neither expose nor control the cross-national transfers of oil or credit undertaken by the largest of the MNC oil "majors." Several governments now believe that there never was a real crisis nor a major interruption of worldwide oil supplies; and that the companies had acted collusively to pass on all of the OPEC price increases—while removing any possible competition on the part of "independent" importers and refiners. Even the special enquiry of the U.S. Senate in 1974 was unable to prove that oil supplies had been so sharply restricted that the MNCs had been justified in fact in stopping gasoline flows and raising retail prices. Certainly, the windfall profits of the MNC "majors" suggested that a new mode in the concentration of international wealth and power had been achieved as a result of cross-national oligopoly operations.

Financed and controlled by parent company headquarters in North America, Europe, or Japan, the MNCs have ranged across the world's markets as if national frontiers, currency controls, and differential tariff barriers were of little consequence. Six hundred of the largest MNCs have established manufacturing affiliates or subsidiary plants in 20 or in 60 countries simultaneously. Combining total asset values worth almost one trillion dollars, these global enterprises have overcome many of the economic defense works of the nation state. In doing so they have revolutionized the dynamics of international capitalism.

Previously it had been assumed by political and business leaders that the national economy would remain subject to the regulatory controls of the liberal, capitalist state. Theorists on the Left shared the same assumption. They believed that they could devise a realistic planning formula for "socialism in one country at a time." Both conservatives and socialists failed to recognize the extent to which vital export and high-technology industries were intricately tied to the international trading system. As the 400,000 workers in European aerospace firms discovered, it is no longer feasible to think in terms of statist autonomy—even in an era in which most firms and airlines were already nationalized and fully subsidized.

In fact, the aero frame and aero engine industries demonstrate the futility of rejecting a multinational pattern of development. The largest companies in Europe, whether nationalized or not, have been systematically undercut by the civilian and military competition offered by American MNCs. Efforts were made by Dassault, Aerospatiale, the British Aircraft Corporation, and a merger of Vokker-Messerschmidtt to build military jets or shorthaul airbuses, as well as the ill-starred Rolls Royce and the Concorde SST. In nearly every case, the U.S. equipment was superior in quality, easier to service and more profitable to operate. Admittedly, there were unfair advantages—such as the subsidized R and D or the Pentagon-financed procurement schedules enjoyed by Boeing, Lockheed, or McDonnell Douglas. Defeated from the start, the European firms refused to rally their separate forces. They competed against each other as national subcontractors to the giant American MNCs and they failed to agree on cross-national modes of financing or development. Strikingly, the $3 billion wasted on the SST could have bought a controlling interest in every major U.S. company outright; and if the British and French had jointly invested in a short-haul airbus, every European airline would have bought it instead of the fleets of DC-9 and Boeing 737 which now fill their crowded airspace. As feuding "National Champions," as Professor Vernon has called them, the European aero companies could match neither the expensive technology nor the economies of scale available to their multinational counterparts from Seattle and California.[15]

The surging expansion of the MNC has seriously encroached upon the planning arrangements adopted by the OECD governments. The "indicative planning" of France, the "industrial compact" of Britain, and Scandinavian or Italian variants of public control and the state capitalism identified with "Japan, Inc." have been radically revised as a result of the long-range planning and resource allocation decisions of the MNC. It was the finding of the U.S. Tariff Commission report on the MNCs that:

> The planning and subsequent monitoring of plan fulfillment have reached a scope and level of detail that, ironically, resemble more than superficially the national planning procedures of communist countries. There are general goals set by top management, against which far-flung affiliates generate detailed operational plans for a year's, five years' or ten years' activity.[16]

The global financial and management decisions of the MNC have focused more often than not upon the needs of parent headquarters in New York, London, Rotterdam, or Tokyo. A dramatic list of examples can be cited. Ford Motor company phased out a major production line in the United Kingdom but opened up new assembly units in Belgium and France. Uniroyal rubber and Atlantic Richfield oil sold their holdings in the United Kingdom to French MNC affiliates while British Petroleum abandoned its refineries in Italy in order to avoid Italian price controls). General Electric relocated its appliance plants from Italy to Spain—where strikes and labor unions are banned. The powerful Rank-Xerox Corporation moved from London to Amsterdam to improve its tax position; and Fiat opened new production ventures in the United States with Allis-Chalmers and in the Soviet Union at Togliattigrad to enlarge its worldwide marketing. Dow Chemical and BASF invested jointly in polyester and acrylic fiber plants in the United States when wage rates in the Rhineland rose sharply. The largest MNC banks in London helped recycle $65 billion (in new petro-dollars) into the expansion of the blue chip MNCs of the developed world; and two French financial giants, the Paribas and the Suez Canal groups, moved credit from Europe (where it was urgently needed) to the United States (where it was relatively plentiful). To achieve sizable economies of scale. Olivetti and Singer closed old plants in Europe to build new installations in Scotland and in the United States. Two French chemical conglomerates, Rhone-Poulenc and Pechiney-Ugine-Kuhlmann, merged or exchanged several foreign affiliates. Volvo bought 75 percent of the Dutch DAF auto firm, Pernod bought a major Scotch distillery in Glasgow, and Japanese manufacturers of TV sets made in Ireland seized valuable markets in West Germany. Monthly analyses in *Vision* attempt to unravel the complex pyramiding of dynamic conglomerates like the Compagnie Financiere de Paris et des Pays Bas (Paribas) which owns a significant share of many competing and collaborating MNCs. Another entrepreneur, the Belgian baron Empain, outflanked the French government in selling a major electronics firm to Westinghouse while licensing his Creusot-Loire nuclear interests to the same MNC; he eventually submitted 22 of the leading 30 French contracts for nuclear power to Westinghouse licensing. His own group employs 100,000 workers outside Belgium, turns over $1 billion a year, and heavily influences steel and ship-building in France, iron and steel in Luxembourg, and merchant banking across Europe. Computer development is as critical to most European governments as promoting nuclear technology; yet Empain might sell his share of CII (the only French computer firm that could be merged into a future European consortium) to an American MNC that has no intention of preserving it for purposes of national prestige.

The employment and the welfare of millions of people have been forcibly changed by the MNCs' creation and transfer of wealth. Since the first devaluation of the dollar in 1971, windfall profits were secured by converting forward purchases of company reserves into German deutsche marks, Japanese yen, or Swiss francs. (In 1972, according to the November 1974 issue of *Fortune,* the Gillette company realized nearly $5 million from hedging against currency fluctuations.) But these momentous transfers also wrecked the short-term liquidity market and helped force the devaluation of key reserve currencies. The managers of the London branches of the great American banks created further havoc in 1974. By recycling Arab petro-dollars through their profitable, near-term accounts, they drained credit from economies that lacked it to those that could amply pay for it. Moreover, by selling short against sterling in Frankfurt or borrowing long in francs in Zurich, they protected their own shareholders against appreciable exchange losses—and thus earned substantial profits for their clients. It remains to be seen whether the multinational usurers of the Euro-dollar market, and their oil-rich followers in OPEC, will eventually abuse monetary speculation to the point of destabilizing the fragile equilibrium of international trade.*

Naturally it is wise for the comptrollers of Rio-Tinto-Zinc, the Deutsche Bank, or Petrofina to move as many assets and credit balances out of lira or sterling as quickly as they can. If, however, they succeed in demolishing the economic defenses of Italy or the United Kingdom in the midst of a balance of payments crisis, the whole structure of international transfers and investments might come down, too.

Suspicion and fear of the multiple product division and of the intra-affiliate transfers of the MNC have become so intense that international, professional, and political organizations have begun to debate the issues raised by this novel form of business activity. None of them has yet seen fit to recommend action, though a few—such as the U.S. Congress, OECD, the ILO, and EEC—have held enquiries and published reports. In 1973, the Public Opinion Research Center found that 70 percent of the Americans whom they polled had expressed distrust of the MNC, whether it was American or not; regardless of income, party affiliation, or occupation, two-thirds said that "something should be done" to curb the potentially footloose or irresponsible actions of the MNC.

Perhaps it is logical that a mass public should view a new and big phenomenon with alarm. The 1973 *U.N. Report* noted that 650 of the largest MNCs command an annual turnover exceeding $773 billion; one-third of them gross more than $1 billion a year. Of the 650 MNCs listed as manufacturing companies, 358 are American, 74 are Japanese, 61 are British, 45 are German, and 32 are French. Many of them now sell more or earn greater profits overseas than at home. In some cases, only the corporate

---

*The growth of consortium banking in the Euro-dollar markets for long- and short-term funds has left a few large banks in a strong position vis-a-vis national governments. For example, one of the groups of European international banks (known as EBIC)—which is unusual in having no U.S. or Japanese members—can command access to the following range of assets (in 1973 $ billion):

Bank	Home Country	Deposits	Loans
Amsterdam-Rotterdam	Netherlands	8.8	5.0
Commerciale Italiana	Italy	16.3	8.2
Deutsche	Germany	22.9	17.7
Midland	Gt. Britain	17.2	10.9
Societe Generale	France	20.9	16.7
Societe Generale de Banque	Belgium	7.8	3.4
Total		$93.9	$61.9

Four of five bank consortia can match or exceed these figures, especially if a mammoth U.S. bank belongs to the group. Of the 137 member nations of the UN, 130 command a GNP smaller than the deposits accessible to the EBIC management.[17]

headquarters has stayed at home while production jobs and earnings were relocated abroad. In others, the skilled and value-added work, R and D, and management prerogatives remained in the parent company but the dirty, unrenumerative operations became the specialty of huge affiliate companies in host countries overseas.[18]

The impact of the MNC can be measured in various ways. First, in terms of the home country's balance of payments, it is notable that the MNC generates an inflow of repatriated dividends, licensing fees, royalties, and earnings on interest—while its outflow of capital is limited simply to the expansion funds needed to supplement the loans or earnings retained abroad. The conventional export earnings of the United States, the United Kingdom, Switzerland, Holland, and Sweden are less significant today than the sales effected by the foreign affiliates of their own MNCs in third country markets. In addition, intracompany transfers (between home or affiliate plants) account for one-quarter to one-third of the entries that appear in the home nation's trading position. That the MNC is vital to the international politics of trade is immediately apparent. Of the 76 MNCs sampled in the Department of Commerce *Studies,* 33 sought to "maintain or increase market shares locally"; 25 reported that they would otherwise be "unable to reach markets from the U.S. because of tariffs, transportation costs, or nationalistic purchasing policies"; 20 went overseas to "meet competition," 15 because of "faster sales growth than in the United States."[19] In May 1974 the *Survey of Current Business* found that 298 firms sampled in 1970 earned higher profits than other forms of U.S. manufacturing at home, largely because of a favorable differential in tax credits and liabilities.

TABLE 2

**Percent U.S. Share of Gross Fixed Capital Formation
in European Host Countries, 1970**

Industry	Belgium and Luxembourg	Canada	France	German Federal Republic	United Kingdom
All manufacturing	14.1	32.2	5.8	12.3	20.9
Food	—	23.5	0.9	2.0	4.4
Chemicals	24.9	68.1	2.1	10.4	17.9
Primary and pre-fabricated metals	—	—	1.0	8.4	21.1
Nonelectrical machinery	12.0	57.8	23.3	27.8	29.0
Electrical machinery Transportation equipment	—	—	9.8	27.8	45.5
All other manufacturing	10.8	13.6	2.8	2.7	18.2

For a second gauge of the MNCs' influence, attention must be drawn to the impact exerted upon the advanced economic structure of a host country through new plant and equipment expenditures.[20]

The implications of the data in Table 2 are closely understood by the planning and Treasury officials of the OECD governments. American expenditures on plant and new equipment in the European electronics, automobile, and engineering sectors are of major significance. Europeans know that 63 percent of Canada's GNP was generated (until 1973) by foreign-owned companies; and that 24 percent of Britain's exports—but 30 percent of Belgium's—are produced by the local affiliates of alien MNCs. However beneficial the MNC role might be, its power can only increase as the economic sovereignty of the host states falls away. The 125 American manufacturing MNCs in the sample accounted for $133 billion of worldwide sales, of which $36 billion or about 27 percent went to non-U.S. customers; their exports ($9.4 billion) represented 25 percent of all U.S. non-agricultural exports, with over 50 percent of them going to their own foreign affiliates. These 125 firms accounted for 40 percent of the book value of all U.S. foreign manufacturing investment and 70 percent of investment outflows in 1970. It would be an unwise government that chose to argue with (or close out) such forces for economic growth.[21]

The impact of the MNC on many developed countries can be critical. Whether the MNCs compete or not, they contribute new skills or hard currencies by promoting value-added exports, as in Belgium where affiliate companies export 63 percent of their output (or 55 percent in Holland). Their capital transfers can bring valuable funds into a foundering economy, such as the British, when credit is scarce and interest rates are expensive. The contribution in job opportunities can be equally striking. Of the jobs created in Belgium by new investment between 1964 and 1968, 70 percent came from foreign firms; and only 2 percent of this figure came from acquisitions rather than newly established affiliates. More important, the MNC affiliates either pay higher wages or they have linked wage increases to productivity agreements, thus improving plant efficiencies and lowering unit costs. Only rarely have labor union relations been sorely troubled. The MNCs usually face fewer strikes and often offer better working conditions, though many union leaders swear that the MNC resorts to tougher bargaining procedures than its local competitors.

Because the MNCs tend to be big, as do their affiliates, they can redeploy their forces and absorb severe product-line losses if market conditions change. In the EEC host countries, the foreign affiliates are often larger than indigenous firms. In the home countries of America, Japan, and Europe, it is the largest companies that become MNC parents and that can afford the $10 billion R and D spent by IBM or GE. It is only the global oil major that can finance the multiple refineries, pipelines, and tanker fleets that are envied by the nationalized or the independent companies. A new MNC competitor/

collaborator, the National Iranian Oil Company (NIOC) has begun to lease drilling fields in the North Sea, tankers in Hong Kong, and refineries in the Caribbean. Like its MNC predecessors, it began life as a cash-swollen entity and by expanding its overseas operations it will increase its wealth rapidly.

The MNCs pose grave problems for developed countries that need to repair their imbalance of payments or to secure an export-led growth. Whether their governments are Left or Right-leaning in policy they must be fearful in dealing with the international sectors of their own economy. If they are too vigorous in regulating import traffic or in levying corporate taxes, they might discourage the implanting or the expansion of foreign undertakings. Labour governments in the United Kingdom and Norway are determined to control—or nationalize—the valuable oil-bearing sites in the North Sea. If they do so, the MNC majors might limit the investment of risk capital that is required, in trillions of dollars, to exploit their urgent natural resources. If the majors should not be restrained, however, both nations will become dependent upon production and the marketing decisions that best suit the MNC oil club. If Britain is to pull its economy out of a historic decline by extracting and exporting North Sea oil, it can not afford to ignore the profit projections already calculated by Exxon or NIOC. It might cost $7,500 to produce one barrel a day of production capacity in the North Sea—as against $1,000 in the United States or $300 in the Persian Gulf. To achieve the U.K. target of two million barrels daily by 1980 will require an outlay of $15 billion; if the target is to double by 1985, the initial investment could be $30 billion. Clearly, the U.K. government cannot find such funds; they equal one year's total public revenue. Exxon, Shell, and BP can tap cash-flow or Euro-dollar resources. No major MNC will rush into new ventures if it suspects that the government will tax 80-90 percent of its profits or nationalize a 51 percent share of any successful venture.[22]

It is not so much the legal issues or the capital-ownership difficulties that need deter governments from grappling with the MNCs. It is the potential mobility of the MNC that must worry even the most circumspect of business-minded cabinets. When foreign affiliates can sway the capital or technology-intensive sectors of the host economy they must be handled with considerable deference. In the pharmaceutical or fine chemicals industries, for example, it would be dangerous to nationalize the equity, or to overburden the tax liabilities, or to restrict the capital exports of the major MNCs. A firm like Badische Anilin and Soda-Fabrik (BASF) owns 289 subsidiaries, many in the lucrative American market; it stockpiles 6,000 products in 100 countries, it shares a giant joint-venture partnership with Dow and other MNC chemical companies, it turns over annual sales of $7.5 billion—exactly double its 1970 income—and it significantly contributes to the balance of payments of the 24 OECD countries. That it might relocate its plant or its third-country exports to other host states is widely feared. In Britain, the Monopolies Commission awarded punishing damages against the Swiss chemical firm Hoffmann-LaRoche for making "excessive profits" in its $500 million a year business with the National Health Service (reduction of drug prices by 60 percent *and* the return of $30 million to the health service). Like its American counterparts that are well established in the United Kingdom, the Swiss firm no longer views Britain as having a "favorable climate of investment" and its expansion plans for the future focus upon more sympathetic and pliant host states.

By and large, the MNCs have concentrated their deployments in those strategic sectors that are programmed to the export thrust and the comparative cost advantages of international trade. None is to be found in the profitless, in the aging, or in the labor-intensive industries; these sectors (coal, steel, transportation, and utilities) have been nationalized—usually without protest—by conservative or liberal regimes. By contrast, Olivetti in Scotland, Volvo in Canada, Sony in Ireland, and the Banque de Paris in Rome have settled in the choice areas where profits rapidly increase and the return on asset worth is often enviable. It would be difficult for these affiliates, however, to be held hostage by a government that needed to reassert its economic authority. If threatened with antitrust action or punitive taxation, they could either relocate their capital assets and their firm-specific technology to a more promising milieu; or run down old plants while expanding production schedules in a third country; or utilize intra-affiliate transfer pricing to avoid the regulatory controls of a *dirigiste* host economy. Each of these stratagems has been successfully employed. The gradual "fade out" of Siemens, GE, and BP from Italy reflects the runaway propensities of even the most respectable of MNCs. It is not only the successful MNC that chooses to redeploy, in the manner of say, GE moving its white goods production from Italy to Spain. When the British firm, Burmah Oil, stretched its tanker charters and overseas loans too far, its $650 million foreign debts had to be guaranteed by the Bank of England. In return, the bank seized its interlocking shares in Shell and BP and insisted that Burmah sell off its holdings in Signal and other U.S. oil companies to keep its North Sea investments intact.[23]

The potential mobility and deployment choices of the MNC cannot be underestimated. Its thrust toward crossnational expansion cannot be ignored. No large firm in the automobile, chemical, electronics, petrochemical, or computer industries can survive simply by servicing the domestic market. The largest non-American computer company, International Computers Ltd. of the United Kingdon (ICL) can never match the product range, the costly R and D, or the location options of IBM or Honeywell. IBM can amortize its R and D against $11 billion sales in 126 countries. It can retain its formidable leadership in the industry by spending $5 billion R and D on a new generation of computers or by diversifying into electric typewriters and computerized data processing. ICL is partly financed by the U.K. government and heavily protected with "Buy British" regulations. Though ICL commands 45 percent of the domestic market, largely due to protection, it cannot afford to spend as much on R and D as IBM spends on advertising. ICL's product range is severely limited and its technology has been largely acquired under expensive licensing and royalty agreements. As a result, it commands only 8 percent of the EEC market for data processing and 2 percent of the world share. It refused to follow the lead of RCA and GE, both of which quit the computer industry when they failed to capture a 10 percent share of the world market. ICL cannot hope to crack the one market that really matters, the lucrative sales arena within the United States. The French and German governments—both of which had invested public revenues in their computer capabilities—still painfully recall that when GE and RCA quit, they undermined the French CII and the German Siemens plants that had licensed much of their costly technology from the two American MNCs.

The case of ICL is in no way unique. Volkswagen has been forced by MNC competition and by rising wage and exchange rates to build its new plants anywhere except in Germany. Lloyds Bank and the Amsterdam-Rotterdam Bank have determined to search for new business and better earnings away from their home base, in California or Abu Dhabi. Michelin and Pechiney are extending from the Rhone Valley to Quebec or Newfoundland; Nippon Steel is building new furnace capacity in Europe and upstate New York rather than at home; Bayer and ICI find no reason to bring more jobs to the depressed areas of Ludwigshafen and Liverpool while building new capacity in the tidelands of Flanders or South Carolina.

Obviously, the MNCs can no longer stay at home, neither can they forsake rich foreign markets while other MNCs quickly move in. It is unfortunate, of course, when host governments become restive. The German cartel office joined the U.K. Monopolies Commission in investigating whether Hoffmann-La Roche was overcharging for patented drugs; but neither could afford to lose the company's local manufacturing earnings and employment capabilities. The EEC investigated GM's transfer pricing of cars in Belgium, an aniline price-fixing arrangement in the United Kingdom and Switzerland, and the conglomerate packaging companies affiliated with Continental Can. In fining the offenders, the EEC revealed that it, too, did not want to stir up trouble for the MNCs (no matter if their home base were in the Community's jurisdiction or outside). Were it to do so, it would be all too logical for the antitrust or protectionist authorities in America or Japan to retaliate in kind—by raising their tariff barriers, import surcharges, cartel investigations, or capital export restrictions.

At the present time there is a momentous struggle between the leading MNCs for the development in Europe of telephone switching and data transmission equipment. Each government is trying to protect its own major entrant (and their foreign affiliates) by fighting over the technical specifications that the nine European PTTs must eventually agree to integrate. Plessey in Britain and CGE in France have teamed up to make a triumphant bid for processor controlled digital telephone equipment. Their European competitors, who also receive government encouragement, are Siemens and Philips. It is likely that the largest contracts will in the end have to go to their American rivals, ITT and IBM. IBM is powerfully established in each one of the nine member nations and it has now entered a satellite communication venture with Comsat—which in turn draws upon the technology of Bell Labs and ATT. ITT, however, owns Standard Telephones in the United Kingdom, Matériel Téléphonique in France, Standard Electrik Lorenz in Germany, and another 40 percent or more of the markets in Italy, Belgium, and Spain. As the EEC moves into the electronics age, at a cost of billions of dollars in procurements, jobs, and R and D, it will probably award the lion's share to IBM and ITT. It would be senseless to ignore their leadership in technology, organizational skills, and crossnational management. Were they to receive these coveted contracts, to run the year 2000, it would once again be shown that the MNCs had succeeded because they were so large and successful.

THE MNC IN WORLD POLITICS

Today, the MNC is viewed with a mixture of suspicion and envy by the managers of power in the public and in the private sectors of the capitalist state. As local nationals, the managers cannot relocate their public revenues or their venture capital to a nearby economy. No matter how faltering may be their return on asset worth or their labor productivity ratings, they are locked in by the political frontiers of the national economy. Whether they resent the incoming MNCs' bargaining maneuvers or whether they need to stem a tidal outflow of capital, they must still accept the MNCs' transfer of funds, its repatriation of licensing fees and dividend payments, and its decisions to phase out jobs or assembly lines. It is not often that the formal authority of the state can be summoned to prevent a takeover or to reverse a transfer decision of a powerful affiliate. Were the state managers to do so frequently, the MNCs would conclude that a favorable climate for investment could better be found elsewhere.[24]

The economic logic of the MNC is impressive in concept, in its profitability and in its mode of operation. By contrast, the political logic of the nation state is static and parochial.[25] Bourgeois political and nationalist forces have been so obsessed in the era of Cold War with military rivalry, welfare budgets, and the trivia of party politics that little attention has been given to the permeable sovereignty of the "free market" model of the nation state. While socialists and conservatives argued about the nationalizing of labor-intensive services and industries, foreign and home-based MNCs consolidated their position in the strategic growth sectors that each nation had tried to nurture.

The most dramatic evidence of the MNC's impact is to be seen in the increasing division of labor between national economies—rather than between competing firms. The MNCs' global transfers have helped destroy both the mechanism and the justification for economic nationalism. They have overpowered the defense works of the industrial state, not by building cartels and restraints of trade but by enlarging their influence over the "commanding heights" of finance and technology capital that characterize the developed economy.

This pervasive new trend has left the OECD state dependent upon remote corporate managements to promote their most expensive or export intensive manufactures. It has left them as supplicants for credit and discount rates to finance their costly fuel imports and to cope with the despairing problems of recession. The strongest of governments need to know how to help, not hinder, the MNC's fixing of prices or its extension of lines of credit. The tax waivers and credits sought by foreign affiliate or by domestic parent firms impact severely upon the cash flow resources of the state. The oil companies alone accounted for billions of dollars that were *not* paid into 1973 taxes—due to depletion and deferral allowances—and that were eventually moved beyond the control of home or host states. It may now be of little consequence whether Britain or Italy elect a Left or a Right-leaning government; but were the eight oil "majors" to shift their short-term lines of credit out of sterling or lira the economy would simply cave in.

Protectionist responses to this new pattern are fervently rejected by most businessmen. They insist that the capital or the technology supplied by the MNC are well-nigh irreplaceable. No uninational or nationalized enterprise can hope to duplicate the research patents or the vertically-integrated assemblies of Toyota, Ciba-Geigy, Philips, or Texas Instruments. Thus, the resort to national planning, protection, subsidy, or legislative controls over the MNC are strongly condemned. At all costs the MNC must be free to maneuver, it is argued. It cannot afford to freeze its production schedules in one country or relinquish its market in another simply to placate parochial political interests. It can not resign itself to poor business conditions or high tax rates at home when better opportunities are available abroad. So long as they observe the businessman's "code of good citizenship," it is urged, the MNC managers will be welcome in all countries but owe their loyalty to none. As a citizen of the single-minded world of business, the manager must be the first to advocate internationalist causes and the global mission of free enterprise. He must be a source of pride to the national elite that fostered his education and career; and a committed spokesman for the multinational management to which his ambitions are bent.[26]

TABLE 3

Foreign Content of Selected Industries in Seven Countries
(percent)

Country	100-75	Foreign Content 75-50	50-25
Canada	Tobacco and cigarettes Chemicals Rubber products Transport equipment Oil refining	Iron and steel Electrical machinery	Wood products Pulp and paper products Metal products Textiles Food
Belgium	Timber processing Automobiles	Plastics	Refining Iron and Steel
France	Electric office equip. Elevators Photographic films Detergents	Mineral oil	Building machinery Gasoline Organic chemicals Pharmaceuticals Food processing
West Germany	Computers and electronics	Food Beverages and tobacco Rubber products Electrical machinery Plastics	Refining Chemicals Stone and ceramics Leather products Pulp and paper products Glass Metal products Textiles Machinery Automobiles
Italy		Cosmetics Rubber products	Wood products Pharmaceuticals Textiles Telecommunication equipment
United Kingdom	Razor blades Typewriters Computers and electronics Boot and shoe machinery Sewing machines Electric razors Spark plugs Breakfast cereals	Frozen foods Tractors Refrigerators	Tobacco and cigarettes Synthetic fibers Soap and detergents Pharmaceuticals Agricultural equip. Elevators Automobiles Dental equip. Plastics Tires
Australia	Oils, minerals Soap and detergents Pharmaceuticals Telecommunication equipment Industrial and heavy chemicals, acids	Printing Iron and non- ferrous metal Musical instruments White lead, paints varnishes, oth- er chemicals	Food Meat freezing Beverages and tobacco Rubber products Glass Iron and steel Agricultural equip. Electrical machinery Electrical appliances

Source: The U.N. Report, Table 23, pp. 164-65. Data for various years 1965-71.

The arguments against this latter-day version of laissez-faire capitalism have been made too frequently to merit repetition. Since the unique circumstances created by the MNC are still subject to debate, it might be useful to summarize the more specific criticisms that have been articulated.

1. *The laws of comparative* advantage and the economies of scale are not always respected by the MNC. Given its oligopoly leverage over the markets in which it operates, the MNC frequently chooses to frustrate the 'international equalization of factor costs' by covertly subsidizing—or phasing out—its affiliate operations.[27]

2. *The welfare economics* of a host or a home country cannot be measured on the profit and loss accounting of a parent company. Some industries, no matter how cost-ineffective they might be, need to be protected for military purposes, to enhance skill training, or to curb monopoly distortions of price; others require tariff or protective supports to preserve full employment policies or a political stress upon job security.[28]

3. *Vertical and horizontal integration strategies* allow the MNC to extend (as Galbraith puts it) the logic of production rather than the sovereignty of consumption. By controlling the sources of supply or manipulating the schedules of demand, the oil majors and the drug or computer companies succeeded in stabilizing prices and negotiating franchises on a worldwide basis.

4. *Cross-national market forces* provide neither a stable base for long-range planning nor an adequate fulfillment of the service requirements of an advanced economy. The state managers of public power are obliged to manage the money supply, the balance of payments the calculus of labor employment and productivity ratios, and the free play of domestic market forces. They cannot do so if the MNC exerts its mobile and oligopoly influence in the most profitable of the growth sectors.

5. *The effective management of national resources* can not be left alone to a laissez-faire administration. The nation state has to police the domestic economy against fraud, monopoly exploitation, the squandering of scarce commodities, the oppression of the weak and the siphoning-off of hard currency reserves. If state intervention in the economy is too fierce, the MNCs will be scared away. If it is too lax, the MNCs will be tempted to raid for short-term profit and abandon depressed sectors to the expense of public support.

6. *The managers of public power are held accountable,* at least in theory, to representative government and to the political process. The managers of the private powers incorporated in the MNC are not. There are obviously occasions on which the retention of national economic controls will be preferable to the free floating benefits that *might* be imported by the MNC. But by surrendering its regulatory authority to control the MNCs' behavior, the capitalist state can only increase its dependence upon their resource and

marketing decisions. Neither the economic wealth nor the political stability of
the OECD world will be secure if the MNCs continue to expand at the rapid
rate that they maintained between 1965 and 1974.

It is difficult to measure the extent to which the MNC has aggravated the
political anxieties of the industrial societies that it has penetrated. Public
opinion polls and politicians' speeches reveal that anxieties have surfaced,
though it is not yet feasible to gauge their gravity. Certainly, in an era of
double-digit inflation, energy scarcities, and balance of payments deficits, the
MNCs' lack of political accountability has begun to appear somewhat
menacing. So far, no determined attempt has been made to define or to cope
with the problem. A formula has not been advanced to reconcile the divergent
interests of nation-bound states and multinational enterprises. That the
breach is widening and will widen further is accepted by all parties. The cause
is obvious. The MNC has become a powerful actor in international affairs. As
the MNC banking consortia in the City of London revealed, the recycling of
petro-dollars and the discounting of short-term credit rates is vital to global
branch banking but terribly menacing to national governments. As the total
sum of petro-dollars (the most volatile of short-term funds) climbs towards
$65 billion a year, the position of the MNC banks and banking consortia
becomes more powerful. Their London branches are called upon to digest
short-term Arab deposits, to advance balance of payments loans to countries
in difficulties, and to provide long-term financing for big industry. Armed
with $170 billion in Euro- or petro-dollars they now maintain a triple balance
between the OPEC sheikhs, the OECD governments and the financial V-Ps
of their largest MNC clients.[29]

It can no longer be expected that a developed economy will seal itself off
from foreign competition and penetration. Strategies of financial protection
and trade subsidization have lost strength and credibility in recent years.
National governments have tried to convince the oil majors, the giant agri-
corps, the nuclear power, and the chemical fertilizer industries that they are
too valuable to society to be run as commercial and stateless entities; the
pursuits of their profit and of the nation's interests are patently not identical.
By and large, the governments' arguments have failed. The MNC is
accountable to its parent shareholders and directors, most of whom reside in a
foreign environment. Its primary concern in any host country is to minimize
tax liabilities, to repatriate dividends and earnings, and to enlarge its venture
partnerships or licensing fees. It cannot be sentimental about bailing out a
country in difficulty, such as Italy or Greece; nor is it likely to concern itself
with social injustices or the wider public welfare. The compliant roles of the
MNCs in South Africa or in the dictatorial regimes of the Greek colonels, the
Chilean *junta,* and the Portuguese gerontocracy have been extensively noted.
In contemporary Spain, the power of the Falange is being weakened by an 18

percent annual rate of inflation and the emergence of illicit labor unions. The strikes and sabotage suffered by GE, Westinghouse, BLMC, and Renault are noted in *Business Week* of November 23, 1974. However, no mention is made of the many affiliate managers who report the leadership of the underground *sindicatos* to Franco's police.

The contemporary nation state, by contrast, is in no way viable as a profit center. It is theoretically concerned with local needs and the popular determination of policy priorities. Its claim to legal preeminence is difficult to contest but its economic authority can be exercised only at some risk. It is no wonder that a conservative economist, Charles Kindleberger, and a Marxist historian, Isaac Deutscher, agree that the decay of the nation state will never be reversed and that its long, historic role is about finished. Their apocalyptic view is not widely shared by politicians, workers, consumers or the mass media. However, it is widely assumed by MNC managers that if the nation state cannot adapt to the revolutionary change in international trade, it will simply decline into a further, futile decay. Barnet and Müller report the enthusiasm of the MNC managers as they envisage the future growth possibilities of the "geocentric," "stateless" "cosmocorp." It is instructive that a liberal nationalist like George Ball could move from his directing role in the U.S. State Department to a similar one in Lehman Bros. Bank, exchanging his public patriotism for the internationalist subtleties of the merchant banker. It is not surprising that MNC directors fulminate against the parochial, bureaucratic, and defensive behavior of state agencies once they desert their cabinet offices for a more expansive board room.[30]

Parliamentary regimes, apolitical trade unions, and Social Democrats express a common apprehension about applying sanctions against the MNC distributors of industrial wealth. Their first fear is that the sanctions might be counterproductive. If popular protest should ever intensify, and if restrictive legislation should be called for, the MNCs would either begin to relocate their factors of production to another country or deflect their new investments and short-term funds to a more hospitable business climate. This could be done in a rapid or a covert manner. By borrowing short and lending long, or by utilizing "leads and lags" in intra-affiliate payments, the MNC can evade capital export controls, import restrictions, and high interest payments. The corporate treasurers can either channel their cash reserves through tax havens and overnight funds in the Euro-market; or they can buy forward purchases of currencies that are likely to appreciate; or they can resort to transfer pricing strategies in order to compensate for any losses incurred in the float or exchange rates. There are ample grounds, therefore, for political apprehension in dealing with the financial maneuvers of the MNC.[31]

Parliamentary regimes fear to abuse the MNC as poor corporate citizens for reasons other than financial anxiety. Were their criticisms to sound inflammatory to a mass audience, protest might soon be directed against *all* corporations, indigenous or foreign. This prospect worries many national elites. A populist complaint against oligopoly power can be quickly aroused in most capitalist societies. In the United States it is known that approximately 200 of the largest firms generate 60 percent of the nation's wealth. In Europe, concentration is even more conspicuous—and thus vulnerable to state action.[32] Were the MNC to become the focus of popular discontent during a severe recession, the resentment generated by the foreign MNC might be turned against other forms of corporate capitalism. Chrysler was aware of this threat when it cancelled plans to fire several hundred workers in France. The company also ignored—for the same reason—the wage guidelines set out by the U.K. government and conceded the steep increase in wages demanded by the more militant labor unions in Britain. It was the least they could do to protect their affiliates' local investments against xenophobic rhetoric.[33]

These first signs of conflict are not marginal to or easily removed by the capitalist state. They are not likely to disappear with the passage of time. The political imperative to defend its economic autonomy and sovereignty is vital to any state, no matter how committed its government might be to the doctrines of liberal capitalism or welfare socialism. On the other hand, the wealth in investments, high technology, and employment opportunities brought by the MNC cannot be underestimated or ignored. As the asymmetry increases between the power of the MNC and the state, the latter will perceive that it can no longer compete in the specialized and demanding markets of world trade without the assistance and the willing compliance of the MNC.

Hope prevails that modus vivendi will continue to be devised and that no nation will need to intervene against another's MNCs. This reflects the conventional wisdom that obtains in most pluralist, capitalist societies. It is widely believed, for instance, that giant corporations are politically neutral in their quest for profit; and that their management cadres are wiser than mass electorates or elected governments in mobilizing national resources for the grim struggle for world trade. Contradictory evidence is abundant and both parties to the argument are becoming angry. That free competition ever existed, or that MNCs are *supposed* to equalize factor costs is not doubted by either faction. But that oligopoly equilibrium will provide a reliable mode of market planning, or that foreign affiliates will promote a host country's national interest is bitterly contested. To construct a viable and systematic alternative to the MNCs' occupation of the international market place provides a challenge that few economists have dared to face. There is a compelling economic logic to explain the past successes of the MNC. What remains to be demonstrated is that their industrial benefits clearly outweigh the political costs that must be paid by home or host states.

Doubt and disaffection began to emerge as the ITT scandals broke. The collapse of several MNC banks that had speculated in foreign exchange added to the hostility generated by the windfall profits of the MNC oil companies.

Previously, Raymond Vernon had suggested that if the MNCs were to flourish unchecked by state power, governments would "be obliged to convert issues they had once thought domestic into issues of international concern." He added that:

> the basic asymmetry between multinational enterprises and national governments may be tolerable up to a point, but beyond that point there is need to reestablish balance.... [There must be MNC] accountability to somebody, charged with weighing the activities of the multinational enterprise against a set of social yardsticks that are multinational in scope... If this does not happen some of the apocalyptic projections of the future of the multinational enterprise will grow more plausible.[34]

No formula currently exists to secure the accountability of the MNC. Certainly, in the absence of any useful "social yardstick," the dogmatism that is all too frequently found in socialist literature must be avoided. It is courageous but not necessarily realistic to insist that:

> the growth of the multinationals must be stopped; the surplus value which feeds [their] growth must be directed to national enterprises instead. If this cannot be done under capitalism, as Canada's experience strongly suggests that it cannot, a further answer follows: national independence and capitalism are not compatible, whereas national independence and socialism are.[35]

This blind faith in socialist theory ignores two salient and costly factors of production: the promotion of R and D and of export earnings that advanced economies receive from the MNC. By the mid-1970s, no state or grouping of states has yet learned to compete with or to replace the unique benefits offered by the MNC. There is no sign that the EEC will correct the asymmetry that Professor Vernon fears. Nor is it likely that international capitalism possesses the self-righting mechanism needed to avoid national rivalries and trade warfare.

Thomas Jefferson noted of the business leaders of 1880 that: "Merchants have no country. The mere spot they stand on does not constitute so strong an attachment as that from which they draw their gains." The axioms of trade have not changed radically in 200 years. It is becoming evident, however, that the MNC must be seen as the logical "next step" in the maturation of international capitalism. Its mobile use of finance capital represents one of the greatest threats that must be faced by a world of economically insecure and intensely competitive nation states. Armed with its patented, global technologies, it has entered into a jurisdictional struggle with the managers of state power. The MNC is not likely to blunt its profit-seeking dynamic. It is hardly about to wither away before the protectionist counterattacks of economic nationalism. It is more likely to succeed in pitting one state against another than to succumb to the lesser weapons—of tariff barriers, capital controls, and export subsidies—that capitalist states or the UN can mobilize against it.[36]

It is impossible to predict whether the system of divided nation-states will fragment or whether the more mobile and flexible of the MNCs will manage to pick up the pieces. That a fast moving MNC like IBM or ICI will collapse like Rolls Royce—or for the same reasons—is highly improbable. That other members of OECD will resign themselves to the dependent status of Canada is far more likely. *Dependencia* and economic interdependence are incontestable facts of life in the wealthier economies of the developed world, though none welcome their further growth. But it remains to be seen what alternative strategies are available to competing states as they attempt to grapple with the factor mobility and the fast-changing profit ratios of the MNC. States are becoming harder pressed by the exigencies of international rivalry and industrial competition. That they will increasingly constrain the agency that can best promote their overseas trade and investment is implausible and improbable.[37]

NOTES

1. The most complete listings of data on MNC assets, operations and growth rates are to be found in the *Survey of Current Business* published by the U.S. Department of Commerce. See vol. 54, no. 9 (September 1974) for the latest figures; and in the U.N. Report, *MNCs in World Development*—hereafter referred to as the U.N. Report—published by the Department of Economic and Social Affairs (New York: United Nations, 1973, ST/ECA/190). A later report collates and interprets the U.N. data. *The Impact of MNCs on Development and International Relations* (New York: United Nations, 1974, E/5500/Rev. 1; ST/ESA/6).

2. Raymond Vernon, *Sovereignty at Bay* (New York: Basic Books, 1971), pp. 4-12; and *U.N. Report*, chap. 1.

3. *U.N. Report* (pp. 10-15 and tables XIII-XVIII). A survey of MNC activities appears in the *Harvard Business Review* articles collected by Louis T. Wells ed., *The Product Life Cycle and International Trade* (Boston: Harvard Business School, 1972).

4. A valuable criticism of the literature on oligopoly theory and MNC expansion appears in Theodore H. Moran, "Foreign Expansion as an 'Institutional Necessity' for U.S. Corporate Capitalism: The Search for a Radical Model," *World Politics*, vol. 25, no. 3 (April 1973): 369-86.

5. Robin Murray, "The Internationalization of Capital and the Nation State," *New Left Review*, no. 67 (May-June 1971): 84-109; Stephen Hymer and Robert Rowthorn, "MNCs and International Oligopoly: The Non-American Challenge," in Charles P. Kindleberger ed., *The International Corporation* (Cambridge: M.I.T. Press, 1970); and Ernest Mandel, *Europe versus America? Contradictions of Imperialism* (London: New Left Books, 1970). A theory of oligopoly competition among MNCs is conservatively stated in Charles P. Kindleberger, *International Economies* (Illinois: Irwin, 1973), pp. 245-78.

6. Jean-Jacques Servan-Schreiber, *The American Challenge* (New York: Atheneum, 1968), p. 9. A critical review of this best-selling polemic appears in Walter Goldstein "Europe Faces the Technology Gap," *Yale Review,* vol. 59, no. 2 (December, 1969): 161-78; and in the tabulated data of Rainer Hellmann, *The Challenge to U.S. Domination of the International Corporation* (New York: Dunellen, 1970; translated by Peter Ruof).

7. John H. Dunning ed., *The Multinational Enterprise* (London: Allen and Unwin, 1971), and *International Investment* (London: Penguin, 1972). Listings of the leading MNCs and of their market positions appear in such European business journals as *Expansion, The Economist, Vision, Management Today,* and *Sucesso;* and in Heinz Aszkenazy, *Les Grandes Societes Europeennes,* and Michel De Vroey, *Propriete et Pouvoir dans les Grandes Enterprises* (Brussels: C.R.I.S.P., 1971 and 1973).

8. Data has been drawn from Eva Thiel, "The Profitability of Swedish Manufacturing Investment Abroad," *Columbia Journal of World Business* (Fall 1973): 87-92; and the *U.N. Report,* pp. 138-59, tables 5, 11, and 19.

9. The confusion on the Left in coping with the threat to national economic autonomy is summarized by the present author in "The MNC and its Challenge to Contemporary Socialism," in Ralph Miliband and John Saville eds., *The Socialist Register, 1974* (London: Merlin Press, 1974), pp. 279-301.

10. A striking collection of pious statements and self-applause on the part of MNC managers has been collected by Richard Barnet and Ronald Müller, "Global Reach," in the *New Yorker* (December 2, 9, 1974).

11. The early history and the expansionist motives of many American MNCs are investigated at length in Mirra Wilkins, *The Emergence of Multinational Enterprise* (Cambridge: Harvard University Press, 1970); in Vernon, op. cit.; and in Edith T. Penrose, *The Theory of the Growth of the Firm* (Oxford: University Press, 1966). Empirical studies of the chemical, electronics, and other manufacturing MNCs are summarized in Moran, op. cit. The emphasis placed by managers of the "technostructure" on growth and oligopoly control is best associated with J. K. Galbraith, *The New Industrial State* (Boston: Houghton Mifflin, 1967).

12. Data on MNC profits, inflows, and outflows appear in the *Survey of Current Business,* vol. 53, no. 9 (September 1973) and vol. 54, no. 4 (May 1974). Balance of payments and currency exchange data appear in vol. 54, no. 8 (August 1974).

13. The *European Community* (Jan-Feb., 1974): 16-19. The draft resolution aims simply to establish an outline approval in principle for the Commission's approach to multinationals by raising several issues:

a. The protection of employees in the case of takeovers or mergers;
b. Common rules for stock exchange operations and investment;
c. Better common information on various aspects of MNC;
d. Common rules on groups of companies.

14. *Vision* (October 1974): 91-93; *Vision* (December 1974): 83.

15. See Christopher Redman, "The European Aircraft Industry," *European Community* (December 1974); and Raymond Vernon ed., *Big Business and the State* (Cambridge: Harvard University Press, 1974).

16. Quoted in Elizabeth R. Jager, "The Changing World of Multinationals," *American Federationist* (published by the AFL-CIO), vol. 81, no. 9 (September 1974): 17-24.

17. *Vision* (December 1974): 83-99.

18. The concentration of giant firms in direct foreign investment is revealed in many different industries in *The MNC: Studies on U.S. Foreign Investment,* vol. 2 (Washington: U.S. Department of Commerce, April, 1973), p. 5.

19. Ibid. p. 6.

20. The *U.N. Report,* op. cit., table 24, p. 170.

21. The success of the MNC in fulfilling its expansion objectives was measured in a special study issued by the Business International Corp. *The Effects of U.S. Corporate Foreign Investment, 1960-1970.* (New York, 1972).

22. For frequent reporting on these threatened measures of the British and Norwegian governments, see 1974 issues of *Fortune,* or *Vision,* or *Business Week.*

23. For a list of the failings or of the forced disposition of other MNC affiliates see Louis Turner, *Invisible Empires* (London: Hamish Hamilton, 1970); for a sceptical view of the MNC as a meddlesome, conspiratorial and untrustworthy agent, see Anthony Sampon, *The Sovereign State: the Secret History of ITT* (London: Hodder and Stoughton, 1973).

24. A review of previous studies and of the testimony given before congressional and business groups appears in Hugh Stephenson, *The Coming Clash: The Impact of MNCs on National States* (New York: Saturday Review Press, 1972). The author has forgotten, however, Professor Kindleberger's awesome conclusion that "the nation state is just about through as an economic unit," in *American Business Abroad* (New Haven: Yale University Press, 1969), p. 207.

25. A strenuous defense of contemporary nationalism is attempted in David P. Calleo and Benjamin Rowland, *America and the World Political Economy* (Bloomington: Indiana University Press, 1973).

26. That social and political elites are likely to collude with corporate interests, rather than to constrain them, is convincingly argued in the 1969 publication of Ralph Miliband's *The State in Capitalist Society.* Since many cabinet ministers have quit the conservative or Social Democrat governments of Europe, Japan, and North America to join the boards of prominent MNCs, their reluctance to sell out national interests to foreign capital should not be taken too seriously.

27. (The "rationalization" planned by Olivetti in the 1960s required the closing of its Underwood subsidiary in Connecticut and the relocation of its manufacture of cheap typewriters to Barcelona. Its new plant in the U.S. produced expensive equipment, unlike its nine plants in Italy and Scotland. These decisions were not dictated by a simple regard for differentials in labor productivity and wage rates. Singer, too, made its cheaper sewing machines in Italy or the U.K.—largely for export—and restricted the manufacturing schedule of its American home base. Had both firms faced strongly competitive conditions they would not have enjoyed the oligopoly ability to redesign their own base of operation.)

28. Neil H. Jacoby, the Dean of the UCLA Business School, provides a determined defense of the MNC, *Corporate Power and Social Responsibility: A Blueprint for the Future* (London and New York: Macmillan, 1973). In applauding the contribution that the MNCs can make to the equalization of factor costs Neil Jacoby insists that it is also a vehicle for public trust and benefit. One wonders what he would make of the campaign of the American Chamber of Commerce in West Germany in 1974. It wanted to release U.S.-based MNCs from the new provisions of the German law for *mitbestimmung* (or workers' control and management). It was accused of an unwarranted interference in the domestic political affairs of the Federal Republic.

29. See the special supplement on Euro-banking, *Vision,* December, 1974.

30. Barnet and Müller, op. cit.

31. Michael Brooke and Lee Remmers, *The Strategy of Multinational Enterprise* (London: Longmans, 1970); and John M. Stopford and Louis T. Wells, *Managing the Multinational Enterprise* (New York: Basic Books, 1972).

32. A listing of Europe's ten biggest companies, measured in sales, profits, and employment, is dominated by the MNCs. *Vision* (October 1974): 92.

33. The defensive actions of Chrysler and other MNCs, that preferred to offend government regulations rather than union negotiators, is investigated in John Gennard, *MNCs and British Labour: A Review of Attitudes and Responses* (London: British-North American Research Assoc., 1972).

34. Vernon, op. cit., p. 284.

35. H. L. Robinson, "The Downfall of the Dollar," *Socialist Register 1973*, p. 443. It is an equally assertive and unrealistic prescription that a socialist regime should establish a state monopoly of foreign trade that can monitor all transfer prices and discriminate among imports and exports according to social priorities. The dictates of giant companies are not susceptible to the welfare arguments of Left regimes intent upon the restriction of finance capital. Nor should it be supposed that companies taken-over by state agencies (such as the IRI in Italy, the IDC in France, or the new IRC in Britain) would be able to operate a MNC with all the subtlety and flexibility of its present managers.

36. The U.N. *Report*, op. cit., pp. 75-105, lists many of the remedies that have been suggested in academic literature or U.N. debates. Few call for anything beside surveillance information. A set of recommendations is also given in Jacoby, op. cit., pp. 119-21.

37. Two different approaches to the development of interdependence in the world order can be found in Johan Galtung, "A Structural Theory of Imperialism," *Journal of Peace Research*, no. 2, 1971; and David Osterberg and Fouad Ajami, "The MNC: Expanding the Frontiers of World Politics," *Journal of Conflict Research*, vol. 15, no. 4 (December 1971): 457-70. Both review the claim that the MNC can serve better than the nation state as an agent of economic integration; for different reasons, both dispute the claim.

7

THE POLITICAL ECONOMY OF GLOBAL CORPORATIONS AND NATIONAL STABILIZATION POLICY: A DIAGNOSTIC ON THE NEED FOR SOCIAL PLANNING

Ronald Müller

A conclusion reached by this chapter is that there is a clear-cut need for explicit public sector social planning in the United States. This conclusion is derived from a diagnostic on the *systemic* impacts arising out of contemporary worldwide conglomerate competition between global corporations, both U.S.- and foreign-based. The need for planning, however, is currently recognized by two different groups of advocates, each having different reasons and goals and, therefore, advocating different planning models. One group proposes transnational public institutions and planning for the international harmonization of nation states' macroeconomic policies. The other group recognizes this need but only as a derivative part of a national social development plan for the United States. The latter plan places a major emphasis on the social control and accountability of large corporations; the former does not.

Before examining these alternative views on planning, however, it is necessary to review the systemic impacts which result from the new competitive operating characteristics of global corporations. More specifically, the analysis focuses on whether the global interdependence of

---

This paper was prepared for the panel on "Alternative Perspectives on Planning and Competition," Association for Evolutionary Economics, Annual Meeting of the Allied Social Sciences Association, San Francisco, December 28, 1974. The valuable assistance of Professors John Lyons and Howard Wachtel is gratefully acknowledged while the final responsibility of this work of course remains only with the author. The American University, Washington, D.C., December 20, 1974.

individual economies resulting from the globalization of their largest private corporations does not have a direct bearing on the growing inefficacy of national macroeconomic stabilization policy to maintain full employment, price stability, and balance of payments equilibrium. This review derives a number of testable propositions which, taken together, lead to the conclusion that since the mid-1960s macroeconomic monetary and fiscal policy for regulating the U.S. economy has had increasingly ineffective and at times perverse results. A direct causal connection is seen to hold between this policy inefficacy and the emergence of global corporations as the dominant actors of the U.S. political economy. And it is this growing policy inefficacy which is an important reason for the need for planning. In proceeding, the reader is warned that what follows is a highly condensed and abstracted summary of a rather vast literature and complex topic. Space constraints, for example, have necessitated the exclusion of instability in U.S. income distribution although it is an important symptom of U.S. corporate globalization and its accompanying twin force, domestic corporate concentration.

A major contention of this chapter is that the globalization of the world's largest private enterprises, industrial and financial alike, represents a structural transformation in the location of their activities and the manner in which they behave as institutions. In turn, this structural transformation has now increased significantly the invalidity of the behavioral assumptions in the orthodox microeconomic theory of the firm, the underlying basis for modern Keynesian macroeconomic theory and therefore policy. Because these corporations account for the dominant share of economic transactions within and between nation states, it is hypothesized that their own transformation has brought about a structural transformation of the national and international economy. This change in the behavior of the U.S. economy including its foreign sector means that it no longer responds in the fashion predicted by the theoretical models underlying policy-making. The major part of this paper will present a range of empirical examples for the verification of this hypothesis. First, however, we turn to the meaning of structural transformation as it relates to our knowledge of how an economy changes its behavior over time.

STRUCTURAL CHANGE AND THE NATURE
OF TRANSFORMATION

This is not the first time that the U.S. political economy has undergone a structural transformation. With the development of a nationwide communications infrastructure after the Civil War, America went from a set of regionally-based economies to that of a nationally integrated economy.

This transformation was led by that of the local regional firm into the large nationwide corporation. Other institutions, however, lagged in this transformation process. Nationwide labor units lagged in their evolution, not receiving final legal recognition until after the beginning of the Great Depression. Public sector regulatory institutions were also slow in responding to the transformation underway in the private corporate sector. Only in the very late 1800s, notably in the field of antitrust after the post-Civil War surge in industrial and financial concentration, was there a significant change in the regulatory functions of government over private business. Yet it was not until the depths of the Great Depression that the public sector completed its own transformation into performing the regulatory and macromanagement functions of the national economy as they are known today. This "structural lag" in public sector institutions also mirrored a lag in economic theory. Again, only when the depression was well underway did economic theory experience its own transformation in the form of the Keynesian "synthesis." This was the last transformation of the U.S. political economy until that of the post-World War II period.

The Present Transformation

The present structural transformation can be identified by two sets of empirical indicators representing the *interrelated* forces of change which have been at work. The first, taking place via its largest banks and industrial enterprises, is the globalization of the economy. Stated otherwise, the U.S. economy has undergone an historic increase in its foreign dependency. The second is the historic upsurge in the industrial and financial concentration of the domestic private sector.

The true extent of the U.S. economy's dependence on foreign operations cannot be gleaned by focusing on exports and imports as a percentage of gross national product (GNP). Note rather that in 1960, the proportion of *total* corporate U.S. profits derived overseas was only 7 percent, with exponential increases commencing around 1967.[1] Today, an estimated 30 percent of total U.S. corporate profits are derived from overseas. Another indicator of the new global dependence of the U.S. economy is the amount of total U.S. corporate investment which goes overseas versus that at home. In 1957, foreign investment in new plant and equipment was 9 percent of *total* U.S. corporate domestic plant and equipment expenditures. By 1970, it had reached a figure of some 25 percent; again, exponential increases occur starting in the years 1965-67. In 1961, the sales of all U.S. manufacturing abroad represented only 7 percent of total U.S. sales; by 1965, the figure had crept up to 8.5 percent; but by 1970, foreign sales were more than 13 percent of total sales of *all* U.S. manufacturing corporations. For the U.S. banking sector, current foreign dollar deposits of the nation's largest global banks are estimated at more than 65 percent of their domestic deposit holdings, up from 8.5 percent in 1960.

With a time-lag, the corporate globalization process has led to an acceleration in the rate of increase in industrial and financial concentration of the U.S. *domestic* sector. Between 1955 and 1970, *Fortune* magazine's top 500 industrial corporations increased their share of total manufacturing and mining employment, profits, and assets from slightly more than 40 percent to over 70 percent. Whereas during the 1950s, the largest 200 were increasing their share of total industrial assets each year by an average of 1 percent, by the 1960s, this annual rate of increased concentration had doubled. For 1947-66, the largest 50 U.S. corporations increased their share of total value added in manufacturing from 17 percent-25 percent; the largest 200, from 30-42 percent. The momentum of cumulative concentration is in part reflected by the corporate merger movement. Of the 14,000 individual mergers during 1953-68, the top 100 firms accounted for only 333, but acquired 35 percent of all merged assets. In the mid-1960s the merger movement accelerated at an exponential rate; almost 60 percent of the $66 billion of total merged assets between 1953-68 were acquired in the last four years of that period. In 1965, for example, the 1,496 mergers were the highest annual increase in the history of the United States.

Increases in banking concentration started somewhat later than in the industrial sector, but by 1970 the top 50 of a total of some 13,000 banks had over 48 percent of all bank assets. From 1965 to 1970, the top 50 were increasing their share of total assets at more than double their expansion rate during the previous ten years. Federal Reserve Board studies show that almost all foreign deposits of U.S. banks are in the hands of the top 20 American global banks, with 4 holding 38 percent of these deposits, and 12 having 83 percent of all foreign banking assets. On the lending side, the 220 largest banks account for virtually all of industrial bank loans. For example, 9 of the largest global banks account for more than 26 percent of all total commercial and industrial lending by American banks. In addition, these same 9 hold 90 percent of the entire indebtedness in the U.S. petroleum and natural gas industry, 66 percent in machinery and metal products, and 75 percent in the chemical and rubber industries.

These indicators are presented as evidence of the structural transformation of the economy itself. Globalization and concentration are not, however, the only indicators of transformation. Others, to be discussed shortly, include money flows and the use of credit. Of significance here is that an analysis of these various indicators shows that they broke their historical trend paths sometime during the mid-1960s. This suggests that the turning point in the structural transformation of the economy occurred somewhere between 1965 and 1967, which correlates well with the beginning of the "stagflation" phenomenon, an occurrence unaccounted for by economic theory and thus far defying governmental policy-making corrections.

GLOBAL CORPORATIONS AND THE NATURE OF GLOBAL CORPORATE COMPETITION: POLICY IMPLICATIONS

To understand the transformed behavior of the economy, in contrast to the assumptions about its behavior embedded in policy-making, it is necessary to review the institutional characteristics of actual corporate behavior, since, as already noted, global corporations account for the majority of the economy's transactions. If in the aggregate we understand the dynamics of the corporate sector of the economy, then we have gone a long way towards understanding the behavior of the national economy and the problems of current policy. We shall proceed by focusing on the transformed goals and the actual operational means (corporate operating techniques) by which global enterprises accomplish these goals. This analysis, however, is only illuminating if done in the context of the global competitive forces that to a certain extent both constrain and determine the individual enterprise's behavior. Finally, our review of global corporate institutional characteristics can explain other aspects of the structural transformation of the national economy not yet discussed.

Global Maximization and National Welfare

1. When a national corporation evolves into a global one, the basic change in goals is that of maximizing the long-run profits of the parent's total global system. There is now abundant empirical evidence to demonstrate that global system profit maximization does not necessarily mean the maximization of each subsidiary's profits, at least in the sense of profits as recorded by national statistics. Thus, for example, transfer pricing permits cost minimization for the global system by shifting profits earned, but not reported, in one nation to another nation with a lower tax rate. The outcome is global tax minimization, one of the key requisites for global profit maximization. A second outcome is the negation of the classical and neoclassical theoretical proof (which underlies much of current policy), to wit: that a national production unit will be operated to maximize profits earned, declared, and accruing to the nation state within which it is located. At the very least, therefore, the operational techniques of managing the multinational economic system of a global corporation make uncertain

whether a parent's operation of any given subsidiary will be in harmony with a given country's national welfare. This uncertainty can be attached to the national welfare implications of both host and home nations alike, since the emphasis is on global system profit maximization which need not be the same as home country profit maximization.

National Policy: Concentration and Globalization

2. Two major and empirically well-established characteristics of global corporations are that: a) most of them are conglomerates; and b) in the many different product groups or industries in which they operate, they compete as oligopolies, not as perfectly competitive firms. In turn, oligopoly competition, as orthodox economics correctly teaches, is characterized not only by nonprice forms of competitive behavior, but, more importantly for our present purposes, by a particular short-run management goal for assessing the stability of the corporations' long-term profit stream. This short-run goal of the oligopoly is minimally the maintenance or preferably the increase in its market shares vis-a-vis its other competitors. When an oligopoly, competing to maintain or increase its market share in one industry, is in fact a subsidiary of a parent conglomerate operating in many industries, the parent can choose to "cross-subsidize" the subsidiary with one or more of its three basic resources: technology (including mechanical, managerial, and accounting), finance capital, and marketing resources. If the subsidiary is competing with other oligopoly firms that are not subsidiaries of conglomerates, then the likely systemic outcome* is that these nonconglomerate firms will eventually experience a decline in their market shares, go out of business, or be absorbed by conglomerate enterprises. This is true because compared to the single industry firm, the conglomerate's sheer size allows it to generate internal economies of scale which over time give it an inherent competitive advantage over smaller concerns. Such internal economies include, for example, easier and usually cheaper sources of external finance, lower effective corporate tax rates, lower input costs (for example, advertising) due to quantity discounts and/or greater expertise, greater financial leverage to sustain cyclical periods of profit decline, and/or more easily sustained losses during short-run price competition at times of initial entry to new industries. If in addition the

---

*By "systemic outcome" is meant the inherent result from the interaction of various institutions with each other within the context of a given socioeconomic system. Systemic here is being used in the same sense as in the works of the classical economists such as Adam Smith and Joseph Schumpeter.

oligopoly competition just described is between the subsidiary of a global corporation, that is, a global conglomerate, and single-industry, strictly national, oligopoly, then the systemic outcome of increasing concentration is even more likely to occur.

In the 1930s, orthodox economics accepted into its fold the field of industrial organization. Since that time industrial organization economists have produced a rich empirical literature to demonstrate that crosssubsidization between subsidiaries of conglomerates is a basic practice of modern corporate life. It is also well known that wherever global corporations expand, there is usually associated with that expansion an increase in concentration. This takes place first in both the more and less developed host countries into which global companies expand through cross-subsidizing their initial foreign entries with the resources of the parent's home network. Later, there is a feedback to increased concentration in the home country. After a wave of foreign expansion, the global corporation can use the added internal economies of scale from its now increased size to supplement its competitiveness at home. That is, globalization leads, with a time lag, to increasing domestic concentration in the home nation. That this proposition on the systemic outcome of global oligopoly competition should be taken seriously is confirmed by recent empirical studies of the changing nature of industrial/financial organization and concentration in the countries of the European Community.[2] These studies show that the only way European firms could stop and/or regain declining market shares, lost during the 1950s to U.S. global corporations, was through a duplication of their American counterparts' expansion pattern of globalization and domestic mergers and acquisitions. Thus by the early 1960s, after recovery from World War II, the European response to the "American Challenge" was to expand first globally and later through mergers and acquisitions in the home territory of the European community.

The timing of the historical concentration increases in the U.S. economy of the 1960s would also appear to be explained by this proposition on the systemic outcome of global oligopoly competition.[3] This concentration spurt occurred after the initial global expansions by U.S. corporations into Europe and the underdeveloped countries in the 1950s. It is in this sense that we can understand why increasing global interdependence and concentration are interrelated aspects of the U.S. economy's structural transformation in the post-World War II period: Interrelated and to be directly associated with the globalization of its largest corporations, mostly conglomerates, increasingly engaged in a new form of oligopoly competition, across nations and industries, with competitors who are more and more themselves conglomerates. Analytically restated, there is in short a *systemic and cumulative* process towards increasing global interdependence and concentration of the national economy.

Given this transformation, one notes some significant structural lags in governmental regulatory institutions and policies. For example, antitrust laws primarily emphasize horizontal and, secondarily, vertical integration, with a relative neglect of conglomerate mergers. (Of the some 14,000 mergers between 1953 and 1968, the government challenged 199 cases, won 90 of these, and required divesture in 48 instances.) In addition, as concentration proceeded over this period, there became apparent a set of "vicious circles" arising out of the impacts of Keynesian monetary and fiscal policy and leading to increasing policy inefficacy. A quantitative analysis in 1974 by Professor John Blair of actual policy impacts verifies the mounting evidence of other econometric investigations.[4] During the boom phase, stabilization policy is aimed at reducing inflation via a reduction in aggregate demand. The findings of Blair and others are revealing however: The more concentrated the industry, the greater has been the occurrence of continuing relative price increases, that is, the opposite of intended policy impacts.

Examining the vicious circles inherent in fiscal and monetary policy is helpful in understanding these unintended impacts. For fiscal policy, it has been shown that tax reductions to stimulate the economy are disproportionately absorbed by the largest firms.[5] (Internal economies of scale can explain much of this result.) On the expenditure side, studies also reveal disproportionate amounts going to the largest firms. In both cases, the effect is to give large corporations a greater expansion capacity than smaller firms, thereby promoting further concentration. In the next round, the increased concentration leads to policy's increased ineffectiveness. The vicious circle is complete. A similar phenomenon takes place with monetary policy. On the borrowing side, during periods of credit restriction, the largest industrial firms do not (or only with a long time delay) respond to higher financing costs since their oligopoly positions permit them to pass on increased credit costs to their buyers. Smaller firms, because of their relatively weaker oligopoly power, must respond immediately and lower their investment demands.

As in the case of taxes and expenditures, these differential structural impacts of aggregate policy promote further concentration. Similarly, on the lending side, vicious circles are at work. Take, for example, George Budzeika's findings on the behavior of the large New York City banks, published by New York University's Institute of Finance.[6] "New York City bank behavior in the past two decades has shown that it is very difficult to control large banks whenever the demand for credit is heavy." The reasons for this again turn out to be the internal economies unique to the large but not the smaller banks which because of a "lack of information and skills prevent them from adjusting quickly to changing levels of monetary restriction." For large banks "the only way to restrain efficiently is to reduce the overall liquidity of the banking system." But since the cost in unemployment of such a strong measure are politically unacceptable, only mild monetary restraint has been pursued. This leads to further bank concentration and makes the next phase of policy restraint that much more ineffective.

Market Policy in a Post-market Economy

3. The conglomerate characteristic of global corporations and the nature of global oligopoly competition explain a third category of structural transformation: That is, that more and more of the private sector's total domestic and international transactions are between subsidiaries of the same parent corporation. Thus the global corporation is largely a *post-market enterprise* since a significant share of its total transactions are not with independent buyers and sellers dealing at arms length through the market. Given the dominance of aggregate global corporate transactions in the domestic and foreign sector, and given the systemic outcome of increasing concentration which results from global corporate competition, it is an empirically verifiable fact that our contemporary national and world economy is becoming increasingly a *post-market economic system*.

Let us be clear what is meant by a post-market economy. It is one in which there has occurred the negation of the social *function* of the market as an institution for equilibrating the economy. Yes, there are markets in the sense of a commodity space indicating the total number of goods produced or consumed. But in the functional sense just defined, which is the meaning of the concept as used in classical and neoclassical economics, the market has largely been negated. The function of the market as a social institution is to generate price signals through the forces of supply and demand as carried out by independent buyers and sellers. In the Keynesian synthesis, these signals are relied upon by private business people, unions and public policy makers as the information for guiding their decisions governing the allocation of resources and the distribution of income. Where the market is operative, these decisions theoretically should result in full employment, price stability, and balance of payments equilibrium. *Systemically,* that is, neither by intent nor design, but by the outcome of modern corporate competition, global corporations are a chief source of market negation; first by the process of increasing concentration accompanying their expansion which, as orthodox theory correctly teaches, increasingly distorts price signals. Second, intracorporate transactions negate the market's social function, by definition, because they completely bypass the market. Market negation is another significant aspect of the post World War II structural transformation of the U.S. political economy. This transformation, however, is still incomplete, for there is a notable structural lag in public sector regulatory institutions and decisions underlying economic policy-making which still assume that the market is as healthy as it was, say, 20 years ago.

One ironic episode of the public sector's lag concerns itself with the price controls used at one point during the Nixon Administration's NEP. Whatever the arguments—for or against controls, should a government employ them,—the chief question is whether they can contain inflation in the short run. It is now a matter of record that controls worked both during World War II and the Korean War. They did not succeed in the 1971 attempt. One reason for this unsuccessful attempt was the simple fact that the administration chose to enforce price controls over a vast number of transactions with a miniscule staff of 300 people, less than 10 percent of whom were trained economists.[7] A second reason deals with the current large degree of intracorporate, nonmarket transactions of U.S. exports and imports compared to the earlier periods of price controls. The Nixon controls did not take this structural change into account. Thus not controlled was the phenomenon of domestic produced goods transacted on paper as exports to foreign subsidiaries and then again transacted on paper as imports back into the United States. Since controls did not extend to imports, there were in effect no controls over these types of goods produced and consumed in the United States. The evidence suggests the phenomenon was widespread in important "linkage" industries such as those for construction materials, semi-processed and processed metals, and fertilizers, as well as agribusiness.[8]

National Policy and Financial Structures

4. Another major characteristic of the post-World War II large corporation is the change in the manner by which it finances its expansion across industries and nations. The sheer pace and quantitative magnitude of expansion has necessitated that global enterprises shift significantly their basis of financing from internal to external sources.[9] This shift was accelerated by governmental capital restrictions such as the U.S. voluntary and mandatory balance of payments program. The latter, of course, was a catalyst to the development of the Euro-currency market, a further important structural characteristic of the new pattern of corporate financing to be discussed immediately below. In addition, the growth of output from this rapid expansion could not be absorbed, given actual increases in consumer incomes. Corporations reacted, particularly in consumer durables, through the establishment of ancillary credit mechanisms and advertising, emphasizing the use of credit, a marketing strategy pointedly and successfully aimed at changing the psychology and propensities of consumers' to incur record-breaking debt increases over increases in current income. National governments correspondingly have provided the liquidity to meet the financing needs of this form of expansion, thus bringing about historic increases in the money supply. This took place at a time when other new structural characteristics of finance (for example, credit cards, "checking

plus," leasing) have contributed further to unprecedented increases in debt and the velocity of money.

From the perspective of current short-run stabilization policy, however, the Euro-currency market is one of the most important structural innovations of the post-World War II period. The justifiable and understandable creation by global banks of the Euro-currency market to meet the needs of global corporate expansion nevertheless was permitted by national governments to evolve without normal public regulatory control. The latter is perhaps one of the most notable indicators of the structural lag between the public sector's regulatory function and a now transformed private corporate sector. The lack of deposit reserve requirements, particularly, has made this $110 billion-plus pool of deposits an incalculable and unpredictable source of further increases to the world money supply. A second characteristic of the Euro-currency market is that U.S. and other global banks operating within its domain regularly violate the first principle of sound banking: never borrow short to lend long. These aspects of the Euro-currency market have led observers like Harvard's Professor H. S. Houthakker to note its impact as a "huge creation of private international liquidity," and in his view, "almost certainly contributes powerfully to the inflationary pressures that no nation has succeeded in keeping under control."[10]

Finally, the intracorporate, nonmarket basis of much cross-nation financial flows, the development of an accounting technology for global optimization of firms' liquid assets, combined with the sheer magnitude and rapidity (relative to the past) of these financial transfers has eroded the autonomy or sovereignty of a nation's money supply, implying the increasing inability of national authorities to control it. "Leads and lags," for example, are standard tools of business, invented long before the age of global companies, to preserve the value of liquid assets during periods of foreign exchange instability. Central bank procedures to account for the effect of leads and lags on the domestic money supply are also age-old. In the 1970s, however, given systemic increases in global concentration and improved accounting technology, these same procedures cannot match the more massive and more rapid liquid transfers by many fewer actors than could have been foreseen a few short years ago.

Leads and lags immediately affect the money supply of a country, yet since they are unrecorded transactions, reflected only in the "errors and omissions" component of a nation's balance of payments account, their actual impact on changing the money stock is discovered by central bankers only after considerable delay. The German experience of the late 1960s and early 1970s illustrates the problem and adds a further reason why current monetary policy has become an unreliable tool for regulating the economy. Studies of the German Bundesbank have found that although its policy led to "complete neutralization of the liquidity inflows to domestic banks ... it does not curb the expansive effects exerted by the inflows of funds from abroad to non-banks on the money stock.[11] Additional work on these nonbank inflows by Michael Porter, published in the *IMF Staff Papers,* showed that the Bundesbank's required reserves policies to control the money supply "were substantially and rapidly offset in their effect on bank liquidity by capital inflows recorded mainly in errors and omissions . . . within one month and by some 80 percent."[12]

This example of the loss of sovereignty over the money supply by national governments is also reflected in the 1968 to early 1969 episode involving the Federal Reserve Bank, U.S. global banks, and the Euro-currency market. The latter two in combination with U.S. global firms has led to what Frank Tamanga, consultant to the International Monetary Fund, has called the "convergence of U.S. multinational corporations and multinational banks into an integrated U.S. economy in exile."[13] This episode involved the attempt to constrain money supply growth by lowering interest rates on certificates of deposit (CDs) with the hope of absorbing these released monies into treasury bills. Instead, these monies were drawn to the higher interest rates of the Euro-currency market. Overnight these liquid assets were brought back into the United States by the intrabank borrowings of global banks from their overseas branches. The U.S.-based parent banks in turn used these borrowed deposits to create additional loans to their largest industrial clients, which, for reasons mentioned earlier, were not deterred by the significantly higher interest costs involved. The then low fractional reserve requirements on borrowed Euro-deposits yielded an actual expansion in the U.S. money supply, the exact opposite of the CD-interest policy's intended result. Here we see how the twin forces of globalization and concentration structurally erode the efficacy of the nation state's aggregate stabilization tools. Although in late 1969 (and again in early 1971), fractional reserve requirements were increased, the inflationary damage had already been done.[14]

Mobility vs. Immobility: The Information Crisis

5. The capstone characteristic of what Professor Scott Gordon writing in the *Journal of Political Economy* has called "one of the most momentous facts of the modern age, the emergence of the corporation as a primary *social* institution"[15] is the structural mobility of this social institution as compared to other primary institutions of our society. As the classical economists from Smith to Schumpeter used the term, structure refers not only to the physical but also to the behavioral aspects of institutions. What distinguishes the global corporation of today from its pre-World War II predecessor is its heightened structural mobility, that is, its increased capacity to change rapidly where and what it produces and an accelerating change in its managerial techniques for controlling that production. And what

distinguishes the global corporation from other social institutions is that the latter are relatively immobile in the physical sense and much slower to adapt or change in the behavioral sense. Thus, for example, government, national business firms, and organized labor are globally immobile, being largely constrained in their institutional jurisdiction to the home nation.

This theme of mobility versus immobility characterizing the structural lag of the noncorporate institutions of the economy has as a major symptom a "crisis in information." That is, information once provided via the workings of the market is today increasingly either missing or unreliable. For the foreign sector, large-scale corporate sampling surveys reveal over 50 percent of total trade transactions are now of the nonmarket intracorporate variety. Yet official corporate disclosure information requirements of the government can account for only about half this number.[16] The use of intraconglomerate transfers and the advent of such substitute financing as leasing, combined with the growth mentality of the 1960s, has led Leonard Spacek, former chairman of Arthur Andersen & Co. to comment that the words "generally accepted accounting principles" on corporate consolidated balance sheets are a "fiction." "My profession appears to regard a set of financial statements as a roulette wheel." David Norr of the American Institute of Certified Public Accounting agrees, "Accounting today permits a shaping of results to attain a desired end. Accounting as a mirror of (economic) activity is dead."[17] Whatever legitimate corporate reasons consolidated balance sheets may serve, from the objective of social purposes, however, they now hide more than they reveal. For instance, a growing number of university studies are now documenting the frustration of unions to make, as a basis of their wage demands, an accurate assessment of the profitability of the particular subsidiary with which they are negotiating, since profits may have been shifted to another part of the parent conglomerate's system.[18] For government policy-making, reported corporate trade flows, profits, and debt burdens are the basis of decisions for managing employment, price, and balance of payments stability. But when the statistical basis of these decisions is unreliable and/or misleading then the outcome of policy is, at best, uncertain, at worst, perverse.

These behavioral aspects are not the only characteristics of the new corporate mobility. There is also the physical dimension. In the 1960s, the pace of global oligopoly competition accelerated with the full-fledged entry of European and Japanese enterprises. Driven by international comparative cost differences in first labor and later in the overvalued U.S. exchange rate and in tax and antipollution costs, American companies offset declining domestic and export market shares by a remarkable mobility in transferring their production facilities to "export platform" facilities in underdeveloped countries. What Boston University's Dean of Business, Peter Gabriel, has termed the "herd instinct" of global corporations showed itself dramatically as the latecomer Japanese and Europeans began to duplicate export platform foreign investments of the pioneer American companies. This pattern, starting in labor intensive industries and quickly shifting to more capital intensive sectors, further reinforced the global interdependence of nations while adding new forms of structural lags and tensions in the home countries. Unions found another aspect of their countervailing power eroded as the threat of strike was effectively offset by the threat of production transfer overseas.[19] Smaller domestic subcontracting firms also felt the impacts of these transfers. In addition, government adjustment assistance programs, designed for times past, are ineffective in correcting the significant regional and industry dislocations in employment and small businesses. While no economist has yet to demonstrate the overall net domestic short-term employment impacts, positive or negative, of the new patterns of foreign investment, the results of structural long-term trend analysis are more pessimistic.

In the static theoretical market world of orthodox economics, changes in international comparative costs, dictating changes in the composition of national output and world trade, should lead to a new equilibrium situation via a path of smooth and rapid adjustments. This model underlying our current policies of course has to assume that factors like labor are domestically mobile and that basic economic institutions like the market and the corporation never significantly change their behavioral characteristics. The real world of imperfect and nonexistent markets, global profit maximization and oligopoly competition, labor and governmental immobility, compounded by rapid changes in certain institutions and none in others, all make, however, for an actual conclusion far removed from that of orthodox theory.

THE DILEMMA OF NATIONAL POLICY-MAKING: THE NEED FOR PLANNING

On the eve of 1975, as this essay was being written, the depths of structural lag in national stabilization policies are profound. Policy makers have yet to comprehend the many interrelated and intersecting forces arising out of the globalization and concentration processes of the corporate private sector. The worldwide complementary planning decisions of global banks and industrial companies have brought with them a convergence or harmonization in the business cycles of advanced nations. The upshot is that the United States can no longer rely, through foreign trade and finance multipliers, on Europe's upswing towards a boom to help bring us out of the declining phase of our own cycle, and vice versa. Today, one nation's deflationary or inflationary surges cumulatively help to bring about and accelerate those of other countries.

The rise of the global bank now finds its impacts in the global interdependence between national financial systems and money supplies, with this web of interdependence feeding unregulated banking transactions of a Euro-currency market. The structural lag accompanying the rise of the first and pioneering post-market global corporations, those of the petroleum sector, and their bargaining power as a buyers cartel to determine terms of trade, has been finally "overcome" on the supply side by a structural phenomenon called OPEC. Yet the lag persists in developing the financial structure to recycle the dramatic new distribution of worldwide liquid assets resulting from the rapid shift in bargaining power and accompanying changes in *real* terms of trade arising out of OPEC and like phenomena.[20] And within this matrix of interdependence stands the obvious lack of a global central bank of last resort to stem the (now recognized) threat of an international spiral of debt liquidation crises triggered through the Euro-currency market.

For those who have been studying the interdependent *structural* changes arising out of the globalization of that "primary social institution," the large corporation, the current economic stability was predictable. For orthodox economists (and, unfortunately, the managers and government policy makers they advise), because of their preoccupation with *functional* studies of changes in aggregate data and their use of a model which assumes that primary institutions are static, the current events of the day have come as a surprise. The former group analyzes changes in *terms of trade* within and between national economies based on changing power relations arising out of the diffusion of new "knowledge" and as functionally constrained at the limits by aggregate supply and demand conditions. The latter group attempts to analyze terms of trade by a functional focus on supply and demand with little regard for changing power relations between primary institutions. The structuralist model incorporates the functional approach.[21] The functionalist model sees as unnecessary, and thereby assumes away, the study of structural changes. Surrounding a period of structural transformation, the current functional model breaks down and so too does the efficacy of its policy prescriptions. At this point the model needs "updating" to bring it closer to the structural reality which it seeks to predict. So it was with Keynes, who, in the midst of the crisis in economics of the 1930s, built upon the work of the Swedish structuralism-functionalism school of Wicksell and Myrdal to derive a new model for policy-making purposes, operative until the next—and in this case our current—period of structural transformation. The present crisis in economics was well summarized by former Secretary of the Treasury George Shultz: "We have come into a very unusual period, where we more or less cast loose from beliefs that we once held to be unarguable. We have cast off from a large number of these old moorings and we have not yet found new ones."[22]

There is neither space left nor is this the place for detailed proposals dealing with the inefficacy of current national stabilization policies. The summary conclusions of this analysis do permit us, however, to point to the chief parameters which will govern policy approaches to the problems of contemporary economic instability. The overall conclusion of this analysis states that the traditionally accepted public sector regulatory institutions for managing the economy are structurally lagging behind the revolution in a basic institution of the private sector. The most notable symptom of this structural lag is an information crisis due to the mutually and systemically reinforcing processes of corporate globalization and concentration as they negate the market's social *function* for providing a reliable guide to policy-making. An additional aspect of this conclusion is that the ultimate result of corporate globalization has been the obviously greatly increased degree of interdependence between nation states. However, the political implications of this interdependence are yet to be sufficiently understood.

On the one hand, there is in fact a clear need in the United States to ask fundamental questions about the adequacy of current public regulatory institutions: antitrust laws and enforcement mechanisms, corporate disclosure laws, accounting conventions, banking and labor relations legislation, and the capacity of the government itself to maintain its corporate tax base. On the other hand, such seemingly national political issues have unpredictable economic impacts in a time of global interdependence. Thus, the modification by only one nation state of the public sector's regulatory function is severely limited unless such modifications are harmonized among all advanced countries. This is true because of the nature of global oligopoly competition and the extent to which national income is now dependent on the competitiveness of home nation global corporations in their overseas operations. If the regulatory institutions of only one country, say the United States, are modified in an attempt to provide more reliable stabilization policies, there is a distinct probability that this nation's national income will suffer. In this case, competitive oligopoly advantages could well accrue to the global corporations of other nations. Thus, the age old dilemma of the oligopolist—"If I do not take advantage of an opportunity my competitors will"—becomes, in an era of global interdependence and corporations, the dilemma of the national policy maker, and the underlying rationale for planned international harmonization. Yet the parameters of planning are obviously never solely determined by the dictates of economic (in this case, global) efficiency but equally by those of politics. This is so, if for no other reason than because nation states have different comparative resource endowments, different levels of development and developmental goals and, therefore, different national interests.

It is within this context that the politics of international harmonization will have to deal with what, in the opinion of this writer, undoubtedly will be basic institutional modifications if world economic stability is to be regained. Thus, from this view of the necessity of planning, two central questions emerge: (a) whether or not global harmonization is politically feasible; and, (b) if it is, for whom will it be economically desirable? These are the prime issues of the national and international "econopolitics" of the years ahead,* even when one looks at an alternative, structuralist view of the need for planning, stemming from the works of such writers as Walter Adams, J. K. Galbraith, John Blair, Barry Commoner, Gunnar Myrdal, and others. Their view brings into focus additional considerations, such as the social—as opposed to the private—efficiency of the current size of large global corporations; the lack of local community input into the private conglomerate's centralized planning on the use and/or discontinuance of a given local subsidiary; and the desirability, let alone feasibility, of maintaining the present *composition* of national output. The advocates of planning only the international harmonization of nation state economic policies assume the social desirability of the competitive dynamics of the present conglomerate system of private control of production. Stated otherwise, their philosophy of jurisprudence assumes the modern conglomerate to be a private, not a social institution. The structuralist view challenges this assumption, and thus advocates different planning parameters. Similarly, the first view recognizes global interdependence while officially believing that the market's function as social regulator is still operative. Those of the alternative persuasion rightly recognize the negation of the market's social function, emphasize the heightened technological interdependence of society but, in my opinion, have yet to grasp fully the depths of global interdependence. Again, the differences between the two groups mean different planning parameters and therefore different institutions for plan implementation.

Should those advocating planning for international harmonization of national economic policy emerge from the econopolitical process as the dominant group, one can derive "positivistically" some hypotheses as to what plan implementation for this purpose would entail: significant replacement of national public sector regulatory institutions by transnational institutions, particularly in the domain of finance, taxes, corporate disclosure, and antitrust. Such an outcome suggests an even further removal of productive forces from local and national social control. To the extent these hypotheses[23] are predictively correct, then this writer as an adherent of the normative tradition of classical political economy must "normatively" judge them as unacceptable. He therefore turns to an alternative set of planning parameters;

*The term "econopolitics" was first coined by former Secretary of Commerce, Peter Peterson, in a similar context.

that is, a social development plan for the United States, a basic purpose of which is to increase the degree of local community and national social control over the economic system.

The purpose of this chapter has been to diagnose current international and domestic economic and political forces and to suggest the need for an explicit public sector planning process, not to detail the plan basis and components of that process. Some suggestions should serve, however, to facilitate the discussion for which this chapter has been written: (1) A major objective of a social development plan is to take advantage of our current knowledge and afford to the American polity the opportunity to decide what type of nation it wishes to be in the future. (2) The necessity for such a step is to avoid what the polity decides are the negative social consequences which can occur out of unplanned development in a nation and world which has become so obviously technologically and globally interdependent. (3) Plan objectives, targets, and strategies, if they are to uphold personal freedom, must be explicitly decided upon through the political process and therefore should form an official part of each political party's electoral platform. The respective parties' social development plans thereby become a significant criterion by which the electorate determines for whom to vote. (4) Major components of the social development plan should include a set of objectives covering the desired degree of income equality, a definition of full employment, the composition of national output, and thus the degree of foreign dependency these objectives necessitate. (5) Because of the problems of current global interdependence diagnosed above, it is necessary to implement transitional planning phases of say four years each, with initial plan objectives targeted for the twelfth year. (6) These transitional phases would lay the groundwork for the realization of subsequent planning processes and plan objectives. For instance, there will be the need to pursue a foreign policy supportive of the plan's objectives, taking into account current levels of global interdependence and pushing for certain types of international harmonization derived from the plan itself. During the transition phases, major legislative decisions should be undertaken, foremost of which could be the legal redefinition of large corporations as social rather than private institutions. From this follows the need to overcome the above-defined corporate information crisis, through such measures as "deconsolidation of consolidated balance sheets" and a recomposition of boards of directors to include elected representatives from the various constituencies which large corporations as social institutions employ and serve. Suggestive of other major legislative questions is that of nationalization including its definition, costs, and benefits, and to which corporations (not necessarily industries), if any, it should apply, and so on. Finally, by way of example, there is the question of whether or not the spatial definition of "local community" necessitates the redrawing of state boundaries into economic, political, and administratively functional regions so as to allow a feasible intermesh between community and national objectives.

These suggestions are admittedly incomplete, crudely formulated, and undoubtedly will shock many who read them. The shock will be of two types. There will be those whose dismay is of a political variant and who perceive the idea of a social development plan as a threat to personal freedom, initiative, and enterprise. They are, however, mistaken since, as shown above, the current lack of social planning would seem to negate the pursuit of individual freedoms for all but the most powerful. Still others will base their dismay on feasibility grounds, perceiving the tasks of plan design and implementation as overwhelming. They too I feel are mistaken, but their reservations are to be taken quite seriously. To restore stability in a world of instability is indeed an enormous task. Yet, it is also a challenging one. For much too long our most basic human resource, new knowledge, has been focused largely on our material domain, on a public-private spectrum that extends from the Manhattan Project of the atomic bomb to the factory production line and on to the managerial and accounting technology for global maximization of private profits. Does not the drift of history suggest it is time to bring science and ethics back together again,[24] to commence, through perhaps a number of Manhattan-type projects, the refocusing of our new knowledge on the idea task of an equitable and stable social organization?

NOTES

1. All data on globalization and concentration indicators are taken from official government statistics and reports as well as studies of Business International Incorporated. Detailed documentation of these figures (Chapter 10 for globalization, Chapter 9 for concentration) is in R. J. Barnet and R. Müller, *Global Reach: The Power of the Multinational Corporations* (New York: Simon and Schuster, 1974).

2. See the papers of H. W. de Jong, K. D. George and A. Silverston, Helmut Arndt, S. J. Prais and C. Reid, and Ronald Müller given at the *Nijenrode International Conference on Industrial Organization,* Holland, August 12-17, 1974 and in H. W. de Jong and A. P. Jacquemin, *International Aspects of Industrial Organization* (Leiden: North Holland Publishing Co. 1975).

3. The feedback of U.S. firms' foreign investment on increasing domestic investment concentration has been verified econometrically in Tom Horst's study for the Brookings Institution, "American Investment Abroad and Domestic Market Power," preliminary draft (Brookings: Washington, D.C., December 1974).

4. John Blair, "Market Power and Inflation: A Short-Run Target Return Model," *Journal of Economic Issues,* vol. VIII, no. 2 (June 1974): 453-77. See also the findings of Otto Eckstein and David Wyss, "Industry Price Equations," *Conference on Econometrics of Price Determination,* Washington, D.C., October 30-31, 1973; and Otto Eckstein and Gary Fromm, "The Price Equation," *American Economic Review,* vol. 58 (December 1968): 1159-83; and Nancy S. Barrett, Geraldine Gerardi, and Thomas P. Hart, *Prices and Wages in U.S. Manufacturing: A Factor Analysis* (Lexington, Mass.: D. C. Heath, 1973).

5. See Charles Vanik, "Corporate Federal Tax Payments and Federal Subsidies to Corporations for 1972," *Congressional Record,* House of Representatives, August 1, 1973; and also his "On 1971 Corporate Income Tax," in *Tax Subsidies and Tax Reform,* Hearing before the Joint Economic Committee, U.S. Congress, 92nd session (Washington, D.C.: Government Printing Office, 1973): 17; and Peggy Musgrave, "Tax Preference to Foreign Investment," U.S. Congress Joint Economic Committee, *The Economics of Federal Subsidy Programs, Part II-International Subsidies,* Washington, D.C., 1972, and her "International Tax Base Division and the Multinational Corporation," *Public Finance,* vol. 27, 1972. For data on the expenditure side, see Barry Bluestone, in his review of the literature, presented in *Testimony* to the Joint Economic Committee, U.S. Congress, February 29, 1972.

6. George Budzeika, "Lending to Business by New York City Banks," *The Bulletin,* New York University, Graduate School of Business Administration, Institute of Finance, nos. 75,77 (September 1971).

7. Robert F. Lanzillotti, "Industrial Structure and Inflation Control: The U.S. Experience," paper presented to the *Nijenrode International Conference on Industrial Organization,* Holland, August 12-17, 1974, op. cit.

8. For the role of foreign-based global corporations and their oligopoly pricing in the U.S. import sector, as it made ineffective the 1971 dollar devaluation, and led to an "overdevaluation" in 1973, see footnotes to, and pp. 287-90, Barnet and Müller, *Global Reach,* op. cit. The impact on price controls is an example of negation of the market's social function via intracorporate transactions. The impact on devaluation policy is an example of market negation via oligopoly distortion effects. Important in the devaluation example is the policy's ineffectiveness in reducing imports but effectiveness in "overstimulating" agricultural exports and the accompanying inflationary impacts of the latter.

9. See footnotes to, and pp. 270-71, Barnet and Müller, *Global Reach,* op. cit., for a detailed breakdown on the various financial and monetary indicators discussed in the text.

10. H. S. Houthakker, "Policy Issues in the International Economy of the 1970s," *American Economic Review,* vol. 64 (May 1974): 139.

11. *Monthly Report of the Deutsche Bundesbank,* March 1973, p. 3; Samuel Katz, "Imported Inflation and the Balance of Payments," New York University, Graduate School of Business Administration, Institute of Finance, *The Bulletin,* nos. 91-92 (October 1973).

12. Michael G. Porter, "Commercial Flows as an Offset to Monetary Policy: The German Experience," *IMF Staff Papers* (July 1972): 395, 415.

13. Frank Tamagna, "Commercial Banking in Transition: From the Sixties to the Seventies," in *Banking in a Changing World,* papers of the 24th International Banking Conference of the Italian Bankers Association, Chianciano, Italy, May 1971.

14. Even in 1973, after further adjustments by the Federal Reserve Bank, financial analysts were still worried about the gap in, and therefore uncertainty of, monetary policy fully "to integrate into its decision-making apparatus the most dynamic and expanding aspect of American banking, the foreign branch operations." See Frank Mastrapasqua, "U.S. Bank Expansion Via Foreign Branching: Monetary Policy Implications," New York University, Graduate School of Business Administration, Institute of Finance, *The Bulletin,* nos. 87-88 (January 1973).

15. Scott Gordon, "The Close of the Galbraithian System," *Journal of Political Economy,* 1968 (emphasis added).

16. See text pages and the footnotes thereto of Barnet and Müller, *Global Reach,* op. cit., pp. 259-61.

17. Leonard Spacek and David Norr as quoted in Adam Smith, *Super Money* (New York: Random House, 1972), pp. 197, 205, 206 (parentheses mine).

18. See the various studies in section 5, of chap. 10, and sections 1 and 2, chap. 11, Barnet and Müller, *Global Reach,* op. cit.

19. Ibid.

20. For the methodology and theory of bargaining power as a component of economics, to analyze changing terms of trade occuring not only in petroleum but other raw materials, manufacturing, and financial sectors of underdeveloped countries, see Ronald Müller, "The Developed and Underdeveloped: Power and the Potential for Change," International Sociological Association, *World Congress of Sociology,* Papers and Proceedings, Toronto: Ontario, August 1974. Also, C. Fred Bergsten, "Coming Investment Wars?" *Foreign Affairs* (October 1974), and his "The Threat from the Third World," *Foreign Policy* (Summer 1973).

21. Ronald Müller, "Structuralism-Functionalism in the Study of Social Change," *Department of Economics Study Paper,* American University, January 1970, with an addendum by Professor Jiri Nehnevjasa, Department of Sociology, University of Pittsburgh, February 1970. See also V. V. Bhatt, "Sterility of Equilibrium Economics: An Aspect of Sociology of Knowledge," Economic Development Institute, International Bank for Reconstruction and Development, Seminar Paper no. 9, February 1974.

22. George Schultz, as quoted in *Fortune* (January 1974), p. 61.

23. The derivation of these hypotheses is outlined in Barnet and Müller, *Global Reach,* op. cit., chap. 13.

24. On the relationships between new knowledge, science, and ethics see, Ibid; Müller, "Structuralism-Functionalism . . . ," op. cit.; and V. V. Bhatt, op. cit.

THE MULTINATIONAL CORPORATION AND DEVELOPMENT— A CONTRADICTION?
Harry Magdoff

Among current ideas about the importance of the multinational corporation for the future of society and the nation state are quite a few flights of fancy indulged in by conservatives and radicals alike. It is time that some of these be brought down to earth, and there is no better way to do this than to examine the roots of this phenomenon historically. As we see it, the multinational corporation can best be understood as a logical stage in the evolution of capitalist enterprise, a stage during which innate tendencies of the capitalist firm come into full flower. This can be recognized most clearly if we begin by taking special note of what Marx considered the mainsprings of capitalist behavior.

Since Marx's central focus was the study of economic institutions as part of an historical process, he separated out of the multitude of operations of capitalist enterprises those features which he considered decisive in determining historical development, or, as he put it, the laws of motion of capitalism. Among the governing principles he selected are those which are also found at the heart of today's multinational firm:

1. The conditions of capitalist enterprise impose on the individual firm the necessity to expand continuously. As Marx wrote in *Capital:* "The development of capitalist production makes it constantly necessary to keep increasing the amount of capital laid out in a given industrial undertaking, and competition makes the immanent laws of capitalist production to be felt by each individual capitalist, as external coercive laws. It compels him to keep constantly extending his capital in order to preserve it, but extend it he cannot, except by means of progressive accumulation."[1] This growth imperative is graphically summarized in Marx's much quoted epitomization: "Accumulate, Accumulate! That is Moses and the prophets!...Therefore...reconvert the greatest possible portion of surplus product, into capital!"[2]

2. The process of accumulation of capital generates, and is in turn further advanced by a growing concentration of capital in fewer and fewer hands. This process of concentration takes two interrelated forms: the spread of large-scale production and the combination of firms through mergers and acquisitions. The organizational instrument most useful for this persistent tendency of capitalist development is the corporation more often called in Marx's day: a joint-stock company.[3]

3. The world market provides "the basis and vital element of capitalist production."[4] In fact, capitalism was born in the commercial revolution of the sixteenth and early seventeenth centuries—a revolution which produced a global market centered on the needs and desires of the nations of Western Europe. The expansion of international trade stimulated the spread of capitalist enterprise, furthered the transition from feudalism to capitalism, and led necessarily to a continuous deepening and widening of the world market.[5]

These three cardinal attributes of business enterprise—investment expansion, concentration of corporate power, and growth of the world market—are eventually uniquely fulfilled in the multinational corporation, but the latter cannot take shape until the concentration of capital reaches the stage conveniently called monopoly capitalism (as distinguished from competitive capitalism), in which competition among only a few giant corporations is the typical pattern in each of the leading industries.[6]

Foreign investment played a relatively subordinate role in the international economy of competitive capitalism, and that role was to aid and support what was of primary concern in that period: the promotion of markets for rapidly expanding domestic industries, and the procurement of raw materials for industry and food for burgeoning urban populations. (This is not to deny the growing importance of foreign investment to the British economy during the period of competitive capitalism: as a most useful component in the maturation of its money markets, and its international financial ascendancy; and as a spur to its metals and machinery industries. Loans and direct investments were useful aids in the acquisition of railway building concessions, and thus they supported the rising exports of iron and steel, railway equipment, and allied capital goods. Capital went abroad, and the resulting profits were reinvested overseas, for a variety of political and economic reasons. Nevertheless, the central integrative factor was the expansion of foreign trade.) In contrast, the economics and politics of the monopoly stage entailed a heightened attention to the spread of ownership, control, and influence over productive activities in foreign lands. The expansion and deepening of the world market was no longer correlated primarily with exports of commodities; to an increasing extent it took the form of transnational migration of capital. This new interest in foreign investment was grounded in the distinguishing features of this new phase of development in the advanced capitalist countries which began to shape up towards the end of the nineteenth century:

1. A host of new industries based on major technological breakthroughs appeared on the scene. Examples are steel, electric power, oil refining, synthetic chemicals, aluminum, and automobiles. Most of these new industries required an unusually large scale of production (along with enlarged, more complex capital markets to mobilize the needed finance) —thus accelerating the trend towards further concentration and centralization of capital.

2. Industrial processes relied more and more on the conscious application of science. This, along with the pressure of competition among giant firms and the urgency to protect large capital investments, encouraged growing attention to research and development for product innovation and improvement in production methods.

3. The new industries created a demand for a wide variety of raw materials, often entailing the discovery and development of new sources of supply in distant lands. At the same time the corporate giants felt an increasing need to own or otherwise control these sources of supply as a form of insurance against being squeezed by rivals, as a means of protecting the huge amounts of capital sunk in the extraction and processing of the needed materials, and in order that the profits of the extractive industries accrue to themselves.

4. Under the impact of the new industries and advances in transportation associated with the new technologies, the world market reached a new high in integration: the remaining self-contained areas were transformed into adjuncts of international markets; a single multilateral system of international payments evolved; and more or less uniform world prices came into effect for the more common commodities of world trade.

5. The state assumed an increasingly important role in stimulating, influencing, and resolving conflicts among the emerging giant corporations. Protective tariffs and other trade barriers—no longer for the protection of infant industries but for the benefit of more advanced, export-oriented manufactures—became the order of the day. Above all, the evolving monopoly phase was tied to the mushrooming of militarism, with the latter performing two indispensable services: (a) a vital and rapidly growing market for the heavy industries, for which government funds were readily available; (b) assistance, via direct military action or the threat of force, in obtaining privileged trade and investment opportunities.

These and related developments both reflected and intensified the pressures on large capitalist enterprises to expand their international operations. While most involvement abroad was at first based largely on loans to governments and industry,[7] equity investment before long began to take a prominent place as the modus operandi of the giant firm in the world market, evolving eventually into the flowering of the multinationals. This evolution proceeded at an uneven pace, influenced by international conditions, the state of the domestic economy, and the organizational strength of the corporations themselves. But the thrust was always toward the expansion of control over production and marketing on a global scale. And from its very beginning, the burgeoning of foreign investment in the late nineteenth and twentieth centuries was closely linked with the maturation of monopoly-type firms and their social and political alter ego, the new imperialism. Capital flowed abroad to gain exclusive control of raw material supplies needed for the new industries, to acquire maximum leverage from technological and other monopolistic advantages, to make the most use of regions with exceptional market opportunities, and to profit from the low wages and favored locations of colonies, semicolonies, and spheres of influence. Moreover, the very obstacles erected in this period to restrict imports and protect domestic industry gave added impetus to the spread of foreign investment as a means of jumping trade barriers.

Another important development of this period was the dramatic shifts in the national sources of capital moving into foreign operations: these changes reflect not only the fluctuating fortunes of the advanced capitalist nations but the essential nature of the internationalization of capital as part of a continuous struggle for power and ascendancy by nations and their industries. Great Britain's headstart in the area of capital exports, stemming from its initiating role in the industrial revolution, its huge empire and dominant navy, and its being the headquarters of the international money market, led quite naturally to its becoming the foremost owner of foreign productive assets. France and Germany, however, were fast on the same trail. Together, the three nations accounted for almost 90 percent of foreign investment at the outbreak of World War I, Britain owning 50 percent, Germany and France 40 percent.

Despite the debtor status of the United States, a number of U.S. firms participated in the new wave, with substantial investments moving abroad before the turn of the century. On the whole, though, the position of the United States was relatively minor compared to the big three, representing only some 6 percent of the total in 1914. All this changed radically as a result of the dislocations of World War I and the subsequent readjustments in power relations among the advanced industrial nations: the loss of Russia as a host to foreign investors; the drastic reduction in Britain's investments in the United States as a result of the liquidation of assets to pay for U.S. exports of munitions; and the declines in Germany's and France's role. Thus, the 40 percent held by Germany and France in 1914 dropped to 11 percent by 1930. At the other extreme was the expansionism of U.S. industry and finance striving to realize its "manifest destiny" in world affairs. Along with other political and military realignments on the international scene between World War I and the Great Depression, including a U.S. bid to take over Britain's paramount position, came the marked rise in the absolute and relative status of U.S. investment activities abroad: the 6 percent of 1914 became 35 percent by 1930.

The impressive forward movement by the United States was speeded up and consolidated in the new world situation arising out of World War II and the postwar arrangements. By the early 1970s, 60 percent of the world's foreign investments were in the hands of U.S. corporations, the result of an unprecedented eightfold growth in this type of capital accumulation by U.S. firms since 1945. Once the Western European and Japanese economies got back on their feet, the reach of their corporate giants also began to extend to capital accumulation across national boundaries. British firms ran a weak second and French firms a much poorer third to the United States; the two combined accounting for a little over 20 percent of total foreign investment in the early 1970s. Germany and Japan, for obvious reasons, were laggards (in 1971 they represented 4.50 and 3 percent of the total, respectively), but their rates of growth hint at probable major changes ahead in their foreign production role. Between 1966 and 1971, Germany's foreign investment increased by 172 percent, and Japan's by 270 percent.[8]

THE RISE OF THE MULTINATIONAL CORPORATION

The groundwork of the clear-cut dominance of U.S. foreign investment that took shape in the post-World War II years was grounded on the overwhelming U.S. military and economic power and the *Pax Americana* which this power sought to establish. As part of the coalescence of these interrelated developments, the multinational firm appeared on the stage as the quintessential embodiment of the innate logic of capitalist enterprise: relentless accumulation of capital on a world scale, aided and abetted by ever greater concentration and centralization of enterprise. As we see it, the main contributing factors to the explosive acceleration of U.S. foreign enterprise and the emergence of a qualitatively new form of international capitalist operation, pioneered by U.S. firms, were as follows:

1. The system of international payments, once focused in the London money market during the British Empire's hegemonic heyday and the predominance of British foreign investment, was reconstituted under U.S. leadership by the Bretton Woods agreements. The enshrinement of the U.S. dollar at Bretton Woods provided the financial framework for the great leap forward of U.S. corporate investment abroad. The international payments system, which provided that the U.S. dollar was as good as gold, and thus created the unique, prolonged deficit in the U.S. balance of payments, made possible the deficit financing not only of the far-flung military bases and

military operations of the U.S. government, but also the sprouting of foreign affiliates of multinational firms. The breakdown of the Bretton Woods system in 1971 proved to be no serious obstacle, for by then the huge float of U.S. dollar liabilities outside the country, the financial assets accumulated in the interim by multinational subsidiaries, and the resulting Euro-dollar market provided the practical financial media for still further international business growth by U.S. firms. (The World Bank—the second institution created at Bretton Woods—also contributed to the spread of foreign investment by, among other things, financing the needed infrastructure.)

2. The prosperity and type of economic development spurred by the Marshall Plan, which had been undertaken largely to rebuild and strengthen European capitalism as a political and military ally, led to an intensification of the kind of monopolistic competition that characterizes the multinational firm. The Marshall Plan, financed and steered by the United States, stimulated the rehabilitation and growth of native giant firms and at the same time prepared a fertile seedbed for the sprouting of U.S. corporate enterprise in Western European countries and their dependencies. In addition, the NATO arrangements, the continuous presence of U.S. military power in Western Europe, and the latter's reliance on the U.S. nuclear umbrella reinforced the special relations within the so-called Atlantic Alliance, which among other things sustained a favorable environment for U.S. business expansion across the Atlantic.

3. Designed to influence and control "safe" and allied nations, the postwar U.S. program of military and economic aid also helped create and support many new investment opportunities. Japan was the notable exception; the Japanese consciously and far-sightedly managed to retain their home market and to limit the encroachment of U.S. foreign investment. Their ability to get the U.S. government to go along with this obstinacy, despite the U.S. military occupation, was perhaps due to the special role assigned to Japan as the primary bastion of capitalism in the Far East and as the major ally of the United States in that area. Not only was the protection of foreign private investment a prerequisite for the receipt of such aid, but energetic encouragement of an inflow of foreign investment was fundamental to the economic development programs designed in response to the advice and pressure of the loan and grant administrators. Perhaps even more important was the proliferation of experts among business, professional, and military personnel engaged in distributing this aid. Increased knowledge of local industrial and financial practices; better acquaintance with indigenous geography, language, laws, customs, and markets; and, above all, close contacts with the "right people" in government and elite circles—all this was, and continues to be, of invaluable assistance to capitalists seeking avenues abroad for the piling up of further investments.

4. World War II and its aftermath introduced and galvanized business and technological changes that primed the rapid growth, and helped develop the distinguishing features, of the multinational firm. War production requirements fattened the industrial giants of the U.S. economy and gave a push to further concentration of economic power. Enlivened by strong direct and indirect government demand for military goods during the war and ever since, the giant firms turned into supergiants. The technological underpinning for the new earth-girdling enterprise was also intimately associated with the militarization of the economy. The heavy expenditure of funds and personnel on weapon development achieved significant breakthroughs in the fields of communication, transport, and computers, which in turn opened up new opportunities for the business community. The technological edge achieved during the war has been further sharpened with the help of continuing subsidies: since the war between 50-60 percent of R and D in the United States is financed by the federal government;[9] an indeterminate additional share is paid for by private industry in anticipation of new products or new technologies that will eventuate in still larger defense contracts. The changes that contributed most to facilitating networks of global industry closely coordinated from a few metropolitan centers were: (a) speeded-up and expanded air transport; (b) vastly improved modes of communication; and (c) sophisticated computers for the amassing and analysis of data needed to plan for global maximization of profit.

The developments outlined in the above four points help to explain what is distinctively new in the latest phase of international capitalist affairs. Previously, foreign investment activities consisted to a great extent in acquiring control of raw material sources, establishment of manufacturing subsidiaries for particular locational advantages, and the spread of international banking largely in colonial and semicolonial nations. These were, as noted above, products of the striving for monopolistic advantage and manipulation by the most powerful firms to divide world markets. While foreign investment as an integral constituent of monopoly capitalism moved ahead energetically, several features of the years prior to World War II limited its rate of growth. Apart from the effect of the Great Depression on the rate of investment, the major restraints were the following: 1. World markets became divided by cartel-like arrangements in a large number of important industries, manufacturing as well as raw material extraction. Spheres of influence were parcelled out. Poaching on each other's territory was prohibited, including curbs on where foreign investment could be located. 2. Nations with colonial empires attempted insofar as possible to keep their colonial possessions as exclusive investment preserves for themselves. This limitation was especially onerous for U.S. business in the light of the small share of the colonial world occupied by the United States. 3. Despite the steadily increasing power of giant firms, few had the financial resources and managerial strength for truly worldwide operations. The typical international enterprise ran to only two, three, or four foreign branch plants. The noteworthy exceptions were the early multinational organizations in the oil industry.

One after another of these inhibitions faded away during and after World War II. Many cartel agreements evaporated during the war. Decolonization created new opportunities for trade and investment competition from metropolitan centers which formerly were excluded or were disinclined to attempt to climb over expensive barriers. The pervasive military presence of the United States around the globe, the strength of this military power, and the design of the imperial world order under U.S. leadership not only opened doors in advanced as well as underdeveloped countries but also inspired confidence in foreign investors—most especially, of course, in U.S. business interests—about the security of their overseas assets. (This is in addition to the influence of U.S. power on the readiness of ruling elites of weaker nations to create an attractive environment for outside capital.) Finally, as discussed earlier, the accelerated concentration of power increased the number of firms able to operate internationally; more and more supergiants, assisted by the new technologies, were capable of exercising central control over a large and geographically widespread number of affiliates.

This extended scope for accumulation on a global scale developed a momentum of its own, especially as the resulting terms of monopolistic rivalry changed. While cartel deals did not entirely disappear, and some new cartels came on the scene, the struggle for markets among giant firms in many industries shifted to producing goods in each other's territory and in the dependencies of the various metropolitan centers. In the very nature of monopolistic competition, as one or more of the giant firms in a particular industry spread its tentacles abroad, competitors were eventually impelled to do likewise. The changeover in the strategy of competition, and the experience gained in the process of running a business on an international scale, kept on strengthening the impulse for, and widening the geographic range of, new foreign locations yielding lower costs of production and /or improved market control. The path, once opened up, became a well-trodden one.

The upshot was an explosion of U.S. foreign production activity, a quickening of the global spread of competing giants from other advanced industrial nations, and the advent of the age of the multinational firm. Thus, within the short span of a quarter of a century, the multinationals reached such a level in the international accumulation of capital that their output away from home base began to outdistance trade as the main vehicle of international economic exchange. The combined sales of foreign affiliates of multinational corporations in 1971 is estimated to have been $330 billion, while total exports of all capitalist economies in that year amounted to $312 billion. It should be noted though that this has come about because of the very substantial excess of output abroad over exports in the United States and Great Britain. Except for Switzerland, and the fast-approaching Sweden, the other capitalist nations still show a substantial excess of exports over their foreign production.[10] (This is aside from the fact that a substantial portion of foreign trade is now conducted between multinationals and their subsidiaries.) As in the past, the modern upsurge in transnational production is also concentrated in the hands of a relatively small number of companies. But in contrast with the former pattern, the leading firms are no longer operating in only one or two foreign countries but have truly spread their wings: for example, two hundred of these companies, among the largest in the world, now have affiliates in twenty or more countries.[11] Moreover, the multinationals, or their prototypes, were formerly for the most part in raw material extraction and to a limited extent in banking. Today's global firms have invaded manufacturing and services, and taken a major leap into international banking. (Note that deposits in foreign branches of the larger New York-based banks compared with their domestic deposits have increased from $8\frac{1}{2}$ to $65\frac{1}{2}$ percent between 1960 and 1972.[12]

SPECULATION ABOUT SUPERMULTINATIONALS

Such rapid and striking changes naturally cry out for new interpretations. Similarly, analyses of international economic events that ignore, or do not adequately reflect, the effects of the multinationals are bound to come a cropper. At the same time, however, it is especially important not to fall victim to oversimplified projections and conjectures or great sounding theories based on speculation rather than fact. For it is in the nature of transitional periods for many sprouts to emerge, some to wither while others mature and become dominant. Simple linear projections, without weighing countertendencies, are therefore unreliable guides. Thus, a frequently met expectation is that the process of concentration and centralization of capital will before long end up with a handful of global companies owning and operating the preponderant part of the capitalist world's enterprise. This is hardly a novel theme. Reading the death of competition into the decline of competition has recurred time and again, ever since the giant corporations loomed on the scene almost a hundred years ago. The onset of the multinational age has quite naturally precipitated a blossoming of such expectations. It is important, however, to distinguish clearly between a steady pressure within capitalism towards more concentration of power on the one hand and the virtual elimination of all competition on the other. While the direction may be persistently towards the ultimate in monopoly, the logical end of this process is never reached because of obstacles arising from the nature of the very forces which propel it forward.

What needs to be understood is that the very process of concentration and centralization of capital is spurred by competition and results in intensifying the struggle among separate aggregates of capital, albeit on a different scale and with altered strategies. As a rule, above average growth of an enterprise, or a merger of two or more firms, occurs in more than one sector of an industry in a given period: the emergency of one focus of power stimulates, by example or by the threat of extinction, reflex convergencies of capital. In addition, contending focuses of financial power generated within the rapidly inflating capital markets associated with the process of concentration, inter-industry as well as intra-industry rivalry, technical innovations and new industries induced by competition, and state intervention to forestall or ameliorate a crisis—all serve to create conflicting blocs of power, no one of which has the strength to win a battle for absolute control or the will to risk the loss of accumulated assets in such intensified economic warfare.

This being the case, as each giant firm holds on to its attained share of the market, the potential for further accumulation of capital within an industry is generally restricted to the growth of demand for that industry's products. Under the impetus of the growth imperative, then, the search for new worlds to conquer generally narrows down to two main channels for accumulation: diversification (development of new products and new consumer "needs" as well as buying into other industries) and conquest of foreign markets. While the entry into the international scene produces new strains and tensions, the underlying reality is still competitive struggle among industrial and financial power groups. In addition, we frequently find state intervention contributing to the perpetuation of monopolistic competition within and between industries. Faced with foreign economic penetration, the advanced industrial states tend to strengthen their own giant firms, and, if necessary, step right into the act themselves through ownership and operation of industry. (Of the leading 211 manufacturing companies in capitalist nations with sales of over $1 billion, at least 12 are state owned.[13] Struggle for markets on a world scale will of course encourage, and necessitate, further mergers and alliances, but these are for the purpose of more effective competition and not its elimination. In this connection, the rise and decline of U.S. hegemony is a useful illustration. American economic dominance was a natural outgrowth of the great disparity of economic strength between the United States and the war-devastated nations. Viewed abstractly and in terms of straight-line projections, many expected this hegemony to grow until the world's productive capacity would be in the hands of a few U.S. firms. But the requirements and side effects of this dominance (the global military stance, the military adventures, the rebuilding of its allies, the European Common

Market, the related unsettling of international financial arrangements) produced its own countereffects, leading to increasing challenges to U.S. dominance from other capitalist nations.

On the international as on the domestic scene, the means and intensity of conflict will vary over time, depending on political and military conditions, particular circumstances in a given industry, and the general state of the market (whether the latter is experiencing stagnation, growth, or decline). Alliances and truces in a particular industry may produce temporary calm, but these generally last only until a new crisis rekindles the flames of competition. For the essential nature of modern monopoly capitalism is restless struggle on the world stage by giants and supergiants which, despite their accumulation of power, are far from omnipotent; indeed, the dialectical interrelation between coalescence and competition of capitals is one of the most important contributors to the dynamics of the economic system.

MULTINATIONAL VS. THE NATION STATE

A second popular line of theoretical projections in the multinational age holds that internationalization requires, and eventually will result in, the decline of the nation state. In part, this type of speculation is prompted by the search of big business for the ultimate in freedom for the international movement of capital, profits, and goods. However, this theory has more objective roots in the supposed contradiction between the evolving global structure and strategy of the multinationals and the restrictions inherent in the nation state. The typical foreign manufacturing subsidiary in the premultinational years was either a plant that merely assembled components sent from the home country or a more integrated duplicate of the parent company adapted to the host country's markets and standing pretty much on its own feet. The strategic difference between such forms of organization and the typical multinational manufacturing organization—in fact, that which gives the latter its uniqueness and novelty—is the high degree of interdependence among the subsidiaries and the kind of coordination needed in the central offices of the parent company in the pursuit of global profit maximization. A classic example of the new level of integration is provided by a former head of General Motors:

> If the South African assembly operation and its recently added
> manufacturing facilities are to function smoothly and efficiently,
> they must today receive a carefully controlled and coordinated
> flow of vehicle parts and components from West Germany,
> England, Canada, the United States, and even Australia. These

must reach General Motors South Africa in the right volume and at the right time to allow an orderly scheduling of assembly without accumulation of excessive inventories. This is a challenging assignment which must be made to work if the investment is to be a profitable one.[14]

We see here not only the shape of the foreign operations of General Motors in today's world but also get a glimpse of the model for which many multinational manufacturing firms are striving. Their ideal would be to maximize overall profits by the highest degree of flexibility in the global movement of capacity and of goods at lowest production and distribution costs—all to be finally planned, coordinated, and directed from one financial center. The realization of such a dream quite clearly would imply the complete removal of all national barriers. And it is therefore not surprising to find that the advanced thinkers and publicists of the business community have sounded the tocsin: the old-fashioned nation state is standing in the way of progress. Reverberations of this theme are heard in both orthodox academic and radical circles, by those who see the free sway of international capital as the wave of the future as well as by those alarmed over its implications.

Implicit in much of this thinking is an oversimplified technological determinism. The assumption is made that the multinational method of integrated global production represents a higher and more progressive stage of industrial organization—one that reaches a new level of large-scale efficiency and is realistically based on the interdependency of the various regions of the earth. It is then inferred that what is rational will prevail: since the system of nation states interferes with an advanced global technology of production and management, the nation state will tend to fade away, with many of its functions being replaced by formal or informal international institutions.

This line of thought has two weaknesses: the assumptions, implicit and explicit, are wrong; and what is most relevant is disregarded. The multinational firm may indeed be a more efficient organism, but the issue is: efficient for what? Its superiority is in the realm of profit-making by oligopolistic organizations designed to exploit to the hilt the existing hierarchy of nations, in other words the imperialist world order. Decisions on location and integration of plants are of course influenced by such technical factors as transportations costs and proximity to raw materials. These are, more often than not, minor inducements compared to more pressing economic and political considerations, which have nothing to do with the design of a superior form of international production, the political climate for foreign investment, low wage rates, tax advantages, and imperatives of monopolistic competition. Nor is the large scale of corporate enterprise in and of itself evidence of greater inefficiency. The scale of organization is not arrived at by purely technical criteria (even if there were such a thing, independent of social values) but with concern for greater effectiveness in the exercise of economic power to protect and control markets.

Furthermore, it is hypocrisy or obfuscation to see any resemblance between the transnational integration brought about by the multinationals and the growing interdependence of the earth's regions. The latter arises from the problems of limited natural resources and the effects of environmental changes in one region on the life-supporting possibilities of other regions. On such matters, the global corporations are the culprits and not the saviors: far from being organisms that have grown out of the *necessary* interdependence of all parts of the world, they have been built to obtain the maximum-profit advantage out of the artificial interdependence imposed by the long history of colonialism and imperialism.

In sum, from the viewpoint of either technology or management, the multinationals are hardly the prototypes of a superior international mode of production, certainly not the mode of production that will cope with the world's problems of hunger, disease, scarcity of resources, and environmental pollution. The multinationals are not basically out of harmony with the system of nation states and the interwoven imperialist network; in fact, these firms—and their so-called global technology and administrative structures—evolved in a system of nation states in a fashion best adapted to struggle for profits and control in precisely that environment.

In addition to speculation about the fate of nations based on technological determinism, there is another trend of thought tending to the same conclusion but based on an oversimplified concept of the relations between the state and big business. One finds, especially among radical critics, the anticipation of a coalition or conspiracy of multinationals which will settle international matters among themselves and then force the nation states to conform to their will. In other words, as the multinationals grow in strength, their common interests will prevail over and hence weaken the nation states. In a certain sense, there has always been a community of interest among capitalists who viewed the world as their playground. This has been the common cause of a class whose success depends upon antagonism against workers and other subordinate classes throughout all capitalist nations, including most assuredly a united front against national liberation and proletarian revolutions aimed at overthrowing capitalist rule. In addition, the interference by foreign capitalists in the affairs of weaker dependent states is central to the whole history of capitalism (the most recent well-documented and publicized example being of course ITT's activities in Chile). But these aspects of capital's unified world spirit are a far cry from the rule, by an international committee of business firms, over the advanced capitalist nations. Such a notion overlooks the essence of the international firms as participants in economic warfare among themselves, in which the gains of one are the losses of another. Even more important, this type of prognostication ignores the underlying symbiosis of monopoly capital and its home state, as for example:

1. Above all, the multinational corporations need social stability in the countries where they operate or expect to operate. For internal stability, a police force is needed; for external law and order, an army, navy, and air force. Business firms will when necessary invest in private armies to guard their property and repress trade unions. They will also devote resources to assure a friendly environment and have a voice in security matters. Thus they will spend money to bribe officials, influence newspapers, radio, television, and other forms of "public relations" and in general on activities that will sustain friendly governments or get rid of unfriendly ones. This type of investment, however, is miniscule compared with the huge sums needed to finance and direct national police and military forces (for example, to finance a navy and air force in the Mediterranean Sea and Persian Gulf). Even the supergiants are not rich or willing enough to use their profits on such activities on the global scale on which their businesses are spread. Nor is it reasonable to expect competing financial groups (conflicted between the need to support a common interest and the perpetual pressure to get an advantage over rivals) to reach agreement on how to maintain security and stability in the absence of a state to knock heads together. The dependence on force as the bedrock of business enterprise acts to strengthen, not weaken, the nation state.

2. It is important to keep in mind that almost all the multinationals are in fact *national* organizations operating on a global scale. We are in no way denying that capitalism is, and has from its very beginning been, a world system, or that this system has been further integrated by the multinationals. But just as it is essential to understand, and analyze, capitalism as a world system, it is equally necessary to recognize that each capitalist firm relates to the world system through, and must eventually rely on, the nation state. Thus, the decisive owners and the headquarters of the multinationals are located in one of the metropolitan centers, and dividends are paid in the currency of that center. No matter how profitable the widespread and integrated foreign affiliates are, their profits have little meaning to owners unless these profits are more or less freely convertible at an advantageous rate in the home country's money. And this assurance can hardly be provided by a council of international firms, for these matters are the product of a multitude of economic activities over which the corporations can have little control. Moreover, there is little reason to expect that the leaders of the multinationals of different countries could reach an amicable agreement on exchange rates, since there is no objective standard of equity. Quite the contrary, an exchange rate that will benefit one nation's economy and its business community will likewise disadvantage another. Foreign monetary exchange relations are therefore focal points of power struggle; and because of the complexity

and diversity of international money transactions they require the active participation of states. Having conflicting interests among themselves in domestic as well as overseas economics, the multinationals are in no position to dictate the terms of the battle over foreign exchange. In fact, neither is there a state that can now dictate in the area of foreign exchange. What the multinationals of each nation expect, and demand, is that the state operate as effectively as possible to represent their common interests in protecting the currency in which profits are ultimately distributed.

3. The more multinationals struggle among themselves for market control, the more they need and rely on active support of the state. As noted above, funds and direct intervention of the state are called for to back up domestic corporations whose stability is threatened by entrance of larger and stronger foreign competitors. Furthermore, rich as these giants are, they nevertheless depend extensively on government support through subsidies for research and development, government purchases of goods and services (notably for the military), and so on. Finally, the giants are far from all-powerful financially. They are subject to the vicissitudes of the market, the perils of speculation, overextension of credit, and other business risks. Even the seemingly strongest of the banks, manufacturers, and public utilities must face the possibility of bankruptcy in critical circumstances. Here again, in the final analysis, they count on the rescue operations by the state, not only because of their influence on the state, but also because the state needs them to keep the economy on an even keel. (The above reasons apply equally to joint ventures and other alliances by firms of different nations. In these situations each participating firm still expects to be paid eventually, in its own national currency, and to rely on its nation state in the event of extreme difficulties.)

NATION STATE SOVEREIGNTY

If, as we maintain, the nation states of the advanced capitalist areas are becoming more rather than less important for the well-being of the multinationals, what are we to make of the widespread claims that these firms are whittling away the sovereignty of the state? Obviously, this question needs to be put separately for the advanced and underdeveloped capitalist nations. With regard to the advanced countries, the argument is made that the operations of the multinationals in parent as well as host country are harmful to the national interests of both insofar as these activities limit each state's ability to keep employment high, maintain a sound currency, and otherwise control the economy for the common good. There are two aspects to this proposition: the definition of national interest, and the ability of the state to control the economy.

What is meant by the national interest? The concept is more or less identifiable when a nation is occupied or indirectly oppressed by a foreign power. In the absence of a palpable common enemy, however, the delineation of the national interest is not so clear-cut. This is especially so if the interests of different classes or sectors of a nation's population are antagonistic to each other. And antagonistic they must be except in an egalitarian society or one working towards such a goal. For when resources are limited, the more one sector of the population gets in the way of assets and income, the less will go to the others. (This fundamental conflict of interest exists at all times, even when the distributable pie is growing.) How resources are distributed depends ultimately on the socioeconomic structure and accordingly on which class owns and controls the bulk of the nation's resources. Under such circumstances, the national interest, no matter how clothed in the ideology of the times, boils down to providing the best environment for the arrived-at socioeconomic structure. Various types of compromise are reached among the classes and among diverse groups within the dominant class, but how far such compromises can go are themselves limited by the constraints of the economic structure and limited resources. Because of these constraints, the national interest becomes equated with the interests of those individuals and institutions who, by virtue of their ownership of the decisive wealth of the community, direct and regulate the allocation of economic resources. From this angle, as the multinationals become the dominant form of business enterprise, the national interest, as long as the capitalist system is operative, is to protect these organizations. As Professor Robert B. Stobaugh of the Harvard Business School put it: "To an important extent, the economic health of the United States depends upon the economic health of its multinational enterprises."[15] Since the success of the state rests on the success of its economy, there is at bottom no contradiction between the national interest and the multinationals: the global corporations need the support of their state and the state needs prosperous multinationals.

The above point may seem to apply only to the parent country and not necessarily to a host country, such as a West European nation, where key industries are in danger of being dominated by foreign enterprise. But here too the national interest assumes the form of supporting an environment best suited to the needs of an economic structure whose engine is fueled by expanding giant enterprises. The struggle among these giants, whether of foreign or domestic origin, must be conducted in accord with the rules of the game. Even in the face of setbacks, it is still in the interests of the host states whose economies are based on monopoly capital to maintain an environment where such battles can take place. Two other factors help keep the door open in Western Europe for U.S. enterprise: (1) the role of the U.S. military in stabilizing the Third World and the trade and investment activities of enterprises based in all the advanced capitalist nations; (2) the huge float of

U.S. dollar liabilities in European markets, the product of U.S. hegemony during the first two postwar decades. There are, to be sure, many sources of friction in these pressure areas just as there are in the competitive struggles of the multinationals. The road is far from smooth and contains many detours, as for example in the recent energy crisis and in the threat of a future world economic depression. But the tensions are best understood within the context of the laws of motion of imperialism rather than in terms of a mystifying abstraction like the national interest.

We come now to the second component of the argument over the decline of state sovereignty: the weakening of the state's capacity to control its interest rates, fiscal policies, and money supply for the commonwealth. Underlying this train of thought is a model of a self-contained economy which can be regulated to keep the economy going at full employment and at a steady rate of growth. Neither of the two aspects of this model is realistic. First, the advanced capitalist nations were never self-contained; they were always part of a world economy, and their strengths and weaknesses were always tied to the financial and industrial problems of operating in world markets. As discussed earlier, the growth of the MNCs is merely the latest emanation of the restless accumulation of capital and the innate drift towards greater concentration and centralization of capital. Second, much of the thinking about the self-regulating potential of government economic intervention is illusory. Whatever limited use the Keynesian tool kit may have, it should surely be evident in these inflationary times that the tools are self-limiting; their effectiveness tends to peter out. Moreover, whatever success government policies do have comes from maintaining or restoring the health of the economy via promoting the power of the giant firms, for without the prosperity of these firms the economy can only go downhill. The basic reasons for the impotence of governments to maintain their economies on an even keel are to be found in the limits and contradictions of monopoly capitalism. In other words, the problems arise not from the evils of the multinationals or the presumed diminution of the sovereignty of the advanced industrial nation states, the problems are inherent in the nature of a capitalist society.

MULTINATIONALS IN THE THIRD WORLD

Where the issue of state sovereignty does assume significance is in the underdeveloped nations. Typically, the balance of economic and financial power in most of the Third World is unequivocally in favor of the multinational firms. So much so that an adverse action of the latter, whether deliberate or arising out of impersonal market forces, can critically affect the whole economy, reducing employment levels, living standards, and export volume, as well as necessitating currency devaluations. But even though in today's environment the multinationals embody the essence of foreign domination, they are not, in our opinion, the only or even the most important determinant of underdevelopment in the Third World. The problem of state sovereignty goes deeper and involves not only countries where the influence of foreign investment is overwhelming, but also those underdeveloped areas where the operations of foreign investment are not necessarily decisive. What really makes the difference in the Third World is that these countries, under the sway of a long history of colonialism and semicolonialism, have evolved a mode of production, a class structure, and a social, psychological, and cultural milieu that are subservient to the metropolitan centers. So long as these conditions prevail, even the removal of the multinationals would not basically change either the sovereignty or the underdevelopment question. In the absence of a fundamental change in economic and class structure, the dependency of these economies, and hence their states also, would sooner or later reassert itself after the nationalization or withdrawal of the multinationals. The reason is that their economic structure, the nature of their international trade, and their wage-and-price relations are all geared to reproduce, through the ordinary processes of the market place, the subordinate condition of these societies.

In marked contrast with this view, the mainstream of Western thought is concerned with how the underdeveloped world can get out of its rut while more or less maintaining the existing socioeconomic structure. In this context, there is much talk about social reforms, accompanied by imaginative economic analysis and advice. But common to all orthodox economic thinking—indeed the kernel of its prescriptions—is reliance on a sufficient injection of just two ingredients: capital (money) and technology. It is therefore argued that even if the multinationals have many undesirable features (repression of sovereignty, distortion of resource allocation, and so forth), they are a necessary evil, for they are the bearers of the money and the Promethean fire that will ultimately set the Third World free.

If there is any validity to this doctrine, it could only be with respect to technology. It is time that the myth about the money-capital contributions of foreign enterprise is put to rest. For the facts on this are crystal clear. First, a substantial portion of the financing of multinationals in the Third World is raised in the host country itself, by loans from local sources and by using part of the profits and depreciation reserves generated within the host country. Second, the aggregate flow of capital *out of* the host country to pay dividends, interest, royalties, and management fees (even forgetting hidden transfers due to overpricing of goods shipped from the parent companies to their affiliates) is in excess of the flow of capital *into* the host countries. In other words the operations of the multinationals, whatever other benefits they may bring, result in a net flow of capital from the underdeveloped to the developed nations.

It is true that the activities of the multinationals, especially those engaged in extractive industries, often contribute to a significant expansion of exports by Third World countries. However, these rising exports are generally offset by (a) rising imports needed to operate and expand the new enterprises and to supply the higher consumption standards of foreign technicians and those nationals who get some of the gravy; (b) the outflow of foreign exchange reserves for the payment of profits, and so on, to foreign investors. These offsets to rising exports usually limit the ability of the host country to import capital goods, and they thus become even more dependent on foreign investment for their capital goods demand. This condition changes of course when host countries take over foreign-owned industry, or, as in the case of the oil-exporting nations, are able to exercise control over the price of their exports.

The question of technology transfer, on the other hand, does touch a vital spot. While real development presumes a wide variety of social and economic changes, there is no doubt that the *sine qua non* of any meaningful progress is a major increase in the output of goods and services. And the extent to which production can advance depends on bringing as much of the population as possible into useful productive activity on the one hand, and increasing the productivity of the employed on the other. The latter requires a stepped-up increase in the use of science and machinery (including improved methods of organization of production).

Taking account of these elementary truths, the advocates of the need for foreign investment build their case on the following assumptions: (a) the science and technology of the industrialized nations can only—or, if not only, most efficiently— be transferred by foreign investors who have a profit incentive to do so; (b) the multinationals are best suited to bring in the needed technology. The first assumption has been proven false by history. Japan, the Soviet Union, North Korea, and China have all demonstrated that an underdeveloped country can speedily (as compared with the most successful industrial nations) obtain, exploit, and adapt modern science and technology without dependence on foreign investment. (To the extent that these countries obtained limited foreign technical assistance from foreign capitalists, it was done with contracts for a specific planned undertaking initiated by the host country, and it excluded long-term or perpetual ownership and profit-taking by foreign entrepreneurs.)

Subsumed in the second assumption is again a crude technological determinism, with overtones of vulgar and distorted Marxism: the belief that technological progress as such is the most powerful driving force of social development, plus a corollary that the most modern technology will inevitably produce the most modern and progressive society. One need not dispute the crucial role of technology to find fault with these oversimplifications. First, it should be recognized that new science and technology will not automatically produce conforming social changes. A social agent is needed for social change: specifically, a class that has both a vital interest in pursuing and utilizing a particular type of innovation, and the will and power to implement this interest. In the absence of such an agent and the proper environment in which it can flex its muscles, the best of science and technology may lie fallow. Second, a distinction needs to be made between past technological change and the fruits of capitalism. In general, the state of the technical arts at each stage of social development determines both the potential and the limits of production. Looking broadly at the long stretch of history prior to capitalism, the "limits" were more important than the "potential." Thus the standard of living of the vast majority of the world's population through almost all of human history was necessarily severely restricted despite the many revolutionary advances in production and transportation. While one can speculate on how much better past societies might have been with better organization of economic activity or with a more equitable distribution of output, the basic reality remains that even with the best will and the most altruistic of rulers, the people's living conditions would not have been altered significantly: the constraints on the production potential imposed by the available knowledge and tools were too severe.

With the industrial revolutions of capitalism, however, the situation changed dramatically. A body of scientific and technological information (not to mention tools and the ability to reproduce the tools on an expanding scale) has been generated which opens up entirely new horizons for the living standards of the people of the world. Limits are clearly and most decidedly present, as no doubt there always will be. The difference today is that the "potential" carries more weight than the "limits": the room for choice has been vastly enlarged. In contrast with the past, when certain types of social development were circumscribed by barriers of knowledge, the limits imposed by the prevailing technical arts are of lesser importance. Society can, if it wishes, select from a wide variety of technologies, with many more degrees of freedom in the choice of priorities. Thus, even though technology still imposes certain limits and restricts the range of choice, what is most important today—in fact, decisive—is the agent of change: who is in charge and for what purpose?

This is the context in which the role of the multinationals as the bearers of modern technology should, in our opinion, be viewed. If the existing class structures in the Third World are to be more or less maintained, if production is to be geared to meeting the effective demand of the top income groups, and if the trickle-down doctrine of economic orthodoxy is to be the reigning rationale—then by all means, the multinationals are doing a necessary and useful job. One might insist, as do so many liberals, that the claws of the multinationals be trimmed and their greed curbed somewhat. But if what is wanted is a technology that will meet the consumer needs of the upper strata, then it is reasonable to expect that on the whole the multinationals will supply in the speediest and most efficacious fashion what the existing host society and its entrepreneurs find impossible to do by themselves. In thus meeting the needs of such Third World countries, the multinationals will select the most suitable way of producing the required goods at the lowest cost (consistent with the special outlays the oligopolists must make to maintain their management and marketing structures). Moreover, this transfer of technology will also multiply opportunities for local elites to enrich themselves. If this gravy is insufficient for the native ruling classes, new sources of profit and capital accumulation can be stimulated by enlarging participation in international trade. And for this the multinationals are also the best bet: their knowledge and influence are invaluable. To widen the scope of international trade for the Third World and its profit-taking classes, the multinationals can be relied on to choose and introduce the best technology and industrial organization for the most effective use of a valuable Third World "asset": its depressed living standards and the accompanying exceedingly low wages. But while recognizing the real and potential contributions of the multinationals in transferring modern technology for these purposes, it should equally be understood that the sectors of advanced industry thereby created will coexist with the traditional miserable living conditions of the bulk of the Third World's population.

Let us suppose, on the other hand, that there is a totally different class structure in the Third World, that the property-owning classes who obstruct social progress have been removed from power, and that the new ruling class (or alliance of classes) insists on an opposite set of priorities, as for example giving first and absolute precedence to improving the lot of the impoverished majority by eliminating hunger and epidemic diseases, raising housing and clothing standards, bringing medical services to the poor and dispersed, introducing education and cultural opportunities for the masses, and so on. The science and technology to achieve these goals exist. This, however, is not the technology that the multinationals have to offer; these firms are not suited to select the most appropriate technology.

The multinationals do of course have a great store of talent and experience which could be put to use in countries operating with a relatively primitive technology. Thus, a few of the large corporations have been experimenting with the mass production of items that are especially adapted for wide use in the less technically advanced countries. However, flexible as these firms may be, their ingenuity and enterprise are necessarily confined to production and marketing items that meet each company's profit objective. And the profit goal is precisely what stands in the way of the multinational devoting itself to the most urgent priorities: the basic needs of the most impoverished masses in the Third World—the poor peasants, the rural and urban unemployed, and the working class.

Before considering the sort of industrial arts needed, we should recall that there are two components of the task of increasing national output: full and nonwasteful use of the labor supply, and increasing labor productivity. Under the first heading the multinationals, to say the least, have nothing to offer. What is needed, if the most urgent priorities are heeded, is a mobilization of the people to lay the groundwork for improving agriculture and health: to undertake water conservancy projects, provide irrigation networks, dig latrines and sewer systems, create roads and canals, innoculate the population against epidemic diseases, install rural electrification, and so on. It is true that modern earth-moving and other machinery could be very helpful, and surely more efficient than hand tools and crude equipment in completing most of these tasks. But the jobs won't get done by waiting and hoping for the best technology, for poor countries haven't the resources to pay for or to manufacture enough of the needed equipment for the amount of work involved in laying the basis for eliminating hunger and reducing disease.

When it comes to the most urgent technologies needed to raise labor productivity and increase agricultural yields, again we find that the multinationals have little to offer. What is most urgently required is not sophisticated electronics or mass production of automobiles or washing machines. Much more pressing is a need for carts, wheelbarrows, and bicycles in vast numbers to replace the movement of goods on head or shoulder; enough cement to waterproof linings of irrigation works, drainage, and silos; pumps, pipes, and sprinkling apparatus for irrigation; supplying the farm population with simple hand and mechanical devices for plowing, weeding, and threshing; and so on. In addition, the standards of industrial organization and efficiency would differ radically from those of the multinationals. Thus the remedy for rural unemployment requires small-sized and diversified manufacturing plants which would be anathema to the cost and profit calculations of big business.

It is not our purpose to outline a plan of development or to deny the desirability and necessity to learn from and borrow the most modern technology available. The intention is simply to insist that the order of precedence in the choice of technologies, their adaptation and mix, will differ depending on the social goals and on which classes have the power to determine priorities. And outstanding among the priorities of a society seeking to solve the most urgent problems of poverty and technical backwardness is for *themselves* to become masters of the industrial and agricultural arts so that they, and not others, may choose and adapt the technology they deem most important, including when needed the most complex modern industries. For this, a complete change in social power and social psychology is called for: to throw off the yoke of subservience to Western technology and culture; to develop self-confidence; to spread respect for, and education in, science, mathematics, and engineering; and to generate in the lowliest peasant the urge to experiment. Such a transformation cannot be ordained from above, it cannot be imported. It can only come through the experience gained in the process of becoming self-reliant, as the mass of the working people in field and factory learn—by doing—to care for and repair machinery, as large numbers of workers and farmers become master mechanics, and as indigenous design and engineering capabilities are aimed for and attained. If ever an adage made sense, it certainly does for the underdeveloped nations: "God helps those who help themselves."

NOTES

1. Karl Marx, *Capital* (Moscow: Progress Publishers, 1957), vol. I, p. 555.

2. Ibid., vol. I, p. 558.

3. Ibid., vol. I, pp. 585-88.

4. Ibid., vol. III, p. 110.

5. Ibid., vol. III, pp. 332-33. Note also Marx's evaluation of the inner drive to world operation in capitalism, *Grundrisse* (New York: Vintage, 1973, p. 308-408, as he explains why, "The tendency to create the *world market* is directly given in the concept of capital itself."

6. While this monopoly phase came into full blossom after Marx's time, he sensed the significance of its early sprouts. An interesting example is found in his discussion of the impact of price fluctuations in the process of circulation: "...the greater the disturbances the greater the money-capital which the industrial capitalist must possess to tide over the period of readjustment, and as the scale of each individual process and with it the minimum size of the capital to be advanced increases in the process of capitalist production, we have another circumstance to be added to those others which transform the function of the industrial capitalist more and more into a monopoly of big money-capitalists who may operate singly or in association."

7. It should be noted that loans to industries (and portfolio investments) at times were as effective as direct investment, in so far as the lenders influenced and controlled production and marketing operations. And there was of course a growing amount of direct investment in extractive and manufacturing industries. But on the whole the composition of transnational capital migration differed significantly before and after the age of the multinationals. For earlier patterns of capital exports, see Herbert Feis, *Europe the World's Banker 1870-1914* (New Haven: Yale University Press, 1931). And for still earlier developments, see Leland H. Jenks, *The Migration of British Capital to 1875* (New York: Alfred A. Knopf, 1927).

8. Woodruff, Bornschier, U.N. report.

9. *Statistical Abstract,* Government Printing Office, various issues, 1973.

10. United Nations, *Multinational Corporations in World Development* (UN: New York, 1973): 159.

11. Ibid., p. 7.

12. Ibid., p. 12.

13. Ibid., p. 190.

14. F. G. Donner, *The World-Wide Industrial Enterprise* (New York: McGraw Hill, 1967), pp. 35-36.

15. *Wall Street Journal,* June 6, 1973. Prof. Stonbaugh conducted the U.S. Department of Commerce study, "Multinational Enterprises and the U.S. Economy."

DAVID E. APTER is Henry J. Heinz II Professor of Comparative Political and Social Development at Yale University, and was formerly director of the Institute of International Studies, University of California, Berkeley. He has been a fellow of the Center for Advanced Study in the Behavioral Sciences, and at All Souls College, Oxford. His publications include *Ghana in Transition, The Politics of Modernization,* and *Choice and the Politics of Allocation.* He is currently completing a manuscript entitled *Founding Myths and Transforming Ideology.* Dr. Apter received his B.A. from Antioch College and his Ph.D. in political science from Princeton University.

LOUIS WOLF GOODMAN is Staff Associate and Director of the Program on Latin America and the Caribbean at the Social Science Research Council. He has been a professor at the Facultad Latinoamericana de Ciencias Sociales in Santiago, Chile, and at Yale University. His recent work has focused on problems of international stratification with empirical studies on decision-making in multinational corporations, and on international medical migration. Dr. Goodman received his B.A. from Dartmouth College and his Ph.D. in sociology from Northwestern University.

WALTER GOLDSTEIN, born and educated in England, came to the United States on a Fulbright scholarship. His graduate work in political science was completed at Northwestern University and the University of Chicago. He has been a professor of political science at the City University of New York and the State University of New York at Albany. He has been a visiting professor at Columbia and New York University. His recent work has concentrated on the political conflicts between multinational firms in the high-technology industries and the advanced industrial states.

HARRY MAGDOFF has been co-editor (with Paul M. Sweezy) of *Monthly Review* since 1969. He received his B.A. in economics from New York University. During the 1930s he was in charge of statistical productivity studies for the WPA National Research Project on Re-employment Opportunities and Technical Development. During World War II he was chief of the Civilian Requirements Division of the National Defense Advisory Commission. Mr. Magdoff's final years in government were spent in the Department of Commerce as head of the Current Business Analysis Division, and as Special Assistant to the Secretary. Since that time he has been a financial consultant, stockbroker, publisher, and university instructor. He is the author of *The Age of Imperialism,* and numerous articles and reviews.

RONALD E. MÜLLER has received graduate degrees from the University of Munich and the American University, earning his Ph.D. at the latter institution where he is now on the faculty of economics. He has been a consultant to private business firms, international organizations, and U.S. government agencies. His articles in the fields of economics, political economy, international business, sociology, and social psychology have been published by journals in the United States and abroad. His recent book (co-authored with Richard Barnet), *Global Reach: The Power of the Multinational Corporations,* represents in part his interest in integrating the social and behavioral sciences into a comprehensive methodology for social forecasting. A further effort in this direction is his forthcoming *The New Geopolitics: Power and the World Political Economy.*

GUSTAV RANIS is Professor of Economics at Yale University. He received his B.A. from Brandeis University and his Ph.D. from Yale. From 1965 to 1967 he served as Assistant Administrator for Program and Policy in the Agency for International Development. Previously he had been Director of the Institute of Development Economics in Karachi, Pakistan. He has served as a consultant for the Ford Foundation, the World Bank, the Treasury Department, and a number of foreign governments. In 1973 he led the ILO Comprehensive Employment Mission to the Philippines. He has written extensively in the field of development theory and policy.

YOSHIHIRO TSURUMI is Visiting Associate Professor at the Graduate School of Business Administration, Harvard University. He has also taught at Queen's University in Canada, and at Keio University in Tokyo. He completed Ph.D. course work in economics at Keio University before obtaining an M.B.A. and a D.B.A. from Harvard. His recent publications include articles about Japan and the oil crisis, and Japanese multinational firms. His latest book, *The Japanese are Coming: Multinational Spread of Japanese Firms,* will be published this year.

RAYMOND VERNON is the Director of the Center for International Affairs at Harvard University. He is also Coordinator of the Multinational Enterprise Project at the Harvard Business School, and is the Herbert F. Johnson Professor of International Business. He received his B.A. from the College of the City of New York, and his Ph.D. in economics from Columbia University. He has worked extensively in developing countries on the problems of foreign investment, generally as an advisor to governments and international agencies.

NATIONAL CONTROL OF FOREIGN BUSINESS
ENTRY: A Survey of Fifteen Countries
Richard D. Robinson

IMPORTING TECHNOLOGY INTO AFRICA: Foreign
Investment and the Transfer and Diffusion of
Technological Innovations
edited by D. Babatunde Thomas

DEPENDENT INDUSTRIALIZATION IN THE
LATIN AMERICAN MOTOR INDUSTRY
R. O. Jenkins

THE NATION STATE AND TRANSNATIONAL
CORPORATIONS IN CONFLICT: With Special
Reference to Latin America
edited by Jon P. Gunnemann

MULTINATIONAL CORPORATIONS IN
WORLD DEVELOPMENT
United Nations Department of
Economic and Social Affairs